A HISTORY *of*

US

CONCISE EDITION

Front Cover

An artist's rendition of Pocahontas, daughter of Virginia's Powhatan chief in the early 1600s

 K12

Compilation Copyright © 2011 K12 Inc.
Text Copyright © 1993, 1999, 2003, 2005 by Joy Hakim
Adapted with permission of Oxford University Press, Inc.

ISBN-13: 978-1-60153-181-0

Printed by LSC Communications, Willard, OH, May 2019.

VOLUME **A**   PREHISTORY TO 1800

Joy Hakim

A HISTORY *of* US

CONCISE EDITION

Editors of the K^{12} Concise Edition

John Holdren and Patricia O'Connell Pearson

Concise Edition Volume A Staff and Contributors

Allyson Jacob, Connie Moy, Jill Tunick *Text Editors*
Suzanne Montazer *Creative Director, Print and ePublishing*
Stephanie Shaw Williams *Print Visual Designer*
The Quarasan Group, Inc. *Interior Design and Composition*
Kim Barcas, Carol Leigh *Cover Designers*
Meredith Condit, Charlotte Fullerton *Picture Editors*
Jean Stringer *Rights Manager*
David Swanson *Cartographer*
Jay White, *Contributing Instructional Designer*
Susan Raley *Senior Manager, Editors*
Candee Wilson *Senior Project Manager*

Maria Szalay *Senior Vice President, Product Development*
John Holdren *Senior Vice President, Content and Curriculum*
David Pelizzari *Vice President, Content and Curriculum*
Kim Barcas *Vice President, Creative*
Laura Seuschek *Vice President, Instructional Design and Evaluation & Research*
Aaron Hall *Vice President, Program Management*

Lisa Dimaio Iekel *Senior Production Manager*
John Agnone *Director of Publications*

About K12 Inc.

K12 Inc., a technology-based education company, is the nation's leading provider of proprietary curriculum and online education programs to students in grades K–12. K^{12} provides its curriculum and academic services to online schools, traditional classrooms, blended school programs, and directly to families. K12 Inc. also operates the K^{12} International Academy, an accredited, diploma-granting online private school serving students worldwide. K^{12}'s mission is to provide any child the curriculum and tools to maximize success in life, regardless of geographic, financial, or demographic circumstances. K12 Inc. is accredited by CITA. More information can be found at www.K12.com.

A Note from the Author

Here is a problem writers have: what to put in and what to leave out. When I began writing *A History of US*, it was supposed to be one book. That one book got fat, so I divided it in two, kept writing, and, to my surprise, ended up with ten books. I was still unhappy: there was so much more I wanted to write about. But I learned that ten books are too much for those who are immersed in other subjects and want an overview of American history. My friends at K^{12} came to the rescue. They made choices and helped create this new four-volume version—something I couldn't do on my own. I'm very pleased with what they've done.

—Joy Hakim

Contents

PART 1

THE FIRST AMERICANS

PART 2
MAKING 13 COLONIES

PART 3

FROM COLONIES TO COUNTRY

Part 1

the First Americans

★

History? Why?

History is the story of US. It tells who we are and where we have been. Sometimes it is so surprising it jolts your mind.

History is full of stories—true stories—the best ever. Those stories have real heroes and real villains. When you read history, you are reading about real-life adventures.

History is a mystery. No one knows what happened in the past—at least we don't know the whole story. We weren't there. Have you ever put a jigsaw puzzle together? That's what learning history is like. You gather pieces of information and try to discover how they fit. Suddenly, when you have enough pieces in place, you begin to see the big picture. That's exciting, and so is studying history, because new pieces of the puzzle keep fitting in.

When we read about *the mistakes people made in the past,* we can try not to make them ourselves. Nations and people who don't study history sometimes repeat mistakes.

History is especially important for Americans. In many nations—Japan or Sweden, for instance—most citizens share a common background. They have a similar look. They may worship in the same church. That isn't true of us. Some of us were once Chinese,

Archaeologists help tell the story of history by examining pieces of the distant past, such as these bones of a huge creature called a mammoth. ▶

or Italian, or Turkish, or Ethiopian. Americans don't all look alike. Sometimes we don't think alike. But as Americans we do share something. It is our history. We Americans share a common heritage. If you are an American, then the Indians, the Vikings, the Pilgrims, and the slaves are all your ancestors. You will want to know their stories.

Before we were a nation, we were ruled by England. Many Americans wanted to be free. So they wrote a Declaration of Independence explaining their goals. It begins: *We hold these truths to be self-evident, that all men are created equal, that they are endowed by their creator with certain unalienable Rights, that among these are Life, Liberty, and the pursuit of Happiness.* It also says that governments derive *their just powers from the consent of the governed.* (What does that mean?)

Consider those words about equality and happiness. In past times, governments didn't worry about things like that. Our Declaration changed ideas. It was written in 1776 and, since then, it has inspired people all over the world in battles for freedom and fairness.

▲ As Americans, we all share a common heritage.

▲ A sculpture in the Rotunda of the U.S. Capitol Building tells the stories of important events in American history, including the arrival of Columbus shown here.

SAVE FREEDOM OF SPEECH

BUY WAR BONDS

▲ The United States—no other nation has provided so much freedom and opportunity to so many people. This poster reproduces an oil painting from the *Four Freedoms* series painted during World War II by Norman Rockwell.

Which brings me to this book's theme. It is this: *I believe the United States of America is the most remarkable nation that has ever existed. No other nation, in the history of the world, has ever provided so much freedom, so much justice, and so much opportunity to so many people.*

That is a big statement. You don't have to agree with it. Arguing with a book's theme is okay.

Some people will tell you of evil forces in the United States. They will tell of past horrors like slavery and war. They will tell of poverty and injustice today. They will be telling the truth.

The United States isn't perfect. Far from it. Being fair to everyone in a large nation is very difficult. (Do you treat everyone you know equally? How about people you don't like?) The U.S. government has made some terrible mistakes. It is still making mistakes. But usually this nation can, and does, correct its mistakes. That is because we are a democracy: power belongs to the people, not the rulers. We are also a nation governed by law, and that is very important. No one is above the law. Everyone—the president, congressmen, congresswomen, and you—lives by the same laws.

▲ In a representative democracy, the people vote for their leaders. Here, people gather at the U.S. Capitol for Barack Obama's inauguration in January 2009.

▲ Symbolizing a nation governed by law, the Authority of Law statue sits on the steps of the U.S. Supreme Court Building.

In the United States you are free to do anything that anyone else can do. You can run for president, be an artist, write books, or build houses.

But being a citizen of a free nation isn't easy. Free citizens are expected to be informed and think for themselves. Having rights means having responsibilities. It means asking questions and learning so that you can vote intelligently. Nations are constantly tested by those who want to upset or criticize or conquer. A good way to handle those attacks is with history's information.

The more you study history, the more you will realize that all nations are not the same. Some are better than others.

Does that seem like an unfair thing to say? Maybe, but I believe it.

I don't believe that people in one nation are better than those in another. Every nation has a mixture of good and bad people.

So why, if people are the same, are nations different?

Ideas have a lot to do with it. Nations stand on their ideas. We're lucky. The architects who designed this nation had sound ideas. They were looking for liberty, justice, and opportunity when they came here. They made sure the United States provided them.

Then they did something never done before: they created a people's government. Some men and women in other parts of the world thought that was impossible. After all, it was an untried idea. But America's citizens proved that government by the people can work. How we did that is a fascinating story.

That's the story of US—the people of the United States—the story you're about to read. It's a story of hunters, explorers, pirates, slaves—the men and women and boys and girls who came to a strange land and made it their own. It's a story with heroes, and villains, and big ideas.

We're going to start that story way, way, way back in time, with some of the first Americans. Read on—there is much to tell.

▲ American history is the story of US—the diverse people of the United States.

In the Beginning

Are you ready? You're about to study the history of US—the people of the United States. You'll need to use your imagination. You can start by climbing into our sturdy time-and-space capsule. Hold on tight; you're going back to the Age of Stone and Ice. You're going to northern Asia, to a place called Siberia. When you get out of the capsule you might shiver a bit; it is cold here in Siberia.

Watch that band of people move across the plain. They look hungry and tired. The tribe is small, just 20 people in all, and only six are men of hunting age. But they are brave and their spears are sharp, so they will keep going. They follow the tracks of a mammoth.

If they can kill the mammoth—a huge, woolly elephant—they will feast for much of the winter.

The trail of the great animal leads them into a wide grassy earth bridge that stretches between two continents. They have come from Asia. When they cross that bridge they will be on land that someday will be called America. The trail of the mammoth leads them from Asia to a new world.

They don't realize what a big step they are taking. They don't know they are making history. All they know is that they have lost the mammoth. He has outsmarted them. But it doesn't matter; the new land is rich in animals and fish and berries. They will stay.

All that happened a long time ago, when families lived in huts and caves and the bow and arrow hadn't even been invented. It was a time when ice blankets—called *glaciers*—covered much of the northern land. We call it the Ice Age. Some of the glaciers were more than a mile high. Nothing humans have built has been as tall.

If you look at a map of the world today, you will find the Bering Sea between Asia and Alaska. The distance is short—just 18 miles—but the sea is icy and treacherous. Now, this is strange, but true: in the Ice Age, that region had a mild climate. And that

During the Ice Age much of the earth's water was frozen in glaciers. The oceans were a lot smaller and lower, so there was more land exposed. The continents and islands were fatter and there were land bridges where now there is ocean.

Bands of hunters migrated from Asia to North America. ▼

18 miles, which is now sea, was land. It was an earth bridge—
1,000 miles wide—with open grasslands, clear lakes for fishing, and
even some forest regions. Much of the earth's water was then frozen
in glaciers, so there was more land and less ocean everywhere.

That long-gone land between the continents is known as Beringia.
About 40,000 years ago—circa 38,000 B.C.E. (*circa* is Latin for

Early peoples migrated at a time when much of earth's water was frozen in glaciers. ▼

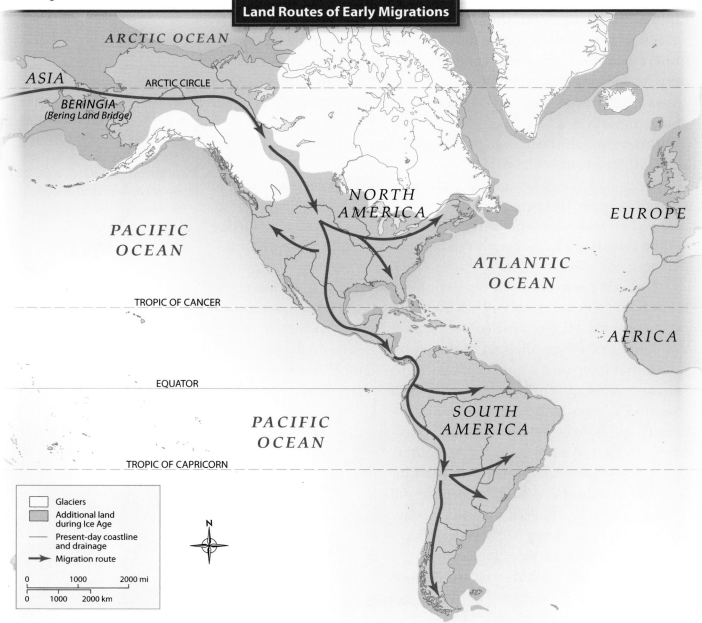

"about")—the land bridge was open between Asia and America, and animals went back and forth on it. Some experts think people did, too, but no one knows for sure. Then the land bridge disappeared. It was covered with water.

About 26,000 B.C.E., Beringia (the land bridge) opened up again. Big animals came to Beringia; and at some point, people came, too. Some of the people walked there; some came by sea. There was lots to eat. For everyday dining, the hunters and the fisherfolk lived on small game and small fish—but they had the skills to kill mammoths and whales, and when they could, they did. The mammoths and giant sloths and camels were plant eaters, and only moderately dangerous. It was the meat-eating animals—the saber-toothed cats, the maned

◀ Early hunters use their spears and skills to kill a mastodon.

lions, and the huge bears—who must have licked their lips after munching on humans. That was the way of the hunting world.

Journeying by sea may have been safer than by land. And these people were very good sailors. In boats covered with animal skins, they could explore and settle the coastline. Gradually, we think, the land rovers and the seagoers took a big step—onto the new continent.

Alaska, where the hunters went, seemed like a fine place. There were seals, bison with big curved horns, birds called ptarmigans, and other good things to hunt and eat. Glaciers covered large parts of North America, but much of Alaska and Siberia was free of ice.

More hunters came with their families. At first there was plenty of food, but after a few years (maybe it was a few thousand years) the land seemed crowded. There was no longer enough game for everyone to hunt.

Each year, when the hunters saw birds fly south, they wished they could fly over the mountains of ice. They watched the animals and found there were ways around and through the thick glaciers. Some of the hunters followed the herds east, into Canada, until they reached some great lakes; then they took those waterways south onto the vast plains of North America. Others may have followed a narrow beach-side path, with high glaciers on one side and the ocean on the other.

It was worth the trip. They found grasses and nuts and berries to eat. They found a hunter's wonderland: there were ox, bighorn sheep, lions, deer, moose, foxes, otters, beavers, saber-toothed tigers, and bison. Some of the animals had come from Asia too, by walking over the earth bridge, or by swimming in the sea.

In America, animals had grown big—bigger than any animals you have ever seen. Some beavers were as large as bears; and birds—great vulture-like teratorns—had wings that reached 15 feet from tip to tip. Lions were huge; moose antlers measured eight feet across.

North America was a hunter's heaven, and big game hunters had arrived. Someday those hunters will be known as Clovis people—because, in the 20th century, their spear tips will be discovered along with mammoth bones at Clovis, New Mexico. Spear points with bison bones—found near Folsom, New Mexico—will indicate that some early Americans hunted animals, like bison, that travel in herds.

These versatile hunters—who also kill and eat birds, fish, foxes, and turtles—will thrive in North America.

Those Clovis people weren't the first Americans. No one is sure who arrived first. Some very old artifacts—about 22,000 years old—have been discovered in Virginia. Their discovery startled archaeologists who thought the earliest humans arrived on the west coast. Virginia is on the *east* coast. So where did those first families of Virginia come from? We don't yet know, but scientific sleuths are trying to answer that question.

Archaeologists (ar-kee-OLL-uh-jists) are scientists who study materials from the past.

We now believe that some early Americans came over the eastern Canadian ice sheets. Others may have sailed directly across the Atlantic, possibly from the Mediterranean world. (On the west coast, some Pacific Islanders may have used the ocean as a direct highway.) We know that ancient humans explored South America down to its tip.

One thing is sure: those who came arrived in waves, over centuries, bringing different backgrounds, different skills, and different languages. The American continents were a good place to live—especially as the climate was changing.

It was getting warmer—slowly. Up north, the big glaciers—which were like seas of frozen water—melted and froze and melted and froze. When they melted, the oceans got bigger and flooded some of the land. The earth bridge disappeared under the sea; then, when the waters froze again, the earth bridge reappeared. The pathway through the glacier closed up, then reopened.

Finally, about 10,000 years ago, things settled down much as they are now. Water covered Beringia. It got very cold in the Bering Sea. When all that happened, the animals and people who had come across to the new land were stuck. They couldn't go back to Asia, and no one could join them. America was cut off from the rest of the world.

The Clovis people made these spear points. ▶

How the First Americans Became Indians

Those first Americans were on their own in the New World. Thousands of years would go by before Christopher Columbus sailed across the Atlantic Ocean from distant Europe. Columbus called the First Americans "Indians" because he thought he was in the Indies—way over by China. That was a big mistake. But it would be a long time before anyone realized how wrong Columbus was. So the name *Indian* stuck. It's what we use most often today.

Some people use *Native Americans* instead of Indians, although the word *native* is confusing. It has two meanings. Anyone who is born in a country is a native of that country, so many of us are native Americans. "Native" also means to have an origin, or beginning, in a country. As far as we know, no people is native to America. Our ancestors all came from somewhere else.

Still, the people who came over the Bering Strait were here long before anyone else. So you can see why it makes sense to call them Native Americans. Indians, First Americans, or Native Americans—they are all good names. (Most Indians call themselves simply "the people" in their various languages.)

Some historians think that by the time Columbus got here, there may have been as many as 75 million Indians living in South and North America. That is a lot of people—almost a third of the population of the United States today. But no one knows what the actual number was.

These handprints on a cave wall in South America are 10,000 years old. ▼

◀ Early American hunters caused animals to stampede into places where they could be easily speared.

If we go back in time 10,000 years, those First Americans, who now were spread out over the two American continents, were beginning to do some remarkable things.

Most of them continued to hunt—they were good at that. They knew how to make animals stampede into deep ditches or watery bogs, where they could be easily speared.

When it came to spearheads, theirs were the best. They made them of flint, a hard stone they chipped at until it was sharp and deadly.

So many animals got killed that some of them became extinct. (That means they all died out.) But, in most cases, their disappearance wasn't because of hunters. The mammoths, for instance, were just too big. After the end of the Ice Age, when the climate warmed up, mammoths couldn't adjust. They drank huge amounts of water; a family of thirsty mammoths could drain a pond. Scientists think they couldn't find enough water to drink or grass to eat.

More than 100 species of animals became extinct between 6,000 and 10,000 years ago. No one knows why all of them died. Perhaps they were infected by germs carried by humans. Maybe hunters killed too many of some species.

A *stampede* is a wild rush of animals.

Species (SPEE-sheez) is the scientific word for groups of plants and animals.

That was too bad, because there was so much food on the land that people could make choices: to catch fish or dig for clams and oysters or gather nuts and berries and roots. And some tribes did just that. They became gatherers.

Others became farmers—among the best in the world. They took wild plants and bred them, and they developed corn, potatoes, sweet potatoes, and squash. They learned to make chocolate from the cocoa plant. They found corn kernels that popped when heated. They discovered plants and herbs that could heal sickness. They grew tobacco and peppers and tomatoes. None of these plants was known in other parts of the world.

Indian basketweavers wove baskets so tight that they could hold liquids and so handsome that people in later generations put them in museums. Potters learned to make sculptured figures and useful pots and bowls. Weavers designed colorful rugs.

Native Americans race canoes on a western river. ▼

◀ A sculpture from ancient times by the people called the Anasazi

▲ No more hunting on foot—in the 16th century, horses changed Indian life.

Native American thinkers created mathematically precise calendars. Goldsmiths made some of the most beautiful jewelry the world has ever seen. Indians invented the hammock, the canoe, snowshoes, and a game called lacrosse. They learned to gather rubber from rubber plants; they made rubber balls and played ball games. They built pyramids and temples and cities.

But no single tribe of Indians did all those things. Native Americans developed different lifestyles and different languages, just as Europeans and Africans and Asians did. It all depended on who their leaders were and where they lived.

One thing Indians never did was to make good use of the wheel. Their lives would have been easier if they had. In Mexico the Indians put wheels on their children's toys, but they never made wheeled wagons for themselves. Perhaps that was because they didn't have horses to pull them.

When people came from Spain to America (at the end of the 15th century), they brought horses and mules and oxen. In the 16th century, horses completely changed Indian life, just as the automobile and airplane changed life in 20th-century America. (Can you imagine hunting buffalo on foot? Now jump on horseback and see the difference it makes.)

When the horse came to America, it was returning home. A tiny horse ancestor had lived in America in Ice Age times. Some of those ancient, dog-sized horses had trotted across Beringia to Asia. In Asia they grew large and galloped on—to Europe and Africa. Those that stayed in America became extinct.

The Inuit

When Beringia, the land bridge, was covered by water, America was cut off. But a few people *did* get to America after water covered the land. They were Eskimos. They came by sled over the polar ice. The Eskimos are thought to have been the very last of the ancient Asians to arrive on the American continent. They stayed in the north country and never followed the others down to the warmer climates.

Eskimos are not Indians, but a separate people with a language like no other. Today, most Eskimos lead modern lives. But a few live—right now—more or less as they have for thousands of years: hunting and fishing near the North Pole and across the arctic and subarctic regions in Alaska, Canada, Greenland, and Siberia.

By the way, the name *Eskimo*, like the name *Indian*, got attached to the people for the wrong reasons. The name many Eskimos use to describe themselves is *Inuit* (IN-yoo-it), which means "the people."

The Inuit who live in coastal villages hunt seals, walrus, and whales. Others, who live inland, are nomads and must move to survive. They hunt reindeer (also called "caribou") and the shaggy musk ox. They fish through holes cut in the ice. They live on land called "tundra" that has no trees and stays partly frozen all year round. The Inuit of central Canada used to build igloos as winter homes. Some still do. An igloo is a domed house made of snow bricks with ice windows. (The word *igloo* comes from the Inuit word *igluvigaq*.)

▲ An Inuit hunter spearing fish

When the Inuit travel in winter, to hunt the fish and marine animals they eat, they live in *igloos*, snow-block houses built on top of the iced-over sea. ▼

Cliff Dwellers and Others

Climb in the capsule and set the dial to the year 1250. You are going to the Southwest of what will someday be the United States: to the place where four states—New Mexico, Arizona, Colorado, and Utah—meet. You are going to Mesa Verde, Colorado.

That's where the amazing Anasazi (an-nuh-SAH-zee) Indians live. But they don't call themselves Anasazi—that's the modern name for them. We have no idea what they call themselves. *Anasazi* is a Navaho word. The Navaho Indians are nomads, wanderers who sometimes raid and steal from the peaceful Anasazi farmers. The word *Anasazi*, in Navaho, means "ancient enemies." Like Eskimo and Indian, Anasazi is another of those wrong names that history sometimes attaches to people. The Anasazi are resourceful people. This should be an interesting visit.

Name Calling

The Navaho nomads, and other tribes called "Apache," are said to have come from western Canada. Someday they will settle in villages and become farmers, shepherds, and silversmiths. Apache means "enemy." Many Indian names used today were given to Native Americans by the newcomers. The Navahos were called the *apache of navahu,* "enemies of plowed fields." Do you think the people we call Apache called themselves that?

◀ Every day the Anasazi farmers climbed to the flat top of Mesa Verde to work in their fields. The low round chambers of the pueblo are special rooms called "kivas."

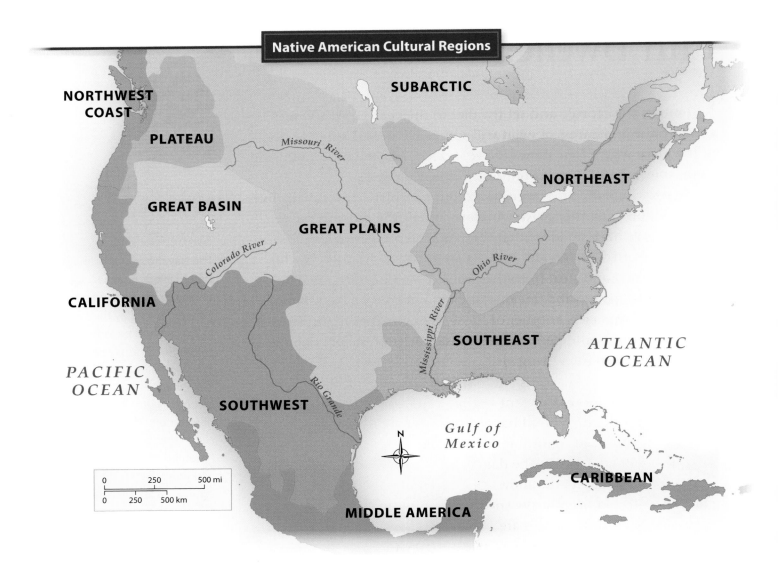

Native American Cultural Regions

NORTHWEST COAST

SUBARCTIC

PLATEAU

Missouri River

GREAT BASIN

NORTHEAST

Colorado River

GREAT PLAINS

CALIFORNIA

Ohio River

PACIFIC OCEAN

Mississippi River

SOUTHEAST

ATLANTIC OCEAN

SOUTHWEST

Rio Grande

N

Gulf of Mexico

CARIBBEAN

MIDDLE AMERICA

| 0 | 250 | 500 mi |
| 0 | 250 | 500 km |

▲ By C.E. 1400, millions of people lived in North America. The geography and climate of the places they settled influenced their ways of life. We divide the hundreds of North American tribes into 12 cultural regions based on the geographic and cultural traits they shared.

The Anasazi are just one of the peoples of the ancient Southwest. The Hohokam, Hakataya, and Mogollon are others. We think the Anasazi's modern descendants are Pueblo peoples like the Tiwa, Zuñi (ZOO-nyi), and Hopi. Some people now call the Anasazi "Ancestral Puebloans," to emphasize their connection to the modern Pueblo peoples.

Imagine you're an Indian boy, not quite a year old. Your mother is carrying you to the fields. You are strapped to a board on her back. Hold still or this could be a real cliff-hanger. (Being strapped to that board will make the back of your head flat. The Anasazi see that as a sign of beauty.)

You've just left your home, which is part of a 200-room apartment house built on a natural stone shelf on the side of a steep mountain.

To get to the cornfields, where she will work, your mother has to go the rest of the way up the mountain—straight up—by pulling herself from one toehold to another. Don't look down: the canyon floor is 700 feet below. (Imagine looking down from the roof of a 70-story building—you would be looking down about 700 feet.)

Usually your mother stays home, takes care of you, cooks, cleans the house, and makes pots out of snake-shaped coils of clay. She uses the sharp leaf of the yucca plant to paint black designs on the white pottery. But at harvest everyone is needed to help gather the corn, squash, and beans that grow on the flat top of the table-like mountain.

This year the skies have been generous with rain. A manmade reservoir is filled with water. The corn is heavy. Soon you will see your first harvest dances: creatures wearing painted masks will jump and dance to the pounding of drums. You will tremble and maybe scream when you see the eagles, wolves, and ferocious giants. You will smile at the dancing corn maidens and butterflies and laugh at the painted clowns. The ceremony is meant to thank the gods for the harvest and to prepare for the hunts and harvests to come. (Only when you are grown will you learn that these dancers are people of the community. Then you will take part in the dance, too.)

You Anasazi are like swallows nesting in the hollow of a hill; you are protected from heavy snows and from human enemies, too. But the stones are damp and the apartments cramped. As soon as you are grown, you will begin to feel the pains and aches of arthritis; you will die before you are 40. (Centuries from now, scientists will study your bones and learn these things.)

Still, it is a splendid home. The mountain site faces south and catches the sun's rays. In winter, with a roaring fire on the town's flat plaza and fires in each house, you are warm even on snowy days.

▲ Southwest cultural region

The Anasazi weren't the only people who died at what we consider an early age. The average lifespan in England or Spain in the 13th century wasn't much longer. People often died from common diseases, or malnutrition, or just by getting caught in a war.

The Anasazi painted black designs on their white pottery. ▶

These are new buildings you live in. Your parents were born in a village on top of the table mountain, a village with fine houses and lookout towers. Your people have lived in this region for hundreds of years. Why has everyone moved to the side of the mountain? (Perhaps you can leave a clue; future generations will want to know the answer to that question.)

It must have been very hard to build these rooms where they are. Building materials had to be carried up, or down, the steep side of the mountain. Your apartment house is a marvel of architecture. It has walls built of heavy stones, held together with thick clay. There are towers too, and many *kivas*. The kivas are round rooms dug into the ground. Men gather inside the kivas to make laws, to discuss problems, to hold religious ceremonies, and perhaps just to have a good time. Sometimes there are games on the roof of the kiva.

Anasazi men would gather in the kivas, round rooms dug into the ground. ▼

Before you leave your teens, a girl will sit in front of your door for four days grinding corn. If she grinds well, and pleases you and your parents, you will marry her. As a wedding gift you will weave yucca fibers into a pair of sandals and put them on her feet. Your parents will give the two of you a blanket of turkey feathers.

But right now your father is waiting for you on top of the mountain. Like most of his friends, he is a farmer. This is a sharing community, and deeply religious. There is no freedom to hold different religious views here—but there is tradition and order and harmony. The priests are the most important people in your town, but day-to-day affairs are run by a council of town leaders. Your father is a member of the all-male council. Of course, you are too young to understand all that, but you are not too young to love music. Your father has a flute, made from a reed, and he plays it sweetly. He is also a good ball-player, and in a few years you will be able to play ball games with him.

Your name is Swift Deer. Your parents hope you will become a fast runner. There are no horses in this land, no animals to ride, so runners are important. But you may surprise your parents and become a mighty hunter and chase and kill rabbits, pronghorn, deer, and elk.

Maybe you will become a trader and travel to a great city in far-off Mexico (where your ancestors first learned about maize). Perhaps you will bring shells home from the western sea. Or will you be a runner after all and take messages to Chaco Canyon? There your Anasazi cousins have built a 2,000-room complex of apartments and official buildings with avenues, like wheel spokes, leading to outlying villages.

Maize (say "maze") is corn.

Is it imagination and artistry that have caused your people to build a great city in a cliff? Or is it a need to feel safe? Can you imagine anyone trying to attack a cliff?

But your cliff home does not keep you safe from drought. In the year 1276, when you are a grown man and a father yourself, terrible times begin. For the next 24 years there will be little or no rain. Your people did not practice conservation during the good years. Many trees were cut and now there is not enough wood for fires. The land has been overplanted, which means that the nutrients in the earth that feed the crops have been used up; harvests begin to shrink. You and your friends go hungry. By the year 1300, when you are in your grave, the cliff will be empty of people.

A *drought* is a long spell of dry weather. It's pronounced DROWT and rhymes with out. We know about the drought in 1276 because scientists have studied tree rings in the area: a wide ring means much moisture, a narrow ring means little.

An artist's reconstruction of Pueblo Bonito, which was located in what is now northern New Mexico. ▶

This pueblo dwelling is located near what is now Taos, New Mexico. The ladder provides access to entrances on the upper levels. ▼

Your children and grandchildren will go south to the great river that will be called "Rio Grande." They will build small villages and live in homes made of clay that is strengthened with sticks and brush.

These clay-plastered villages are called "pueblos" (PWEB-lowz). The sun-dried clay mud is called "adobe" (uh-DOE-bee). A flat-topped mountain is called a "mesa" (MAY-suh). *Mesa Verde* (VAIR-day) means "green table mountain." Those are all Spanish words. (Keep reading this book, and you'll find out how the Indians met the Spaniards.)

To see a pueblo in your mind, imagine rectangular rooms made of clay. On top of one is a smaller room set back a bit, then another on top of that, and another. Picture stairs. The roof of one house is the foundation and front yard of the house above. There are no doors on the ground floor of the houses. To enter you must climb a ladder and go through a hole in the roof. When enemies approach, the ladders can be raised. Put a lot of the houses together, like town houses, and you get the idea of a pueblo village. It is an efficient way to build.

The Southwest is a hard place to grow crops; it is too hot and too dry. Yet Pueblo Indians, more than any other Native Americans, depend on farming. Those who live near the river irrigate their fields with carefully constructed ditches that bring water from the river. Usually they survive dry times, but in the desert region it is never easy.

The Show-Offs

In case you forgot, you're still in that time-and-space capsule, but you're not a baby anymore. You're 10 years old and able to work the controls yourself. So get going; we want to head northwest, to the very edge of the land, to the region that will be the states of Washington and Oregon. The time? We were in the 13th century; let's try the 14th century for this visit.

Life is easy for the Indians here in the Northwest, near the great ocean. They are affluent (AF-flew-ent—it means "wealthy") Americans. For them the world is bountiful: the rivers hold salmon and sturgeon; the ocean is full of seals, whales, fish, and shellfish; the woods are swarming with game animals. And there are berries and nuts and wild roots to be gathered. They are not farmers. They don't need to farm.

These Americans go to sea in giant canoes; some are 60 feet long. (How long is your bedroom?) Using stone tools and fire, Indians of the Northwest Coast cut down gigantic fir trees and hollow out the logs to make their boats. The trees tower 200 feet and are 10 feet across at the base. There are so many of them, so close together, with a tangle of undergrowth, that it is sometimes hard for hunters to get through the forest. Tall as these trees are, they are not as big as the redwoods that grow in a vast forest to the south (in the land that will be California).

These Native Americans carve animal and human figures on tall fir poles, called "totem poles." The poles are painted and are symbols of a family's power and rank. The Indians' totem poles are colorful but rough; finer poles will be carved after the Europeans come and bring metal knives.

> The names of some of the Northwest tribes are Kwakiutl, Tsimshian, Tlingit, Nootka, Chinook, Makah, Haida, Okanagon, Spokane, Quinault, Kalapuya, Kalispel, and Shuswap.

This modern totem pole continues a long tradition of displaying symbols of family power and rank. ▶

Taut means tight. It rhymes with "caught."

▲ Northwest Coast cultural region

The word *potlatch* is from a Nootka word, *patshatl*—"giving." Perhaps members of the Haida clans gave away things as beautiful and costly as this Chilkat blanket. ▼

Because food and wood are so easy to gather, the Northwest Indians have much leisure time. Their lives are full of playacting, dancing, and singing. In times of celebration, relatives and friends come from far villages. They beat drums made of animal skins that have been heated near a fire and then stretched taut across a frame of birch. These people of the coastal forests gather in circles and dance and sing of the fish and animals they will hunt. They also sing of their ancestors, and of their fears and hopes, and they pray to the animals for forgiveness and for good luck in the hunt. Sometimes they have wrestling contests. Often they wrestle just for fun. Sometimes the best wrestler gets to marry a special girl.

Many Indians elsewhere in North America live in communities where almost everything is shared—sometimes even leadership. That is not true here. These Indians care about wealth, property, and prestige (press-TEEJ—it means "importance and reputation"). They value private property, and they pass their property on to their children and grandchildren. They own slaves and sometimes go to war with other Indians just to capture slaves. People are not treated as equals in this society. They are divided into ranks, or classes. There are slaves, commoners, and nobles. In times of strife, many of the men become warriors and wear wooden helmets and wood slat armor.

These Indians of the Northwest Coast like to pile up their goods and show off. They have good taste. They weave handsome blankets, make beautiful baskets, carve fancy wooden bowls, and fashion spoons of decorated animal horn. Their dress-up clothes are gorgeous. Their houses are spectacular. Sometimes several families live together in a large house built of wooden planks with carved and painted walls and posts.

They take pride in other possessions, too—in furs, copper shields, and fancy hats.

These Indians are big party givers. Sometimes they spend years planning fabulous parties called "potlatches." There is much feasting at a potlatch. The party may go on

▲ Guests arrive by canoe for a potlatch, an extravagant party that ends with the host giving away his finest possessions.

for days. Then the host gives away his finest possessions; sometimes he gives away everything he has.

Have you heard of people spending years planning a wedding? Do you know of people who spend more money on a party than they can really afford? Perhaps these Indians are just vain and boastful, like other people in other times and places. Perhaps there is an important reason for the potlatch.

Some of the guests at the potlatch will plan their own parties and try to make them bigger and give away more things. The bigger the party and the more that is given—or sometimes even thrown away— the more prestige the giver has.

Was the potlatch a way to gain power? Or to show off? Or something else? No one really knows.

Life on the Northwest Coast

◄ A Bella Coola mask

The Bella Coola used masks for ceremonies where they danced to honor their gods. Some of the masks have movable parts, some have masks within masks. The Bella Coola are Nuxalk people who live on a beautiful river high in the Rocky Mountains in British Columbia, Canada.

This Haida village looks rundown, but in its 19th-century heyday it must have been splendid. The Haida were known for their fishing skills, for their potlatches, and for their warring nature. If you were captured by a Haida tribe you were likely to become a slave.

▲ A Haida village

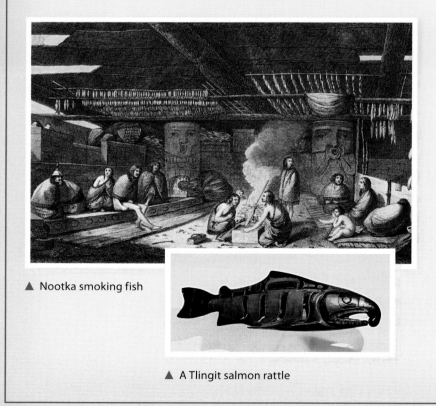

▲ Nootka smoking fish

▲ A Tlingit salmon rattle

These Nootka, from the Pacific Northwest, are smoking fish. Of course they ate salmon (everyone did) but not everyone could hunt whales. The Nootka did, and moved seasonally following their prey. They lived in long wooden houses, carved elaborate totem poles, participated in ceremonial dances, and celebrated with potlatches. See if you can find Nootka Sound on a map; it was a center of the worldwide fur trade.

The Tlingit are Native Americans who live in Canada and Alaska. When the first Europeans met them they were astounded by their beautiful wooden homes and canoes. This carved object in the shape of a salmon makes a rattling sound.

CHAPTER 6

Taking a Tour

In this chapter we're going to move in time and space. You'll be busy working the controls of the capsule. So get ready. We need to take a spin around this land to see the big picture. Remember, we were at Mesa Verde in the 13th century and in the Pacific Northwest in the 14th, so let's try the 15th century for this trip across the continent.

It will help if you are good at learning languages, because the Indians living in North America speak at least 250 different languages. That's a big problem. The tribes often don't get along well because they don't understand each other. (Do you think that happens with nations today?) Don't look for a typical Indian; there is no such thing. Indians live differently in different environments.

> A *tribe* is a community, sometimes of several villages, all sharing a common ancestry. A *people* is a larger group, often including several tribes, all speaking the same language.

A satellite-image map offers a big picture of North America. ▼

Some redwoods in the forests of the West Coast are as tall as 300 feet. ▶

Take us up high over the continent. Are you looking down? Does what you see look a little like the maps in your schoolbooks?

No? You're right, it is much prettier.

Start over there, on the West Coast, where we just left a tribe having a potlatch. Then you can head south, along the foggy coast. Notice the sandy beaches and the rocky cliffs that drop right down into the ocean. Watch out! Don't fly too low or those redwood trees will scrape the bottom of this space vehicle. Some of them are 300 feet tall. If you look carefully, you will see tiny orange-and-blue specks at the feet of those giants. The specks are tiger lilies and iris, and they thrive in the moist soil under the towering trees.

We are still on a course south and heading into the sunshine of the land that will someday be California. It is a land of plenty. Look below. Most of those California Indians you see are easygoing, gentle people. Some tribes have lived here for thousands of years. The women weave colorful designs into watertight baskets and then use the baskets to gather acorns.

Native Americans were the world's most productive farmers. They developed many of the major food crops eaten worldwide today. Cotton was first raised by Americans. And—this is not so good—American farmers domesticated tobacco and coca (the source of cocaine).

Early Americans process cotton. ▼

The acorns are ground into meal that makes nourishing bread. There are many different peoples in this region speaking many different languages. Mostly, the tribes live peacefully with each other. The trade routes between the villages are well worn. Because food is plentiful, these people have much time for games, music, storytelling, and religious festivals.

Look at the steam coming from that building! Is it a health club? Inside, men sit and sweat. Soon they will dive into a cool stream to bathe. The steam huts are something like the kivas we saw in the land of the Anasazi: they are both social halls and spiritual centers.

Now put the capsule on a course east. That flat land, spreading back from the coast, will someday make fine farmland. Even from here, way up, we can see wildflowers—fields of orange poppies, purple thistles, and flowering mustard the color of canaries. You may have to zoom close to see how rugged the mountains are. Wait until the pioneers try to cross those snow-coated California mountains with their covered wagons! They will need ropes to pull the wagons up one side and ropes to lower them down the other side. They are formidable peaks—steep, rocky, and hard to climb.

The desert, which we are now approaching, isn't easy to cross either. Notice the cactus: its red and gold flowers match the reds and golds of the desert sun. Indians eat the giant cactus and often rest in its shade, but if anyone makes the mistake of leaning against a cactus—ouch!—he'll never do it again.

You can slow down a bit to see the soaring Rocky Mountains. Pull up, high, so we get a look at the two continents. Can you see

▲ These giant cactus plants can be both useful and troublesome for desert travelers.

Snowy Range

The Spanish were the first Europeans to arrive in California. So it's not surprising that a lot of place names around California are Spanish. Those snowy mountains are called the "*Sierra Nevada.*" In Spanish, sierra means "range"; what do you think Nevada means? (The state of Nevada was named after these mountains—but, unlike them, the state is mostly desert, hot and dry.)

This rugged peak in Montana is part of the Rocky Mountains, which stretch from Canada down to the tip of South America. ▼

that the Rockies are part of a backbone that runs from Canada all the way down to the tip of South America? Those Rocky Mountains are the rooftop of this continent. But a flat area—called the Wyoming Basin—cuts through them. People on foot will find that path and follow it. So will animals.

The mountains are teeming with life: with tiny shrews, soaring falcons, fat grizzly bears, lordly elk, hardworking beavers, and nimble mountain goats. And talk about wildflowers! We'd better not.

So on we go, over the windy high plains—full of gophers and buffalo and noisy magpies—until we reach the flat lowland in the middle of the country.

Once all this was a shallow inland sea, but that was long, long, long ago. Slowly the sea disappeared, a tropical forest rose on the land, and dinosaurs played in the mud. Then, still slowly, the land grew cold. Ice blankets thousands of feet thick pushed south from Canada, leveling this middle land. When those glaciers melted, they left thick, rich soil where prairie grass began to grow. Can you see the grass? Well, if you were on the ground you wouldn't be able to see over it; most of it is higher than your head.

A field of grain on the wide open American prairie ▼

▲ The mighty Mississippi, which in the Ojibwa language means "big river"

Let's go on, over the broad river the Native Americans call Mississippi (which means "big river" in the language of the Ojibwa tribes). Some Indians call the Mississippi the "Father of Waters." It is the largest river in North America. Mississippi is easy to spell. Just say out loud: *M, I, double S, I, double S, I, double P, I.*

Did you ever before see a river from up high? Notice that it looks like a tree, with a fat trunk and many branches. A tree grows from its roots toward its top, but a river flows from its tiniest branches down to its base. The Mississippi has two huge branches: one, the Missouri River, flows from the west, the other—the Ohio River—flows from the east. Someday a big city, called St. Louis, will be built near where the branches come together. The M-I-double-S-I-double S-I-double-P-I splits the land in two—but not in half. The western part is twice as big as the eastern part.

Up there in the northland, near where the Father of Waters begins (it is called its "source"), it looks as if someone spilled five buckets of shining blue paint. Those five blue puddles are lakes— enormous lakes. If you were a fish swimming in the middle of one of them, you would think you were in an ocean. That is how large they seem. They are called Great Lakes, and that is what they are. (All are Indian names, except the largest. What does its name mean?)

We haven't finished this trip. We're still heading east, over rolling land and rivers, over the

What's in a Name?

The Missouri River is named after the Siouan (soo-un) tribe that lived along its banks. But Missouri is not a Siouan word. How did that happen? The Illinois, an Algonquian tribe, called the Sioux "owners of big canoes." The word for that, in their language, was Missouri (or something close to it).

A satellite image of the Great Lakes ▼

ancient Appalachian Mountains, over trees that are 1,000 years old and seem to hold the sky in their branches. From the Mississippi east to the ocean, much of the land is covered with a carpet of trees.

And those trees, right now, with the first chill of fall, are like an artist's palette filled with brilliant reds and yellows and golds. Traveling across the land we have seen natural wonders: towering redwood trees, snow-topped mountain peaks, awesome stone spires in the desert, crashing waterfalls—but nothing is more remarkable than this wondrous display of seasonal color. Here the sky is so full of birds—thousands and thousands of them in flocks that stretch for miles, all heading south to their winter homes—that you need to watch the capsule or you could have a collision.

On we go. Now that we have cleared the Appalachians, there are smaller hills, called foothills, then rich, flat land dotted with Indian

In eastern North America, the Appalachian Mountains extend from southern Quebec to northern Alabama. ▼

▲ On the mid-Atlantic coast, low marshlands characterize the Chesapeake Bay area.

farms, and then low coastal lands with swamps and marshes where water rises and falls with the ocean tides until, finally, we reach the ocean itself, and the beaches it licks. Here, on the mid-Atlantic coast, a Chesapeake Indian girl and boy pick delicate sassafras plants. Their parents will brew the roots into a healing, pungent tea. Bright red berries dot the glossy green leaves of holly bushes here, and perfumed blossoms fill the branches of the shiny-leafed magnolia trees. (The boy picks one of those big, creamy blossoms and puts it on his sister's head; it fits like a cap.)

Here, by the sea, the aromatic leaf of the bay tree is prized for the flavor it brings to meat stews. Here wild roses flower and long-necked white cranes pick crabs from the shore waters. Someday, when sailors come from Europe, they will tell of smelling the fragrant land before they see it. What a place this is, and how fortunate are the people who live here!

Southeastern Native Americans prepare for a feast. ▼

Plains Indians Are Not Plain At All

The very center of the North American continent (that's not the same as the center of the United States!) is at Rugby, North Dakota.

Some of the Plains tribes are the Comanche, Sioux, Omaha, Arapaho, Kansa, Iowa, Missouri, Cree, Osage, Cheyenne, Wichita, Crow, Ojibwa, Blackfoot, and Mandan.

Remember how the First Americans found a hunter's paradise in North America? Then the climate changed. Many animals, like the mammoth, became extinct. Much of the land dried up. Life became hard for the people who were hunters. They had to adapt, to change their ways. They had to hunt new animals, gather new foods, and learn to plant crops.

Let's zoom back to the center of the continent. It is the year 1000. If you look out the window, you can see people gathering nuts and grasses and berries. It is summer and the sun is shining on the flat plains that make a wide ribbon across America. That ribbon stretches from Canada south to Texas, and from the Rocky Mountains east to the woodlands near the Mississippi River. Mostly it is windy land, and dry, with extremes of heat and cold. If we get out and stand for a while, you'll see for yourself the vast, open landscape. Wherever you look, the sky touches the earth, and neither mountains nor forests block your view.

The people here live in a region with blizzards, tornadoes, icy cold, blistering heat, droughts, floods, and sometimes nice, balmy days—like this one. Some of the Plains land is prairie. Tall grasses grow on the prairie, and animals feed and hide in the grass. In some places, rivers web through the Plains. Where there are rivers there are trees and, often, Indian farms. But much of this land has only scruffy growth. There are few trees. Farming is difficult.

Most of the people we see are nomads who keep on the move following the trail of the animals. It isn't easy, hunting on foot. These Plains Indians use their brains and their courage and stampede animals into traps. They use bows and arrows. All that helps, but not enough. These are among the poorest and hungriest of the Native Americans.

Some live in tepees made of animal skins. It is the job of the Indian woman to put up and take down the tepee. She can do it in about an hour. If you watch, you'll see that in summer some tribes move almost every day.

▲ Great Plains cultural region

A bow and arrows used by Plains Indians ▼

▲ The Plains Indians knew how to stampede animals, such as buffalo, into traps.

Mostly they hunt buffalo. Buffaloes are fine for hunting for three reasons: they are good to eat and rich in protein; there are millions of them, perhaps 100 million in North America. Buffalo are not smart animals. That helps the men who hunt them.

While you are controlling the capsule, how about zooming ahead to the 16th century? Do you see those men down there, right where Dorothy and Toto will live one day? (That's Kansas, of course!) They are Spaniards. One of them, who travels with an explorer named Coronado, keeps a journal. In the journal he describes what the Indians of the Plains do with a buffalo after they finish eating the meat.

Some people actually think that all Indians used to live in tents (called "tepees"). You know that isn't true. Some did live in tepees, but others lived in ice houses or wood houses or clay houses—or houses of thatched grass, like this in a Wichita village in the plains. ▶

Sinews are tendons—tough, elastic strings—that connect muscle to bone. Animals have sinews, and so do we.

Awls are small tools for making holes in leather.

Dung is animal droppings.

The best Indian knives are made of a dark volcanic glass called "obsidian." They are sharper than steel knives and keep their edges longer. But in the 16th century, Indians want white men's knives. Steel knives glisten; they are new, they are different, and they seem better.

Hunting on horseback— horses allowed Indians to hunt, travel, and make war more efficiently. ▶

With the skins they build their houses; with the skins they clothe and shoe themselves; from the skins they make ropes and also obtain wool. With the sinews they make threads, with which they sew their clothes and also their tents. From the bones they shape awls. The dung they use for firewood, since there is no other fuel in that land. The bladders they use as jugs and drinking containers.

From your capsule, you can see the pale-skinned men trading with the darker-skinned men. They give the Indians horses and knives. Soon those Indians will not be poor anymore. Horses will change their lives. (Think about facing a herd of buffalo on foot!) They will be able to gallop across the plains. They will hunt more efficiently. (They will also make war more efficiently.) They will travel great distances and trade with faraway peoples. They will feel free—and powerful.

Now, how about setting the controls for the 18th century? See those handsome Indians on horseback with feathered headdresses? They are Plains Indians. Some are people of the old tribes, and some are newcomers who have moved from the eastern woods. They have created a great, new Indian culture full of ceremonies, dances, horsemanship, costumes, warfare, and elegant crafts.

▲ The artist George Catlin painted Native American life as he saw it in the 19th century. Here he shows Indians hunting buffalo. That's Catlin (on the right) and an Indian friend camouflaged in animals' skins. It was one way Native Americans were able to sneak up on the buffalo before they had horses.

▲ Indians used buffalo and other hides to record their stories. This 19th-century Shoshone painting on elk skin depicts a buffalo hunt.

With horses and rifles (they trade buffalo skins for guns) these Plains Indians hunt and kill large numbers of animals. No longer do they have to use every part of the animal; they have become wasteful.

Now that they can hunt so effectively, they farm less. Do you see those huge herds down there? Buffalo—millions and millions of them—stretch for miles across the level land. The Plains Indians depend on the buffalo for food and clothing. It is hard to believe, but by the end of the next century, the 19th, the buffalo will be almost extinct. And the Plains Indians will be in trouble, too.

Put your mind on the navigation controls, because we're going to zip around in time and space. Set the time back to the beginning of the 11th century. We're heading east, to the woods that stretch from the Mississippi River to the Atlantic Ocean, home of the Woodland Indians.

Mound for Mound, Those Are Heavy Hills

Great Snakes

The Serpent Mound in Ohio was one of the United States' first-ever conservation projects. It was discovered in the 19th century, just before the Civil War (do you know when that was?). A tornado mowed down the forest that had kept the mound hidden. Farmers wanted to plow it up. Some society ladies in Boston wrote about the danger the snake was in; people sent money to help save the mound as a national monument.

Do you see the Mississippi down there? Now look up, down, around the river, and way to the east—to the mountains and even beyond. We're going to check out Mound Building Indians, and this is the region where they live. These First Americans have fine cities, well-organized governments, beautiful art objects, and successful businesses. It is their mounds, however, that you may never forget.

Mounds? Yes. Imagine thousands and thousands of Indians carrying baskets of dirt and dumping them to make hills. Skillfully shaped dirt mounds were all over the place when Europeans and Africans arrived in America—hundreds of thousands of dirt mounds.

What were the mounds for? Some mounds were graves. These Indians made a big ceremony of death, just as the ancient Egyptians did. (The pyramids in Egypt are burial mounds.) But some Indian mounds were used as platforms for temples and leaders' palaces, and some may have been religious symbols.

If we fly into the present time—right now—near Cincinnati, Ohio, we can see a huge curving snake. It is an earth mound that coils for a quarter of a mile. Amazing, isn't it? It may be more than 2,000 years old. What is the purpose of the snake? Or of a mound shaped like a turtle? Or of some of the other animal mounds? No one today is quite sure. Perhaps someone in your generation will figure it out.

We know quite a bit about some Mound Builders because of a 19th-century farmer named M. C. Hopewell. Hopewell found 30 mounds on his farm in Ohio. He had archaeologists (ar-kee-OLL-uh-jists) dig

◀ A ceramic head made by mound-building people of the Mississippi

▲ The great snake of the Serpent Mound is over 1,300 feet long. The snake was built by people of the Adena culture.

▲ A figurine made by the builders of Serpent Mound

carefully into them. Archaeologists are scientists who are trained diggers. From pieces of pots and bones and throwaway things they can tell a lot about the past. Historians would be lost without archaeologists.

The archaeologists on the Hopewell farm found more than just old pots and bones. They found copper, pearls, shells, mica, soapstone, and obsidian. They found teeth from sharks and teeth from grizzly bears. Most of these things had come from far away: the shells from the Atlantic coast, the obsidian from the Far West, the copper from mines near Lake Superior. So we know the Mound Builders were great traders; we think they used a kind of relay system to get goods to and from distant places.

Now let's fly in our capsule, through a thousand years of time, to the year 1000, until we reach the Indian city of Cahokia (kah-HO-kee-ah). We are near three great rivers: the Mississippi, the Missouri, and the Illinois. This is a marvelous spot for a trading people to place a city. (Someday a city named St. Louis will sit across the Mississippi from here.)

Do you see the mounds? One Cahokian mound is as tall as a 10-story building. Its base is broader than that of any of the pyramids in Egypt. The mounds look like flat-topped pyramids with temples and public buildings and statues on their summits. All those people in the streets are going to markets and schools and businesses.

◀ This mica ornament in the shape of a bird claw comes from the mound-building Hopewell people.

Cahokia covers six square miles. About 25,000 people live here; another 25,000 people live in nearby villages.

Cahokia isn't a democracy; it is a slave society with a powerful ruler who is called the "Great Sun." He is thought to be the earthly brother of the heavenly sun.

Cahokia was big and thriving, and then something happened. It disappeared as a great city. Why?

Some experts think it may have grown too large. They say the inhabitants may have destroyed the nearby forests to get firewood, and without wood, their city couldn't survive. Maybe the sanitary system wasn't good and people got sick. Perhaps enemies attacked. Perhaps the people got tired of the slave society. No one knows for sure.

The Mound Builders' snakes and bears are not the only things of their kind. Other peoples have drawn or dug enormous pictures or monuments on the earth. Such designs can be seen fully only from up in an airplane. Why do you think people would make designs that they could never see properly themselves?

◀ An artist's reconstruction of what the city of Cahokia might have looked like a thousand years ago

Indians of the Eastern Forests

▲ Northeast cultural region

We're still zooming around in that time when the Native Americans shared two continents with no one but animals. We're flying low—between the Atlantic Ocean and the Mississippi River—and looking down at a sea of treetops. So thick are the trees that a squirrel might go from the Atlantic Ocean to the Ohio River and even beyond—jumping from tree to tree—and never touch the ground.

It is a fine place to be a squirrel, and not a bad place for humans either. The woods are filled with good food for animals and people. Passenger pigeons fly in formations so dense they darken the sky. When a flock lands, its weight bends trees low and men reach up and grab birds for their dinner. They are a treat, these passenger pigeons, sweet and juicy, and so abundant that the men net them and waste them. How can they know that someday the pigeons will be extinct and that most of the great trees will also be gone?

Some of these trees measure 30 feet around. Look at your belt. Now imagine a rope 30 feet long. Make it into a belt, and you get an idea of how big the trees are.

If we land the capsule and take a walk in the woods, you'll see that the Indians have cleared away the brush with fire, so the forest—with only tall trees and high grass—seems like a cool, sun-speckled park.

The openness of the forest, and the tenderness of the grass, make it inviting to animals. The woods are filled with beaver, deer, raccoon, possum, and bear. The hunters have an easy time of it. See? Over there? A hunter is wearing deer's antlers on his head. He walks softly in deerskin moccasins, pretending to be a deer himself. He is teaching a boy some tricks with the bow and arrow. The boy is his son, and they will have a good day and drag a heavy deer home with them.

They are Woodland Indians, as are all the Indians of this region; some are grandchildren of the great Mound Builders. They have heard stories of a glorious past, of temples and pyramids. But now the tribes are small and so are their mounds. Still, life is good. The men hunt in the woods and fish in the streams. The women who wait for them at home are farmers who grow corn and beans, squash and pumpkins.

The Woodland Indians knew how to combine foods in nutritious ways. Beans, corn, and squash give more protein when they're eaten together than by themselves. So these forest Indians invented the dish of mixed vegetables that is still called by its Algonquian name—*succotash*.

Some Europeans who came to America in the 1500s and 1600s painted Indian ways of life. Artists like Englishman John White and Frenchman Jacques LeMoyne are important because their pictures show how Indians lived before foreigners changed things forever. LeMoyne made this picture of deer hunters in the late 16th century. Do you think the deer were fooled by the men under the deerskins?

The women and children gather wild grapes, pick nuts from the trees, and sometimes dig clams on the beaches.

Our hunter's wife, who is mother to the boy, is the best cook in their village. She knows 40 different ways of cooking corn. She will stew the deer meat and season it with the vegetables she grows.

The men have cleared trees so the village can sit in the sunshine with open fields for growing crops. They get rid of trees by "girdling" them. That means they cut the bark all the way around the trunk. That kills the tree, although it takes some time for it to die. When it happens, the tree falls down and can easily be split for firewood.

Now that our hunter is home, he has taken the antlers from his head. He isn't wearing much else, just a strip of leather that goes between his legs and hangs, front and back, from a belt. In winter the hunter will add a shirt and leggings—both fashioned from animal skins. On special occasions he will bedeck himself in a fancy robe of turkey feathers. His wife wears a wraparound skirt made of deerskin.

Slash-and-Burn

The Woodland Indians practiced a kind of farming called "slash-and-burn." First they cleared the trees from a piece of land. Then they burned the branches and leaves, and hoed the ash into the ground to fertilize it. Here is a description, written at the time (in the late 1500s):

▲ Indians cultivate their cleared land.

The Indians till the soil very diligently, using a kind of hoe made from fish bone fitted to wooden handles. Since the soil is very light, these serve well enough to cultivate it.

After the ground has been well broken up and leveled, the planting is done by the women, some making holes with sticks, into which the others drop seeds of beans or maize.

His son, who is the oldest child, dresses as his father does. What do the small children wear? Why, nothing at all. (In winter, too? Of course not!)

These people, who live in the warm South, are like people everywhere: they care about the way they look. Their clothing may be simple, but their makeup and jewelry are elaborate. Tattooed designs cover most of their bodies. Today our hunter will paint himself with bright colors to celebrate the hunt. He makes his skin glisten by rubbing it with bear fat. Because he is handsome and a bit vain, he will blacken his teeth with tobacco ash. It is the fashion.

He grooms his hair carefully. People across the world are inventive with hair, and the First Americans are no different. Our hunter shaves his head with a sharp shell, leaving an island of hair on top to which he ties feathers. He leaves another island over one ear and makes a thin braid with those hairs.

The hunter wears strings of pearls around his neck. His bracelet is of polished deer ribs that were bent and shaped in boiling water.

He and his family live in a one-room house made of narrow tree limbs lashed together with vines and covered with bark. It is called a "wigwam." The house has a round roof thatched with strong reeds. It is similar to the other hundred homes all clustered around a central square. Do you see those children turning cartwheels down the village street? And the others playing a game of ball? It would be fun to stay and watch the game, but we need to head north.

From the capsule we can see Indian villages dotting the forests and coastal lands. Most of them belong to Indians who—like our hunter and his family—speak Algonquian (al-GON-kwee-un) languages. That doesn't mean all these villagers speak the same language. It means their languages are related—and most of their customs, too. Many of the Algonquian tribes trade with each other and are friends.

They have enemies who speak a different language. The Algonquians call them "terrible people," or "frightening people," or sometimes "rattlesnake people." In the Algonquian languages the name of those enemies is Iroquois (EAR-uh-kwoy).

They are unusual, these "terrible" people. They believe in peace and brotherhood, but when they fight they are fierce and cruel. Their name for themselves is Haudenosaunee (ho-dih-no-SHAW-nee),

The Abenaki, Ojibwa, Mahican, Massachuset, Narraganset, Powhatan, Blackfoot, Delaware, and Cree are a few Algonquian-speaking tribes.

We're going to use the name *Iroquois* for the Haudenosaunee—it is the name most used today. Remember, names can get chosen for the wrong reasons—then they stick. *Iroquois* has become a name the Haudenosaunee use proudly.

▲ Among the Iroquois, extended families lived in dwellings aptly called longhouses.

▲ Longhouses could measure over 150 feet.

which means "people of the longhouse." It is a descriptive name. Their houses are long, sometimes 150 feet long—sometimes longer. The longest—said to be 334 feet long, even longer than a football field—was built by men of the Onondaga tribe.

Do you see that longhouse above? Twenty families live there. Actually, they are all one big family headed by a grandmother, with brothers, sisters, aunts, uncles, cousins, and other relatives. (No one ever has to hire a babysitter.)

The Iroquois have formed a league of Indian nations and wish to bring the Algonquians and other Indians into that league. They say it is a league of peace. The Algonquians want no part of the league. They do not want an Iroquois peace. They don't want anything to do with their ancient enemies.

The Iroquois have no written language; that doesn't mean they have no history or government or records. Chiefs called "sachems" (SAY-chums), and other leaders of memory and wisdom, are keepers

The original nations of the Iroquois League were the Mohawk, Cayuga, Seneca, Oneida, and Onondaga. A sixth, the Tuscarora, joined the confederacy in 1722 when they were driven from North Carolina by white settlers. The Iroquois were not the only Indians to form a league. The Huron did, and in the south, the "C" nations—Creek, Choctaw, Cherokee, Chickasaw—had an ancient bond.

▲ An Iroquois wampum belt

of the people's past. They have a memory aid—a kind of picture writing—done with thousands of tiny shell beads. The beads, called "wampum," are strung on cords and woven into designs. Often they are sewed on deerskin belts. Wampum is valuable and is sometimes used as money. The designs tell stories. Some record treaties; some tell the history of a clan.

The Iroquois have much history to remember and a remarkable form of government. Here in America, in the 16th century, the Iroquois have fashioned a democratic league of five Indian nations (a sixth will be added) with leaders who are expected to serve the people. It is a confederacy (kon-FED-er-uss-ee), which means each of the nations has its own identity and laws, except in matters of war or common concern. In those cases, a council of all the tribes makes decisions. All this has been organized in a plan of government that has been woven in wampum and memorized by the sachems.

Fifty male sachems, 10 from each nation, sit on the council. The sachems are chosen by women who head family clans. In the Iroquois world, women are much respected. Perhaps that is because the Iroquois depend on their farm crops, and it is the women who do most of the farming. The Algonquian peoples are hunter-gatherers who do some farming. These Iroquois are farmers who do some hunting and gathering. The Iroquois women are excellent farmers.

The Iroquois have a matrilineal (mat-truh-LIN-ee-ul) society. That word begins with a Latin root. The Latin word for "mother" is *mater*. In a matrilineal society your descent is traced through your mother. Iroquois women are leaders of family clans. Our society in America is patrilineal: our names usually (but not always) come from our fathers. (What do you think *pater* means in Latin?)

Let's Turn North

The first Europeans to discover America came from the lands of the north. Called Vikings or Norsemen, they were the terror of Europe. Their ships were fast, their seamen brave and bloodthirsty.

Viking means "sea raider" or "pirate," but not all Vikings were pirates. Most were farmers who kept cattle and sheep. Historians think that during the 9th and 10th centuries their homelands in Scandinavia became crowded, so Vikings set out for other places. Some sailed in search of loot, but others looked for fair lands and good fishing.

Scandinavia is northern Europe: Norway, Sweden, Finland, and Denmark.

Loot is stolen goods, also called "booty."

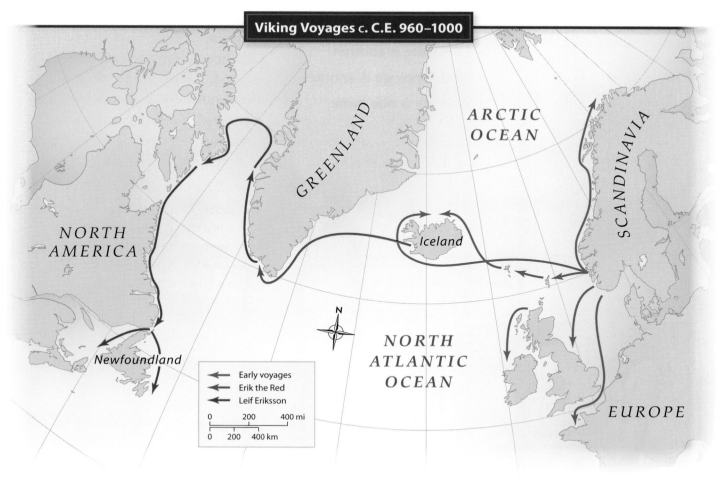

Viking Voyages c. C.E. 960–1000

ARCTIC OCEAN

GREENLAND

SCANDINAVIA

NORTH AMERICA

Iceland

Newfoundland

Early voyages
Erik the Red
Leif Eriksson

0   200   400 mi
0 200 400 km

NORTH ATLANTIC OCEAN

EUROPE

▲ The work of archaeologists and anthropologists has confirmed ancient stories of Viking voyages to North America around C.E. 1000.

Greenland, far to the north between Canada and Europe, is the world's largest island. It is still in the Ice Age. Much of it is covered by a glacier that is two miles thick.

The first Viking ship arrived in America by mistake. A Norse sailor was on his way to Greenland when the wind blew him off course. We think that was in the year 986. He went home and told his people what he had seen. One of his friends, Leif Eriksson, decided to explore the new land. Leif (LEEF) was called "Leif the Lucky" and was the son of Erik the Red, a famous explorer who had discovered Greenland (and had red hair).

Leif landed in a place he named Vinland because it had wild vines. Vinland was probably Newfoundland, which is now part of Canada. (The vines were most likely berry bushes, not grapevines as people once thought.)

How do we know all that? Historians have many ways of finding out about the past. Like detectives, they search for clues. They use tools to help them solve mysteries.

- Archaeology is one tool.

- Literature is another.

- Anthropology is another.

- Zoology is one more.

Vikings landing at the place they named Vinland, which was likely Newfoundland, now part of Canada ▼

◀ A 10th-century depiction of a Viking ship

In 1961 archaeological diggers found a Norse settlement on the northern coast of Newfoundland. It proved that Vikings once lived in America. The archaeologists dug up part of a spindle for spinning wool. Now they knew that women had lived in the settlement. (Why would a spindle tell them that?)

Sometimes archaeologists dig up old bones and bits of pottery. Those bones and the way they are buried can tell us much about the way people lived. We have found mammoth bones together with Indian bones and spearheads in North America, so we know Indians hunted mammoths. So far we have not found Viking bones. Can you guess what old pieces of pottery might tell us?

Literature helps with clues about history. A very old book, *The Saga of the Greenlanders*, relates the story of Leif and his voyages. It gives exact dates. The dates match the archaeologists' findings.

Anthropology (an-thruh-POL-uh-jee) is the study of people and how they develop. Anthropologists study fossils and living people. They study history, languages, and the ways people live. Anthropology is very helpful in understanding the past.

Zoology (zoh-OLL-uh-jee) is the science of animal life. Can that help historians? You bet. When diggers found a strange sea snail in the Viking settlement, they gave it to zoologists to study. The zoologists said the snail was a native of Scandinavia: it had never been found in America before. They believe it must have come over as a hitchhiker in the damp bottom of a Viking ship. It was another clue to prove that the Vikings had been to America.

In the 1960s, archaeologists found the remains of eight Viking houses and four boat sheds at L'Anse aux Meadows on the northeast tip of Newfoundland, Canada. They reburied the original foundations in order to preserve them. Then they built houses of sod and fences of wood to show how the Viking settlement probably looked in the year 1000.

Many historians say that after the days of Leif the Lucky, the Norsemen stopped coming to North America. Other historians think they are wrong. Clues seem to say that the Norsemen kept coming to the new land in order to get furs and timber and fish. Vikings may have settled in New England but no one is quite sure of that either.

Historians, archaeologists, anthropologists, and other scientists still have work to do to solve all the mysteries of the Vikings in America.

▲ A fossilized fish

Fossils are old bones or traces of ancient plants or animals.

A Boy Named Christopher Has a Dream

For most people, before the 15th century, Europe was a place of superstition and poverty. For most it was a place of war and disease.

Then things began to change. In Italy, poets and painters and sculptors began creating new works of art. It was called a Renaissance (REN-uh-sahnce), a time of rebirth. Ideas seemed to be in the air, and inventions, too—like the compass.

Actually, the compass had been around for thousands of years. The ancient Chinese discovered that a magnet, swinging freely, will always point north. Arabs brought that knowledge to Europe. But early compasses were not always reliable. In the 15th century (the years beginning with 14) the compass was improved; it could now be depended upon at sea.

Having a little needle that always pointed north meant new worlds could be discovered. Imagine you're in a small ship in a great ocean. You can't see land—just water in every direction. If you don't have a compass, how do you know which way to go to get home?

Understanding Centuries

Do you know that when you see "12th century" it means the years that begin with 11? The numbers are always 100 years behind the centuries. It's a bit confusing, but once you have it, it's easy. If something happened in 1456, it happened in the 15th century.

Columbus knew all about Marco Polo's travels. This scene, from a Catalan world map drawn in 1375, shows Marco Polo with his father and uncle and their Mongol escorts crossing Asia on horseback. Camels carry their goods. (In the Middle Ages, the Catalans of northern Spain were among the best navigators and geographers of Europe.) ▶

If you know the stars, and most good sailors do, you can wait until nighttime and let the stars guide you. But suppose—just suppose—it's cloudy and stormy. No stars can be seen. Maybe it's cloudy for a week. Your little ship can't carry much food. You might sail in the wrong direction and run out of food before you find your way back—if you get back. Storms at sea are tough to survive. All of which explains why ships stayed close to home before the compass was perfected.

In the 15th century, many Europeans wanted to sail to China and Japan and India because those lands were thought to be the world's most advanced civilizations, and because they held gold and jewels and spices.

Most Europeans were wild to find a way to reach the Indies. (*Indies* was a catchall word for all the lands of East Asia.) And mostly because of a book. The book was by Marco Polo, and it told of his trip to China (back in the 13th century). It told of golden palaces and jewels and wonders beyond imagining. Marco Polo had done some exaggerating—still, a few traders had been to China and brought back silks and spices and tales of splendid cities.

Whoever could find a fast, safe way to get to the Orient (another word for East Asia) would become rich and famous. Everyone agreed about that. But the only way to get there was by land, through Turkey and the Middle East. That route had become dangerous: rival Islamic empires were fighting for control of the region. In addition, there

Gutenberg's Printing Press

In 1456, a German goldsmith named Johannes Gutenberg (GOOT-en-burg) invented an efficient way to use a printing press. He did it with movable type—letters that could be used over and over again. The Koreans and the Chinese had been using movable type for centuries, but Gutenberg reinvented the process and made it usable in Europe. There, before 1456, most books were copied by hand. Gutenberg's printing press helped turn the late 15th century into the first Information Age. Travel and scientific books became best sellers.

An early printing press ▶

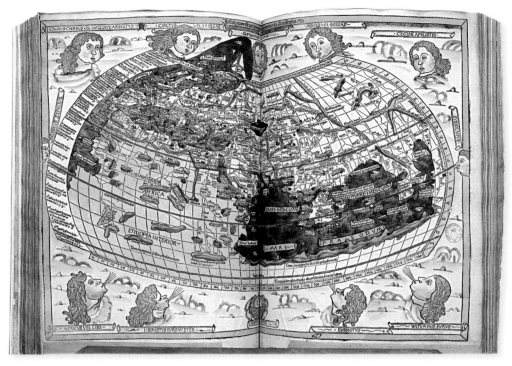

▲ This German map from 1482 is the kind of map that gave Columbus his ideas about how the world looked. The original was drawn by the Greek astronomer-geographer-mathematician Ptolemy, who lived in Egypt in the second century. Maps like this one were very much out of date when Columbus came along. (Columbus was born 13 centuries after Ptolemy died.) Still, they were the maps almost everyone used.

were thieves who preyed on merchant caravans. (That doesn't mean they got on their knees to God. If you want to say that, you spell it *prayed*. If you spell it with an *e*, it means they robbed the caravans.)

Portugal's Prince Henry, who was fascinated with sailing and mapmaking, was determined to have his sailors get to Cathay (China) by sailing around Africa, and finally the Portuguese did it. But one man dreamed of reaching China and the Indies by another, even faster, route. His name was Christopher Columbus.

When Christopher Columbus was a boy he had two dreams. One was to go to sea; the other was to get to China. When he grew up, he thought he had done both.

Columbus was born in Genoa, an Italian city on the Mediterranean Sea. Genoa was prosperous because of the sea trade, and many Genoese boys wanted to be sailors. Columbus became one of the best the world has ever known.

Columbus knew about China because he had read Marco Polo's book. He had read it carefully. His copy of the book is full of notes.

Most people in the 15th century couldn't read. That meant they were ignorant of many things. A few believed the world was flat. They thought if you sailed too far you'd fall off the edge. But people who could read, like Columbus, knew that wasn't so. Scientists had proof that the world was round, and they told about it in books.

There was a problem, though. No one was quite sure how big the world was. So no one knew how far you would have to sail to go around it. One way to try and figure that out was by measuring lines of longitude and latitude.

Longitude and latitude are very useful lines. They are drawn on maps to help measure the earth. The lines that run horizontally (across) the globe show latitude. The vertical lines (up and down) show longitude. To tell where you are on earth, you need two numbers: a latitude and a longitude. Washington, D.C., is at about 39°N (latitude) by 77°W (longitude). Lines of latitude are also called "parallels." Lines of longitude are also called "meridians."

If you know longitude and latitude, you can always tell where you are, on land or sea. Latitude is easy to figure out if you can read the stars, or if you measure the angle of the sun at noon with an instrument called a sextant. But longitude isn't easy, especially on a ship. You need to know exactly how far you have traveled from where you started. You probably know the math: distance equals speed multiplied by the time taken.

A seaman could make a crude guess at his ship's speed by watching its hull cutting through the water. But to calculate exactly the time you've taken, you need a really accurate clock that keeps very good time. To tell time in the 15th century, ships had hourglasses filled with sand, which you turned over every half hour when the sand ran out. If the sailor who turned over the hourglass dozed off—well, you can see how easy it was to make mistakes. So ships at sea hardly ever knew exactly where they were. (That problem wasn't solved until the 18th century, when very good clocks began to be made.)

▲ None of the many portraits of Columbus was made during his lifetime, so no one knows what he really looked like.

All through history people have been sure they "knew" the truth, but often they were wrong.

For a long time men and women "knew" the world was flat. After all, that was what their eyes told them. Everyone laughed at the first people who said the world was round. "What a silly idea!" they thought.

When people think they are sure of something, they stop asking questions. That can be dangerous. Don't ever be afraid to ask questions.

Most seagoing peoples feared sea monsters, such as this man-eating serpent, which was believed to be real. ▶

Columbus did not worry. He knew Spain and Japan were on the same line of latitude—so if he could just stick with it, he figured he'd land in Japan. And he would have—if the American continent hadn't gotten in the way. Columbus figured the earth was much smaller than it is. He also figured that Cathay was much larger than it is.

Now, as you know, people who could read knew the world was round. They understood that if you went west from Europe you would finally get to Asia. But no one wanted to try going that way—it seemed too dangerous and too far. Most people believed there were ferocious monsters in the deep waters. Every sailor knew the dangers of storms at sea.

Because Columbus believed the earth was small and because he was a superb sailor, he thought he could make it to Cathay.

So he went to Portugal to ask for help. The Portuguese were world leaders in exploration and navigation. But the Portuguese weren't willing to take the risk. They turned Columbus down.

So did almost everyone else. Columbus took his ideas to one person after another. Each one said

The Spanish Inquisition

The Iberian Peninsula (today Spain and Portugal) was a collection of kingdoms in the 15th century. Isabella was queen of powerful Castile. Ferdinand was king of neighboring Aragon. They married, combined their lands and forces, and drove out the Muslims who had long controlled much of the region. Their new Christian kingdom was called Spain.

Ferdinand and Isabella brought to Spain a Catholic court called the Inquisition, which tried people for their religious beliefs, and tortured and executed many. The Inquisition often forced people who weren't Catholic to convert or leave the country. Some Jews, Muslims, and (later) Protestants chose to convert, but many refused and were driven from Spain.

▲ Columbus meets with Ferdinand and Isabella.

"sorry," except King Ferdinand and Queen Isabella of Spain, who said "perhaps." Maybe they were just being polite, because they seemed to forget all about Columbus. Years passed. He asked them again; this time they said "no." One thing you can say for Columbus: he never gave up. He was on his way to see the King of France when a messenger called him back to Spain. Finally, Ferdinand and Isabella had agreed to help. They gave him three small ships and some sailors, and sent him in search of China and Japan.

Finding Their Way at Sea

In the 15th century, new and improved navigation instruments made it possible for people like Christopher Columbus to dream of long ocean voyages.

Tools that had been available since ancient times, like the compass and astrolabe, were improved and fine-tuned. Sailors would hold an astrolabe up to the sky to help them estimate their latitude—their north-south position. Longitude wasn't as easy, and some ships were lost because they couldn't figure their east-west location. Still, astrolabes and other navigational equipment let explorers keep more accurate records, which helped later sailors follow the same routes.

Sextant

Astrolabe

Mariner's compass

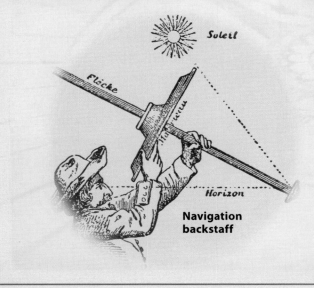

Soleil

Flèche

Horizon

Navigation backstaff

▲ For many years, sailors feared leaving sight of the shoreline, but new and better navigation instruments made it possible to venture out on the open seas.

CHAPTER 12

A New Land Is "Discovered"

It is August 3, 1492, and three tiny ships—the *Niña*, the *Pinta*, and the *Santa María*—set sail from Palos, Spain. Columbus, on the *Santa María*, is 41 years old and commodore of the three-ship fleet and its crew of 90 men. In his pocket is a letter from King Ferdinand to the Grand Khan, the ruler of China. On board is a learned man who speaks Arabic and Hebrew; Columbus thinks those languages will help him talk to the people of Cathay. When the sailors cast off, it is with a feeling of excitement. They know that if they make it, this will be one of the great voyages of all time. They hope to return with gold and spices. Spices make food taste good even if it is a bit spoiled. In these days before refrigerators, spices are very valuable.

In 1492, the *Niña,* the *Pinta*, and the *Santa Maria* head out into the unknown ocean. ▶

The ships stop in the Canary Islands for supplies and perhaps courage; then, on September 6, they head out into the unknown ocean. It is frightening to go where no one has gone before.

In mid-September they come to what seems to be a meadow of grass in the middle of the ocean. It is the Sargasso Sea—an area of thick green seaweed. The sailors have never seen anything like this. They are afraid the ships will get tangled in the green muck. But soon they are out of it and into the open sea again. Now there is a fierce storm with waves that rise higher than the church towers in Palos. The ships are sturdy and the seamen skilled, so they survive the tempest. But the sailors are discouraged and fearful. The sea seems endless. On October 9, they say they will go no farther. Columbus pleads for three more days of sailing. Then, he says, if they don't see land they may cut off his head and sail home in peace.

Three days later, on October 12, a lookout high on the *Pinta*'s mast yells, *"Tierra! Tierra!"* It is the Spanish word for land. The Bahama Islands are straight ahead.

▲ Columbus and his crew arrive on shore at an island he names San Salvador.

They have made it to the Indies! Columbus was right after all, or so they think. Columbus names the island where they land San Salvador; that means "Holy Savior." He plants a cross and a Spanish flag on San Salvador. Columbus is a religious man; he believes it is God's wish that he sail and conquer in the name of a Catholic king and queen.

Soon he knows he is not in China. That doesn't bother Columbus. Marco Polo wrote that there were thousands of islands in the Indies. San Salvador must be one of those islands. Japan, China, and the rest of the Indies are sure to be nearby. The island is small but splendid, with tall trees, gorgeous birds, a beautiful beach, and friendly people.

Mutiny—it means "revolt" or "rebellion." Some sailors talked of taking over the ship and heading back to Spain. That would have been a mutiny.

▲ The Taino, who fashioned this figure of wood, were peaceful fisherfolk.

Immunity (ih-MYOON-ih-tee) means resistance to infection.

Columbus calls the people Indians. He is puzzled when they don't understand Arabic. Actually, the language they speak is Arawak. They are members of a Taino (TY-no) tribe, although soon others will be calling them Indians. Columbus says of them: "They remained so much our friends that it was a marvel…they came swimming to the ships' boats, and brought us parrots and cotton thread…and many other things, and in exchange we gave them little glass beads….Finally they exchanged with us everything they had, with good will."

The Taino are peaceful fisherfolk. They welcome the voyagers who have come in bright ships and brought shining beads that seem to capture the sunshine. But what must be in the Indians' minds when they first see these men? Do they think it strange that they wear heavy clothing in a warm land? Are they surprised that the strangers have skin the color of melons, or that one—a black man from Africa—is dark as chocolate?

The Taino don't realize that they do not have long to live. Columbus will kidnap some and take them to Europe as trophies of his voyage. He will help turn many of them into slaves. Soon all the Arawak-speaking tribes will be dead—killed by European weapons, slavery, and diseases. Those diseases—like smallpox and measles—are new in this hemisphere. The natives have no immunity to them.

But that is to come. At first the Taino help Columbus. He is determined to find gold and the Grand Khan. The Taino take him to a huge island they call Colba. It is Cuba. Here there are many natives, and some wear ornaments of gold! Yet the Grand Khan is nowhere to be found. (Columbus is not discouraged: China and Japan must be nearby.) These Indians put a smoking weed in their mouths. It is the first time the Spaniards have seen tobacco.

There are pearls on Cuba, and enough gold ornaments to take samples to please King Ferdinand and Queen Isabella. Columbus sails home to Spain with brightly colored parrots, Indians, and gold trinkets. Now he is a great hero. The king and queen name him Lord Admiral of the Ocean Seas.

From Columbus's Pen

These are the actual words of Christopher Columbus, written in a letter in 1493 to Luís de Santangel, Treasurer of Aragon, Spain, telling of his discovery:

...I write this to tell you how in thirty-three days I sailed to the Indies with the fleet that the illustrious King and Queen, our Sovereigns, gave me, where I discovered a great many islands, inhabited by numberless people; and of all I have taken possession for their Highnesses....

[Hispaniola is] full of trees of endless varieties, so high that they seem to touch the sky, and I have been told that they never lose their foliage. I saw them as green and lovely as trees are in Spain in the month of May. Some of them were covered with blossoms, some with fruit....There were palm trees of six or eight varieties....There are wonderful pinewoods, and very extensive ranges of meadowland. There is honey, and there are many kinds of birds, and a great variety of fruits....Hispaniola is a marvel....

[The Indians] are well-made men of commanding stature, they appear extraordinarily timid. The only arms they have are sticks of cane,...with a sharpened stick at the end, Sir; and they are afraid to use these. ...they are so unsuspicious and so generous with what they possess, that no one who had not seen it would believe it....

In the first isle I discovered, I took by force some of the natives, that from them we might gain some information of what there was in these parts; and so it was that we immediately understood each other, either by words or signs.

They...believe that I come from heaven...wherever I went...[they ran] from house to house and to the towns around, crying out, "Come! Come! and see the men from heaven!"

As for monsters, I have found no trace of them except at the point in the second isle as one enters the Indies, which is inhabited by a people considered by all the isles as most ferocious, who eat human flesh. They possess many canoes, with which they overrun all the isles of India, stealing and seizing all they can.

—*Christopher Columbus*

The Next Voyage

On his first voyage Columbus set up a base on the island of Hispaniola. (The island is now divided down the middle into two countries, which we call Haiti and the Dominican Republic.) He thought the base would become an important trading post when he found the Grand Khan.

Hispaniola was the first Spanish settlement in the Americas—and it flopped. As soon as Columbus sailed back to Spain for more ships and men, the settlers he left behind started fighting over gold and

On his first voyage, Columbus set up a base on the island of Hispaniola. When he left, the settlers began to fight among themselves and with the Indians. ▼

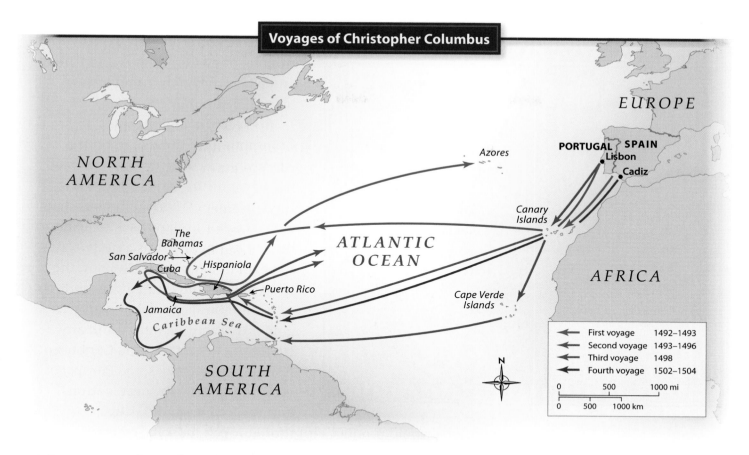

Voyages of Christopher Columbus

EUROPE

PORTUGAL SPAIN
Lisbon
Cadiz

NORTH AMERICA

Azores

Canary Islands

ATLANTIC OCEAN

AFRICA

The Bahamas
San Salvador
Cuba
Hispaniola
Puerto Rico
Jamaica
Caribbean Sea

Cape Verde Islands

SOUTH AMERICA

	First voyage	1492–1493
	Second voyage	1493–1496
	Third voyage	1498
	Fourth voyage	1502–1504

0   500   1000 mi
0   500   1000 km

N

▲ Between 1492 and 1504, Christopher Columbus made four voyages to the Americas. He believed he had reached Asia and never knew that he had come upon lands previously unknown to Europeans.

Indian women. Soon they were killing each other. The Indians—who must have been angry at the way they were being pushed around— killed most of the rest of them.

While this was going on, Columbus was in Spain being a hero. Now Isabella and Ferdinand were happy to give him ships and men. After all, he had found the Indies; he was sure of it. "It's just a matter of getting past those outlying islands to reach Cathay," he must have said.

His second trip was to be the payoff voyage. Now that he knew the way, it wouldn't be difficult to cross the ocean. This time he had 17 ships and 1,200 men. He took horses and armor and European goods. Everyone was sure Columbus would meet the Grand Khan and come home with boats full of gold and silk and spices. So adventurers from some of the most important families in Spain went with him.

Europeans called America a "new world"—but it was another old world with its own ancient civilizations and peoples. They were just different from those in Europe.

▲ An old woodcut print depicts Indians fleeing Columbus in fear.

The adventurers were nothing but trouble. They expected to find China, and when they didn't find it they blamed Columbus.

To keep the men happy, Columbus gave them land on the islands he discovered. They soon began capturing Indians and using them as slaves. Then Columbus sent a boatload of Indians back to Spain to be sold as slaves. It was a nasty way to begin in a new land. Besides, the Indian slaves often ran away, or died.

Columbus kept searching for gold mines, but he didn't find any. He never guessed that the Caribbean Islands would make some Europeans very rich—but with sugar, cotton, and tobacco, not gold. Huge plantations would produce crops for Europe's markets, creating enormous wealth.

Because workers are needed to grow crops, and because Spaniards didn't want to work in the fields—and the Indians were dying— black people would be brought from Africa to be field workers. The first Africans came in 1503; by 1574 there were 12,000 Africans on Hispaniola—and that was just on one island. It was the beginning of black slavery in America.

Learning from Mistakes

Around 1500, slavery was common everywhere, and it didn't seem wrong to many people: not to the Portuguese or the Arabs or the Dutch or the Spaniards or the Africans—who were all involved in selling human beings as slaves.

How could people behave that way? Were they different from us? Not really. Slavery has been around for a long time. It is always easy to do and think as everyone else does. Which brings us to one of the most important reasons for studying history: to learn from the mistakes of others.

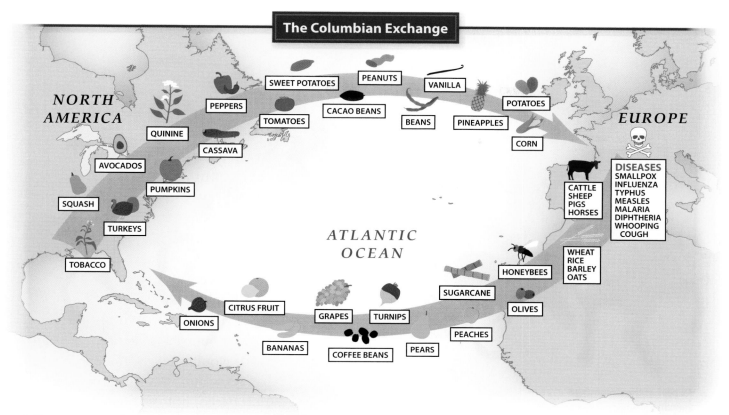

The Columbian Exchange

NORTH AMERICA

SWEET POTATOES
PEANUTS
VANILLA
PEPPERS
CACAO BEANS
TOMATOES
BEANS
PINEAPPLES
POTATOES
QUININE
CORN
CASSAVA
AVOCADOS
PUMPKINS
SQUASH
TURKEYS
TOBACCO

EUROPE

DISEASES
SMALLPOX
INFLUENZA
TYPHUS
MEASLES
MALARIA
DIPHTHERIA
WHOOPING
COUGH

CATTLE
SHEEP
PIGS
HORSES

ATLANTIC OCEAN

HONEYBEES

WHEAT
RICE
BARLEY
OATS

SUGARCANE

CITRUS FRUIT
GRAPES
TURNIPS
OLIVES
ONIONS
PEACHES
BANANAS
COFFEE BEANS
PEARS

▲ The movement of goods and people from Europe to the Americas and back again, by the process that came to be known as the Columbian Exchange, changed the course of human history in both the Old World and the New.

Columbus did something important that no one noticed at first: he helped start an agricultural revolution. Before long, American corn, peppers, beans, pumpkins, and tomatoes were growing in Europe. One plant—the potato—proved more valuable to the Old World than all the gold in both the Americas.

The exchange went both ways. Columbus brought oranges to the West Indies, where they were

The Columbian Exchange

From the Old World to the New World:

Horses, cattle, pigs, sheep, chickens, honeybees, wheat, Asian rice, barley, oats, soybeans, sugarcane, onions, lettuce, okra, peaches, pears, watermelon, citrus fruit, rye, bananas, olives, chickpeas

From the New World to the Old World:

Corn, potatoes, tomatoes, peppers, chocolate, vanilla, tobacco, beans, pumpkin, cassava, avocado, peanuts, cashews, pineapples, blueberries, quinine, sunflowers, wild rice, squash, marigolds, petunias, turkey, sweet potatoes

▲ As part of the Columbian Exchange, horses came to the New World from Europe.

unknown. Cattle, sheep, horses, and pigs were sent to America from Europe.

That transfer of plants and animals provided a way to feed bigger and bigger world populations. Corn was soon a basic food in Africa, as were potatoes in Ireland. The American sweet potato became important in China. Italians took the tomato and created a new sauce for spaghetti.

But nobody back in Spain was thinking about agricultural revolutions. It was gold and spices that they wanted. So Columbus was no hero when he returned from his second voyage. He had a few gold pieces, but he hadn't found a source of gold, and he hadn't found China either.

Still, if Columbus had stopped then, he could have retired with wealth and honors. But he was the kind of man who never stopped. That's what made him a great explorer: he kept going.

He made two more voyages—four trips in all. He discovered more islands and the mainland of South America. He never did reach North America.

And he was always convinced he had found Asia.

What if Columbus Had Reached Cathay?

Most of what Columbus knew of Cathay came from Marco Polo's book, and it was old knowledge. If Columbus had got to Cathay, he would *not* have met the Grand Khan. There was no Grand Khan. The Grand Khan and his family had been replaced in the 14th century by rulers of the Ming family. The word *khan* was no longer used in China. Columbus even had China and India confused.

In 1492, China was the most advanced civilization in the world. Its people were better fed, better housed, better clothed, and better educated than people anywhere else on the globe. Most Chinese lived in family-centered farming villages. An emperor was the head of state. Tax collecting and other government duties were carried out by officials who had to pass a series of strict exams based on the Confucian classics.

Chinese technology was way ahead of that of the West. The Chinese had been printing books for centuries. Chinese mathematics, astronomy, ship design, and navigation aids were more sophisticated than anything the Spanish or Portuguese had developed. The great admiral Zheng He, a Chinese Muslim, sailed across the Indian Ocean to Africa 60 years before Columbus's voyage. Zheng He commanded a fleet of more than 100 junks carrying 25,000 men. His treasure ship was 400 feet long. Compare that with Columbus's *Santa María*, at 85 feet.

If Columbus had made it to Cathay, he probably would not have been allowed to see the emperor. The Chinese would have thought him a barbarian. Columbus, with his tiny fleet and his scruffy sailors, would not have impressed them.

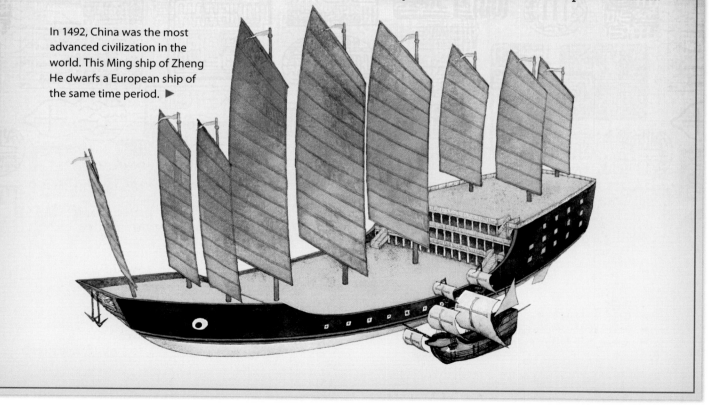

In 1492, China was the most advanced civilization in the world. This Ming ship of Zheng He dwarfs a European ship of the same time period. ▶

Finding the Pacific and Sailing Around the World

It was only after Columbus died that people began to realize the value of his discoveries. The most important thing he did was to sail into the unknown. That took great courage and skill. Once he showed it could be done, others followed.

Among them was Giovanni Caboto (jo-VAH-nee kah-BOE-tow), an Italian who went to England, where he was called John Cabot and given a small ship. Cabot sailed across the Atlantic in 1497 with only 18 sailors. He had to be very brave to do that. He landed in Newfoundland, where the Vikings had first landed 500 years earlier. Later the English claimed all of North America because of Cabot's voyage.

Thirst for knowledge and wealth, religious fervor, and improved technology spurred Europeans to explore the globe throughout the 16th century. ▼

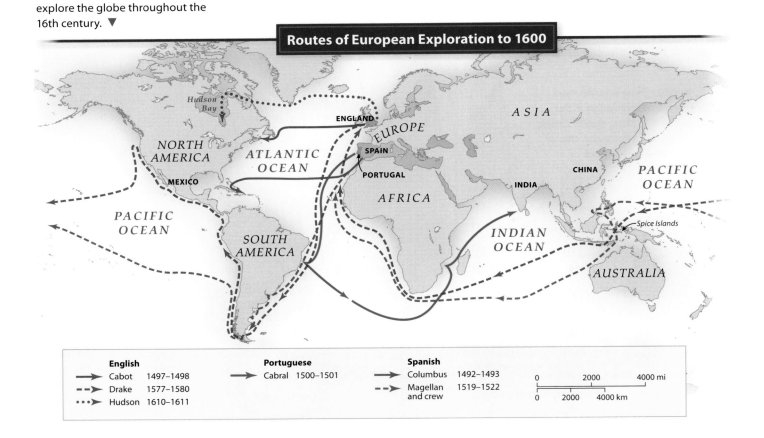

Routes of European Exploration to 1600

Hudson Bay

ENGLAND
EUROPE
SPAIN
PORTUGAL

NORTH AMERICA
ATLANTIC OCEAN

MEXICO

AFRICA

ASIA

CHINA
INDIA

PACIFIC OCEAN

PACIFIC OCEAN

SOUTH AMERICA

INDIAN OCEAN

Spice Islands

AUSTRALIA

English		Portuguese		Spanish	
Cabot	1497–1498	Cabral	1500–1501	Columbus	1492–1493
Drake	1577–1580			Magellan and crew	1519–1522
Hudson	1610–1611				

0   2000   4000 mi
0   2000   4000 km

Naming America

One famous historian (his name is Samuel Eliot Morison) had this to say about how America got named: "America was discovered accidentally... and most of the exploration for the next fifty years was done in the hope of getting through or around it. America was named after a man who discovered no part of the New World. History is like that, very chancy."

Not that Amerigo Vespucci (vess-POO-chee) wasn't a good guy. He was. And quite an adventurer, too. He made several trips across the ocean and went way down the coast of South America. On one of his trips to South America, Vespucci and his companions became the first Europeans to lay eyes on the Amazon River.

But what made him famous was that he wrote about his trips. His letters were so fascinating that everyone wanted to read them. And, thanks to Gutenberg's printing press, many people did. Amerigo Vespucci did something else that was important. He understood that there was a huge continent over here, a continent new to Europeans, and he said so in his writings. He called it a "New World." Actually, he called it a

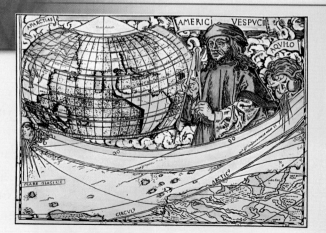

▲ America—named, sort of, for Amerigo Vespucci

novus mundus because, like educated people of his time, he wrote in Latin.

A printer and mapmaker named Martin Waldseemüller (valt-ZAY-mew-ler) actually named America. In 1507 Waldseemüller printed a huge world map, and on it he put a new continent. He used information from the voyages of Columbus, Cabot, and Vespucci to make the map. He decided to put the name AMERICA on the southern continent, since Amerigo had written about it.

The name stuck. Amazing, isn't it, how fickle history can be?

Vasco Nuñez de Balboa (VASS-ko NOON-yez day bahl-BOE-uh) was one of the greatest of the Spanish explorers. He was a stowaway, which means he hid on a ship. The ship was heading for Darien (now called Panama) to search for gold.

Balboa and other Spanish explorers were *conquistadors* (kon-KEES-tah-dors). It is a Spanish word that means "conqueror."

In 1513 the ship landed in Darien. Balboa established the first permanent European settlement in the Americas. That would have been enough to get him into the history books, but it wasn't enough for Balboa. He wanted to find gold. It wasn't gold that made him famous, though. Balboa was the first European to see the Pacific Ocean from the American continent. He "discovered" the Pacific for

> When Columbus arrived in San Salvador in 1492, he set off a cultural tornado. He, and those that followed, brought ideas, technology, and germs that overwhelmed the lands they invaded. In that way, they did make a New World.

▲ Ferdinand Magellan—the surviving members of his crew circumnavigated the globe, which means they sailed around the world.

The Pacific Ocean covers a bigger area than all the earth's land combined. It stretches across more than a third of the globe. *Pacific* means "peaceful" or "peace-loving." Naming an ocean "pacific" is an example of what's known as wishful thinking.

the peoples of Europe. (Before Balboa's discovery, Europeans thought there was only one ocean. They called it the Ocean Sea.)

Exploring can be a dangerous business. It certainly was dangerous for Ferdinand Magellan (muh-JELL-un). His voyage was perhaps the most remarkable of all. Magellan was the explorer who actually found China by sailing west from Spain. He discovered a passageway—a strait—near the tip of South America, sailed through it, and went on across the Pacific Ocean. That southern passageway is so treacherous and stormy that even now only the most skilled sailors attempt it. It may be called a strait, but it is crooked, with steep, rocky walls. It took Magellan 38 days to get through the strait that was later named for him.

But the worst was yet to come. No one guessed that the Pacific was as huge as it is. Magellan headed on, right across that ocean. His expedition would make it around the world.

But that wasn't what he intended when he left Seville, Spain, in 1519, with five ships and about 270 men. He was heading for the Spice Islands. The Spice Islands are also known as the Moluccas (muh-LUH-kuz). If you look at a map, you'll see them in Indonesia, just south of the Philippine Islands and west of New Guinea.

Europeans had been to the Spice Islands by heading south, going around the tip of Africa, and then sailing east. Magellan was convinced he would find a shortcut if he went in the other direction—west—away from Africa and across the Pacific. He thought the Pacific was a calm ocean, much smaller than the Atlantic. Magellan's original plan was to go to the Spice Islands by the new "short" route, across the Pacific, and then turn around and come back the same way. (The best maps of the day showed Japan a few hundred miles west of Mexico.) Magellan was in for a big surprise.

Look at a map of the Pacific Ocean. Now imagine yourself in a small ship, perhaps 70 feet long, heading west from the tip of South America and not knowing where you are going.

When Magellan realized the vastness of the ocean he was crossing, he didn't change his plans. He decided to go for it. He decided to sail around the world.

Like it or not, his crew was stuck with his decision. It was a terrible voyage. The course they steered missed every island between South America and Guam. By the time they reached land, near China and the Spice Islands, most of them were almost dead of hunger. Many did die. They ate rats and chewed leather straps and drank putrid water.

Putrid (PEW-trid) means disgusting or rotten.

Finally, they landed in the Philippine Islands. Magellan realized he had crossed the Pacific! In the Philippines, Magellan had many adventures, and he died there in a battle.

Few men could have accomplished what Magellan did. Some of the voyagers who had set out with Magellan finally returned to Spain— 18 men on one battered ship. (How many men and ships were there when Magellan started out?) They had been gone almost three years and had circled the globe. Imagine a ship from a distant galaxy landing on earth today. That was how amazed people were in Spain when Magellan's ship returned.

◄ Magellan dared to cross the vast and not-so-peaceful waters of the Pacific.

About Beliefs and Ideas

In 15th-century Europe most people were Roman Catholic. There were some Jews and Muslims, too, but no Protestants. (The Protestant churches hadn't been founded yet.) Roman Catholicism and Eastern Orthodox Catholicism were the only Christian religions.

The center of Roman Catholicism is in Rome, Italy; the religion is led by the pope. The Eastern Orthodox Church is divided into regional churches led by *patriarchs*. The leading Orthodox Church is in Istanbul (formerly called Constantinople), Turkey.

The Protestant religions would get started in the 16th century when a man in Germany named Martin Luther protested and tried to reform the Catholic Church.

Those who agreed with Luther were called "protesters." They started new Christian religions: *Protestant* religions. (Here are the names of some Protestant religions today: Presbyterian, Episcopalian, Baptist, Congregational, Lutheran, and Methodist.)

Because the protesters thought of themselves as reformers, the time they lived in is often called the Reformation. (A *reformer* is someone who wants to change the world and make it better.)

Unfortunately, the clash between Protestants and Catholics led to centuries of hatred and violence in Europe. Instead of talking calmly about their differences, Protestants and Catholics fought about them.

Aztecs being baptized—Europeans sought to convert Indians to Christianity. ▶

◀ Martin Luther

There were terrible wars that split towns and families. Neighbors and relatives killed each other because they thought differently about religion, and yet all of them claimed to be Christian.

Remember 1492? That was the year Columbus made his first voyage to the New World. Columbus and most Spaniards believed their religion was the only true religion.

Some explorers thought they could serve God by converting the Indians to Christianity and, if the Indians wouldn't convert, by killing them.

Reading history, you will learn about many well-meaning people who did terrible things to others. Often, they believed they were doing good. Does that excuse them? Does it make a difference to the victim? Is it right to force others to think as you do? Is it possible?

New Spain

In Europe the year was 1519. In the New World, the Aztec Indians of Mexico had their own calendar. It was even more exact than the calendar in use in Europe at the time. The Aztec calendar predicted dire events during this year.

The Mexican prophets said that Quetzalcoatl (ket-zal-KOH-atl) would come from the east—from the rising sun—to take back land that was his. Quetzalcoatl, a feathered serpent, was a god-hero of the common people. It was said that when he appeared in human form, kings would fall. The prophets even predicted the exact day he would come. So when the Spanish explorer Hernando Cortés came on that very day, many believed he was the god whose coming had been foretold.

Hernando Cortés was carried on a ship with sails as bright as birds' wings. Strange animals came with him, and men sat on their backs. Never had anyone seen a man on horseback. Some thought that horse and rider, both wearing glistening armor, were one creature.

There were 16 of those animals and they snorted and bellowed, and when they ran, their hooves made the earth tremble. As to people, there were close to 900: 550 soldiers, 100 sailors, 200 Cubans, some Africans, and a number of women. All had come on 11 ships. Natives called them "small mountains floating on the waves of the sea." When Cortés arrived with 11 ships carrying hundreds of soldiers and sailors, the natives sent word to Moctezuma, ruler of the great Aztec kingdom.

At first, Moctezuma was sure Cortés was the great god Quetzalcoatl, so he sent gifts of gold and precious jewels. The next day he wondered: perhaps they weren't gods. Reports from the scouts made the strangers seem like men. Moctezuma hesitated. That was his mistake.

Mexico is an Indian word meaning "the place of the Mexica." The people we know as Aztecs called themselves Mexica.

Moctezuma II was the ninth Aztec ruler and the most powerful leader in North America; more than 10 million people were his subjects. His name meant "angry lord." The Spaniards could not pronounce it properly, so they called him "Montezuma."

▼ An Aztec calendar—it was more exact than the calendar used in Europe at the time.

Cortés was not a man to hesitate. He marched toward Moctezuma's capital. When some of his men were fearful and wanted to turn back, Cortés sank his own ships. Now there was no way to go but forward.

Cortés marched through a countryside filled with people and villages and cities. An Indian woman marched with him; she had become a Christian and taken the name Doña (DON-ya—it means "lady") Marina. "She was a princess…as her appearance and bearing clearly showed," wrote a soldier who was with Cortés. Doña Marina could talk to the Indians, and so, through her, could Cortés. "The help of Doña Marina was of the highest significance to us," the soldier added.

Cortés was heading for the greatest city in the Americas; the Indians called it Tenochtitlán (tuh-nock-tit-LAN).

As he nears the city he can hardly believe what he sees. Tenochtitlán is more beautiful than any city on earth, he says. It is an island city, five miles square, surrounded by a glistening lake. More than 200,000 people live in Tenochtitlán. They are artisans, warriors, priests, merchants, and government officials. Farming is done on the surrounding lands.

Cortés and his men are dazzled. The lake shines turquoise in the morning sun. Houses and public buildings are chalk-white or earth-red. Some are gilded, as if made of the gold the Spaniards covet.

The Aztec empire is glorious. It encourages art, music, poetry, and crafts. But it has a terrible flaw: the flaw is a religion that demands

Artisans are craftspeople: potters, weavers, metalworkers, woodcarvers, basket makers.

To *covet* (KUV-it) means to want something badly.

The Aztec ruler Moctezuma II greets Cortés and his men near Tenochtitlán. ▼

the sacrifice of thousands of people each year. The stones of the Great Temple are stained black with their blood.

The Aztecs believe that some of their gods demand what is most precious—life. So they kill people and give their hearts to the gods in religious ceremonies. They think the gods will bring earthquakes and other disasters if they aren't fed enough lives. It is the sons and daughters of their neighbors whom the Aztecs sacrifice to the gods. That is why these neighboring peoples hate the Aztecs and are eager to help Cortés defeat them.

Cortés captures Moctezuma and holds him hostage. Then, because Cortés intends to conquer this nation, he fights. He has guns and the Indians don't. And there is something else: the Europeans have brought smallpox germs with them. When the Indians catch smallpox, they usually die. Those who are left are weak and sick.

At its height, Tenochtitlán, the Aztec capital, was a beautiful and busy city of more than 200,000 people. ▼

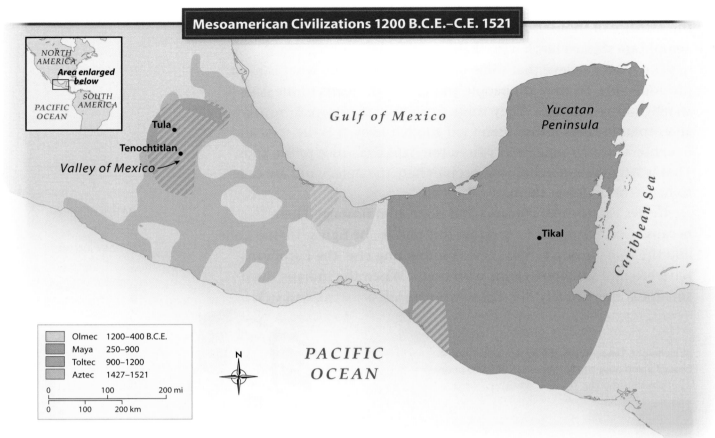

NORTH AMERICA
Area enlarged below
PACIFIC OCEAN
SOUTH AMERICA

Tula

Tenochtitlan

Valley of Mexico

Gulf of Mexico

Yucatan Peninsula

Caribbean Sea

•Tikal

	Olmec	1200–400 B.C.E.
	Maya	250–900
	Toltec	900–1200
	Aztec	1427–1521

| 0 | 100 | 200 mi |
| 0 | 100 | 200 km |

N

PACIFIC OCEAN

▲ Mesoamerican civilizations flourished in present-day Mexico and northern Central America from 1200 B.C.E. to 1521.

A terrible epidemic rages in Tenochtitlán, yet the Aztecs fight on. Most would rather die than give in to conquerors who intend to destroy their empire and the world they have known. Soon there is almost nothing left of that world.

Moctezuma is dead. Tenochtitlán is leveled.

The Spaniards build a Catholic cathedral where an Aztec temple stood. They fill the lake with earth, proclaim Tenochtitlán a Spanish possession, and call it Mexico City. They send Mexican gold and silver back to Spain—boatloads and boatloads of it. From Mexico, which is now called New Spain—Nueva España—the conquistadors subdue South America and eventually explore North America from California to Virginia.

Why did they destroy a great empire? Why did they steal a nation's riches? Were the Spanish evil and ruthless?

Life in the 16th century was cruel, and punishment was often swift and horrible. That was true all over the world—in America, in Europe, in Asia, and in Africa. The piles of skulls in Tenochtitlán—left from the sacrifices—horrified the Europeans. They said that was the reason they had to destroy the Aztec empire. Was it a good reason—or just an excuse?

Reading history is not always easy. It is hard to make judgments about the past. But it is worth trying. It helps us make judgments about the world we live in.

The Aztecs often crafted gorgeous works of art in the figure of a serpent, like this one made of turquoise. The serpent was the god Quetzalcoatl's symbol of power. ▼

A Very Short History of Mesoamerica

The Aztecs were the last of a remarkable series of Middle American (Mesoamerican) civilizations that began with the Olmecs about 1200 B.C.E. (It was the same time that Moses is said to have received the Ten Commandments on Mt. Sinai.)

The Olmecs sculpted 20-ton stone heads, carved fine masks and figures, played ritual ball games, domesticated maize (corn), and created a sophisticated society with priests, warriors, traders, and a strong ruler.

The Maya were an advanced civilization in Middle America long before the Aztecs came to power. The spectacular Mayan civilization (circa 250–900 C.E.) stretched from Mexico's Yucatan Peninsula to the Pacific coast and included at least 60 city-states, a knowledge of astronomy, an elaborate calendar, and math that made use of zero. (Zero was known in Arab lands but wasn't used in Europe until later.)

The Maya developed a system of writing that was partly *pictographic:* the symbols on the page stand for sounds or ideas or things. This system allowed the Maya to record events, give directions, identify objects, and tell stories. It was harder to learn than a system that uses an alphabet—but it worked well enough to help the Maya develop a complex culture. The Aztecs used Mayan writing as a guide.

The warrior Toltecs settled down in the city of Tula and built monumental pyramids. The rough Mexicas moved from the north, conquered, traded, learned from their neighbors, and became Aztecs.

The Mayan Temple of Kukulkan, located in the northern Yucatan Peninsula ▼

◄ The Olmecs lived in Mexico way back between 1300 and 400 B.C.E. Their ceremonial centers held huge altars, thrones, and colossal stone heads. We think the heads are portraits of their leaders.

CHAPTER 16

Ponce de León, Pizarro, and Spanish Colonies

Juan Ponce de León (hwahn PON-say day lay-OWN) heard the stories of Cortés and his great success. He believed he, too, could find kingdoms of gold, and he thought he knew just where to look.

Ponce de León was related to Spanish kings. He set out to find adventure in the New World. On the island of Puerto Rico he found more than adventure; he found gold. He conquered Puerto Rico, became its governor, and made a fortune in gold, slaves, and land. But Ponce de León wasn't finished exploring. He heard tales from the Indians of a magical spring that cured illnesses and made old men and women young again. He set out to find that Fountain of Youth.

He failed to find it. Instead, in 1513, Ponce de León discovered a new land. The new land, which was North America, was filled with beautiful flowers. Ponce de León called it La Florida. In Spanish, *florida* means "flowery."

But Ponce de León still wasn't satisfied. He wanted to surpass Cortés. He wanted to find something even greater than Moctezuma's kingdom of gold, and he was convinced he would find it in Florida. In 1521 the king commissioned him to conquer and colonize "the island of Florida." (No one knew it was more than an island.) Ponce de León set out from Puerto Rico with two ships, 200 men, and

▲ At its peak, the Inca Empire stretched nearly the entire length of South America.

El Dorado—in Spanish it means "the golden one"—was a long-lived legend among the Europeans who first reached the New World. The Spaniards believed that somewhere in the Americas was a place where gold was as common as sand. For years explorers sought it fervently. Many died looking for it.

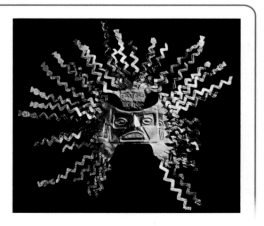

An Inca sun mask made of gold ▶

50 horses. Unfortunately for him, all he found in Florida were Indians who shot poisoned arrows. One arrow entered Ponce de León's thigh, and the poison began to work. When that happened his men fled from Florida back to Cuba, where the tough explorer died. He was buried under a stone that says, "Here lie the bones of the brave lion." (In Spanish, *león* means "lion.")

However, Ponce de León was right. There was another kingdom of gold—it just didn't happen to be in Florida. Francisco Pizarro headed down the west coast of South America and found golden treasures beyond anything anyone had ever imagined. He found them in Peru.

Pizarro's capture of Peru, in 1532, was perhaps the most daring and terrible of all the Spanish conquests. With just 180 men, 67 horses, and three big, noisy guns, Pizarro defeated the powerful Inca empire.

▲ Inca artifacts made of turquoise and gold

▲ Inca gold figurine

▼ Ruins of the ancient Inca city Machu Picchu, near Cuzco, Peru

Land of Gold

The words of 16th-century German artist Albrecht Dürer, on seeing gold objects from the Incas:

Then I saw the things which were brought to the king out of the new Land of Gold… all sorts of marvelous objects for human use which are more beautiful to behold than things spoken of in fairy tales…. and I marveled over the subtle genius of those men in strange countries.

▲ The Inca ruler Atahualpa

When Pizarro arrived in the Inca capital, Cuzco, he captured the ruler, who was known as the Grand Inca. Pizarro promised to release the Inca, whose real name was Atahualpa (at-tah-WAL-pah), if his followers would fill a huge room with gold. They did, but Pizarro killed Atahualpa anyway.

As you can see, Pizarro and his men were not exactly honorable. In fact, they were deceitful and treacherous. Soon they were fighting among themselves for gold and power. They ended up killing each other. Pizarro was killed, too. Some say Atahualpa's ghost got revenge on Pizarro. Things got so bloody that finally the king of Spain took over. He didn't mind at all. Spain was going to grow rich on the gold and silver from the mines in Peru.

The Incas fought to save their city from Pizarro and his men. But they were beaten by guns and greed. ▼

▲ A silver Inca figurine of a pan-pipe player

Sometimes historians say they want to cry when they think of Pizarro's conquest. Remember that room the Incas filled with gold? Well, it wasn't just gold; it included silver, too, fashioned into beautiful jewels, carvings of animals and birds, and gorgeous household items. It was the artwork of a civilization. Almost all of it would be destroyed. Pizarro melted all the gold and silver into bars. It was lost to history forever.

The Spaniards did that kind of thing many times over. Their religion told them the Indian civilizations were pagan and therefore false, and that their symbols should be destroyed. Because they believed their religion was the only true religion, they thought they were doing the right thing when they forced it on others.

Spain and the other European nations had guns, powerful crossbows, ships that could sail into the wind, and printing presses that made the exchange of ideas easy. Sometimes they acted as if that strength gave them the right to bully other peoples. Some Europeans said, "Might makes right." Many Spaniards believed that their nation was best because it was strongest.

A few people questioned those ideas, but most did not. When leaders say something is all right, most people agree, without thinking for themselves.

The Spanish and other Europeans came to America to expand their world and to enrich themselves. They came as conquerors and colonists.

A colony is a region controlled by a foreign country. The conquerors saw themselves as parents and their colonies as children. Spain became a "mother country." Mexico was its colony. (The Mexicans didn't think they were children, but no one asked how they felt.) Mexico was ruled by Spain in a way that was good for the parent, but not always good for the child.

Spaniards brought their religious faith and their architecture to Mexico and South America. They brought their language, their arts, and their elegant manners. They brought

The Incas valued the alpaca's fur too much to eat its meat. This model of an alpaca is made of silver. ▼

A *pagan* (PAY-gun), in Pizarro's time and until very recently, was anyone who was not a Christian, Muslim, or Jew.

Today South America is mostly filled with separate Spanish-speaking countries. But the people of Brazil, the largest country in South America, don't speak Spanish. Because Brazil became a colony of Portugal, Portuguese is the Brazilian language. People in three small countries on the northern coast of South America speak three other languages. See if you can discover the names of those countries and their languages.

learning: the first printing press arrived in Mexico City in 1539, and a university in 1551. They built magnificent churches and palaces.

They tried to make America Spanish. But the nations they created were neither Spanish nor Indian. They were a hybrid; that means "a mixture." Soon these people were living together in Mexico, Peru, and other Spanish colonies, though they were not friendly with one another.

Devastating Diseases

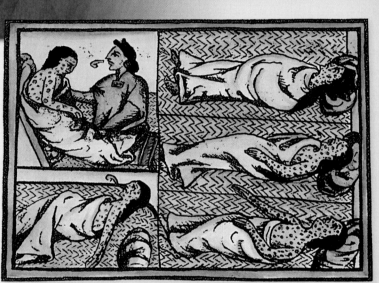

▲ Smallpox killed many Native Americans, who had no immunity to the disease.

Historians guess there were at least 20 million Indians in Mexico when the first Spaniards arrived. No one knows how many died after the Europeans came, but almost everyone agrees it was more than three-quarters of the Indian population. Imagine: if you were a Native American living then, three out of every four people you knew would be dead.

It was an accident that did most of the killing—the accident of disease. No one intended it. Millions of Indians were killed by the germs that came with the Europeans and Africans. Some say only two million Mexican Indians survived. European diseases had a similar effect on Native Americans everywhere. Few people understood the importance of cleanliness or how to combat infections.

People were used to epidemics. They just shrugged their shoulders and called them "God's will." In the 14th century Europe suffered a terrible plague called the Black Death. Europeans looked on helplessly as one out of every three of them died.

The Black Death raged through Europe and Asia in the 14th century and killed more people than any war. It began in China and spread west. One estimate says at least 40 percent of the population of Asia, Europe, and North Africa died in 20 years. About 90 percent of those who got the plague died. The same kind of thing happened when smallpox germs came to America. Today, with antibiotics, the death rate from these diseases is about 5 percent, and smallpox seems to have been eradicated (which means "wiped out," or "eliminated," or "finished").

Looking for Cíbola with Coronado

The Spanish might have made all of North America a colony if they had found gold in the north. They didn't, although they tried hard enough.

Everyone knew there was gold in the north—there had to be. The wise men of Europe said so. For a long, long time, Europeans had been searching for seven fabulously rich cities, called the seven cities of Cíbola (SEE-boe-la). Explorers had looked for the cities in Africa. Then they thought they might be in Asia. But now everyone was convinced they were in North America, especially when they heard the Indians talk of seven cities. Oh, how they tried to find the seven cities of the legends!

Everyone knew that Cíbola existed. No one questioned that. The stories of the riches of those fabled cities grew and grew—and grew.

Francisco Vasquez de Coronado (VAS-kes day kor-oh-NAH-doe) would find Cíbola; everyone agreed about that. He was a fine soldier and an able leader of men.

▲ This treasure map of western North America shows the fabled seven cities of gold.

◄ Coronado and his followers set out to find gold and adventure.

▲ Spanish explorers conquered the Zuñi Indian village of Hawikuh.

The year is 1540. Coronado has gathered his followers together, near Mexico's Pacific coast. He is preparing to set out on one of history's great adventures.

We are with him. If we choose to be Spaniards, we will wear plumed helmets and shining armor. Most of the 300 Spaniards are on horseback and expect to find great riches. We will be exploring lands new to Europe. We will be making history.

There are some black people and more than 1,000 Mexican Indians on this expedition. Some explorers treat Indians like animals, making them carry heavy loads. Coronado is not like that: he has mules and horses to carry equipment. Animals also drag heavy cannons. Coronado wants to be prepared for any emergency.

Look at a map. Do you see the southeastern corner of Arizona, right next to New Mexico? That is just about where Coronado goes. Then he heads due north, for Cíbola.

Take a finger and slide it up the border between the two states. When you hit Zuñi, in New Mexico, you may stop. Coronado stopped near there, too, at the Indian village of Hawikuh. Can you believe what you see? This is supposed to be one of the seven cities of Cíbola! But Hawikuh is a pueblo, not the city of legend, not the golden

Pedro de Castañeda, one of Coronado's soldiers, wrote of the Zuñi Indians of Hawikuh: "They are ruled by a council of old men. They have priests…whom they call *papas* (elder brothers)… there is no drunkenness among them…nor sacrifices, neither do they eat human flesh or steal, but are usually at work."

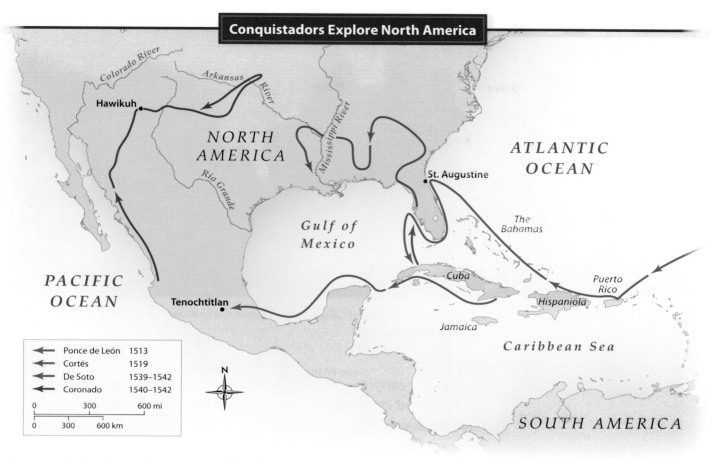

Conquistadors Explore North America

Colorado River

Arkansas River

Mississippi River

Rio Grande

Hawikuh

NORTH AMERICA

ATLANTIC OCEAN

St. Augustine

The Bahamas

Gulf of Mexico

Cuba

Puerto Rico

Hispaniola

Jamaica

PACIFIC OCEAN

Tenochtitlan

Caribbean Sea

SOUTH AMERICA

←	Ponce de León	1513
←	Cortés	1519
←	De Soto	1539–1542
←	Coronado	1540–1542

0   300   600 mi

0   300   600 km

N

▲ Stories of gold and other treasures spurred Spanish expeditions into lands that are now part of the United States.

Cíbola. Coronado calls it "a little, crowded village…all crumpled up together."

By this time a year has passed. Food has run out. Everyone is hungry. One of the hungry Spaniards writes, "We found something we prized more than gold or silver—namely, plentiful maize and beans, turkeys, and salt." To get that food, the Spaniards kick the Indians out of their pueblo. The battle doesn't take long. The Indians fight with rocks and arrows; the Spaniards have guns and crossbows.

Coronado is still sure he will find Cíbola. But it isn't easy. There are no maps to tell him where he is.

One exploring party heads west, to Arizona. They come upon a canyon so vast that some have called it a mountain in reverse. At its deepest it is a mile down; at its widest it is 10 miles from rim

Maize Miracle

Maize is corn. The Taino word was *mahiz;* the Spaniards soon said *maíz.* Some say that corn and potatoes may be the most important products ever to come from the North American continent. They became staple (basic) foods in many Old World countries. Can you figure out why? (Hint: The old staples were wheat and rice. But wheat needs very good soil and rice needs a lot of rain.)

▲ The awe-inspiring Grand Canyon—one Spanish explorer described it as "impossible to descend."

Coronado and his party travel across New Mexico. Coronado never found any cities of gold and went home empty-handed. ▼

to rim. The canyon—with stone towers that look like castles or ships or enchanted creatures—has a tumbling river at its base. This is the Grand Canyon. The conquistadors try to reach its bottom. They get partway down and give up. It is too deep and too dangerous.

The sun reflecting on the icy mountain peaks is so bright that it hurts the explorers' eyes. In Europe the landscape is small-scale. There, trees and hills and houses block the view. Here, broad plains stretch on and on. Mountains rim the plains; their rocky layers tell a story of volcanoes and mountain uplift. Men and women feel small as ants. The conquistadors don't like it at all.

As for Cíbola—Coronado reports in 1540, "The Seven Cities are seven little villages."

Coronado and his party head home, discouraged and disappointed. They have been gone for two years and have traveled more than 7,000 miles. They have marched over land that holds gold and silver and copper—but it will take future generations to discover that.

Conquistadors: California to Florida

The race was on! Whoever found Cíbola would become rich and famous. If you lived in the 16th century, would you have set out to find Cíbola? Many Spaniards did just that. They were willing to risk everything in the hope of finding the treasured cities.

A decade is 10 years. During the decade of the 1540s—from 1540 to 1549—while Coronado was searching in Kansas, some Spaniards went looking in California for the seven golden cities. Others looked in places from Florida to Texas.

Back in Spain, Hernando de Soto (air-NON-do day SO-toe) heard Florida described as a "land of gold." De Soto had been in Peru with Pizarro and had become immensely rich. When he decided to explore La Florida, there was much excitement in Europe. Men sold all their possessions to buy a place on his expedition. An engineer came from Greece, a longbowman from England, and four fortune seekers from Africa. From Spain came knights, priests, artisans, and adventurers. More than 500 people signed up; two were women.

All of them expected to find wealth and fame. Besides gold—and Cíbola—they were also looking for a waterway that would take them on to China and Japan. No one had any idea of the size of the land they called Florida. They thought it was an island, like Cuba, only bigger. It seemed logical that Japan was the next island they would find. No one guessed that the lands Coronado was exploring were part of the same continent as Florida.

It is 1539. Let's watch as de Soto, his men, and their horses clatter off the boats in Florida. They are in a holiday mood. De Soto is a brilliant leader; he has trained them well and kept them enthusiastic. Their armor shines, the horses are frisky, flags fly overhead, and all are anxious to

▼ Hernado de Soto heard Florida described as a "land of gold."

use their weapons and show how brave they are. It isn't long before they have a chance. They learn of an Indian village and, according to an expedition member, "gallop their horses...lancing every Indian encountered on both sides of the road."

Since they have guns and horses, and the Native Americans don't, they capture an Apalachee village. The Spaniards find corn, beans, and pumpkins, and have a feast. But the Indians, who are "very tall, very valiant, and full of spirit," don't give up easily. They set fire to the village and ambush Spaniards who wander away from the camp. It is a tactic that will be used against Europeans as long as they fight Native Americans.

De Soto has come to conquer. He encourages the Spaniards to torture, burn, and kill the Indians they capture. He has brought a pack of snarling attack dogs with him and he throws captives to the dogs. Word of his brutality spreads from tribe to tribe. Some Indians flee as de Soto and his men march through the country, but others give him the food and slaves he demands. They have little choice: if they don't give him what he wants, de Soto takes hostages. Usually he captures Indian chiefs.

▲ Spanish conquistadors such as de Soto were called *adelantados*. It means "advancers." The Spaniards didn't advance the Indians' life much. Here, de Soto and his men surround an Alabama Indian village.

▲ A painting from 1585 of a Native American man of Florida

Explorers and Conquistadors

1492 Christopher Columbus reaches the Bahamas. He makes three more trips, in 1493, 1498, and 1502.

1497 Vasco da Gama rounds the southern tip of Africa and calls at its eastern ports.

1497 John Cabot reaches Newfoundland, off Canada.

1500 Pedro Alvares Cabral reaches Brazil.

1507 Amerigo Vespucci and others explore the coast of South America.

1508 Ponce de León claims Puerto Rico for Spain. In 1513 he lands in North America and names it La Florida.

1510 Vasco Nuñez de Balboa reaches the Isthmus of Panama. In 1513 he is the first European to see the Pacific from its western side.

1519 Hernando Cortés lands in Mexico.

1532 Francisco Pizarro invades Peru.

1540 Francisco Coronado leads an expedition through Arizona and New Mexico.

1610 Henry Hudson sails across the Atlantic, landing in what would become New York City.

▲ Hernando de Soto at the Mississippi River

Picture this procession through the woods. First come proud conquistadors on horseback holding long lances; sturdy foot soldiers march behind them. Then come African slaves; then, Indian guides. Next come chained Indian slaves hauling supplies; then, squealing pigs and their herders, and, finally, more conquistadors.

De Soto and his followers slog through swamps, cross rivers, climb mountains, and push through jungles and forests. They build rafts of wood and bridges of rope.

Finally, de Soto and his men (both women have died) reach America's greatest river, the Mississippi. It's an important discovery, but they don't care about rivers. It is gold they seek. After almost two years of exploring, they have found nothing that they value. De Soto will not stop. The river is almost two miles wide and full of treacherous logs and huge fish. (Some Mississippi catfish weigh more than 100 pounds.) De Soto builds four boats and ferries men, horses, and hogs across the broad Mississippi. Indians, watching, make the Spaniards nervous, but don't stop them.

Now on the west side of the river, they head on: through marshes, bogs, canebrakes, and bayous where resting alligators look "like stumps of trees." In Texas (or what will be Texas), Indians tell them of other men who speak as they do. The Native Americans are describing Coronado and his men, although de Soto does not know that. (At this very time, in 1542, Coronado is on his way back to Mexico.) What if the two armies had met! They would have understood that New Mexico and Florida were part of the same land.

De Soto pushes on. He seems to think he is superhuman. But he is not.

He has been able to bluff and bully his way across half a continent. But when he catches a fever, it is all over. Hernando de Soto—the brave, mean, tough, brilliant conquistador—is dead. Now, his men are terrified. The Indians feared the cruel Spaniard and believed he had magic powers. Will they attack if they know he is dead? De Soto's men don't want to find out. At night they bury him in the middle of the river. Then they flee. They are happy to escape from the wilds of America.

Of those who made this trip, 311 return to safety. They have been gone for four years. When they tell their story, most Spaniards decide that North America is not a very promising place.

California Missions

In 1542, exactly 50 years after Columbus landed in the New World, some Spanish adventurers reached what is now the state of California. The name *California* came from a book that told about a wild land, called California, at "the right hand of the Indies," full of gold and treasure. When the Spaniards did not find gold, they left California. It took the Spaniards more than 200 years to return to California as settlers. That was 1769, when priests and soldiers led by Father Junípero Serra founded Mission San Diego de Alcalá. (You can still visit it in San Diego.) It was the first of 21 missions.

Father Junípero Serra oversees the building of a Spanish mission in California. ▶

A Place Called Santa Fe

After the decade of the 1540s the Spaniards forgot Cíbola. Well, maybe they didn't forget it—they just gave up looking for it. Fifty years passed. Then, in April of 1598, they tried again.

Watch as eight men and their horses stagger to the Rio Grande (the great river that separates Mexico from Texas). They have been five days without food or water.

They are a scouting party sent ahead by Juan de Oñate (hwahn day oh-NYAH-tay). Oñate's wife is the granddaughter of the great Cortés and the great-granddaughter of none other than the Aztec Emperor Moctezuma. Oñate has become rich by mining silver. If anyone can find Cíbola, it should be Oñate and his wife.

> Like Oñate's wife, many Mexicans are part Spanish and part Indian.

But Cíbola doesn't exist, so of course Oñate can't find it. He doesn't find gold either, although he will travel farther than Coronado did searching for it. What he does do is start a Spanish colony in New Mexico, a place where Spanish men and women make homes. "I take possession, once, twice, and thrice...of the kingdom and province of New Mexico," says Oñate.

Inscription Rock, at what is now El Morro National Monument in New Mexico, was named for the numerous inscriptions carved at its base where a spring supplied water to travelers such as Juan de Oñate. ▼

89

▲ Acoma Indians prepare to resist the Spanish invaders.

With him are 400 men, women, and children and 7,000 animals. Goods are carried in 80 wooden wagons with iron-rimmed wheels. The wagons are called *carros* and are heavy and expensive. Each is pulled by eight mules (with another eight tagging along in reserve). Oñate has paid for all this himself. It takes about a year and a half to make the slow trip from Mexico to New Mexico. Supply wagons will not come often.

Oñate is a dreadful man. He seizes food from the Acoma Indians. When they protest, he slaughters or enslaves them. That's just the beginning. Things get so bad that most of the Spaniards are ashamed and horrified. But they are like sailors on a ship: Oñate is their captain, and they are not free to leave. Still, in 1601, when Oñate is off hunting treasure, some of them flee. Word of his behavior reaches the government in Mexico City. Finally, the Spanish court recalls him and takes away his title.

The New Mexicans start a new settlement on a cool plateau; they name it Santa Fe. It is 1610, and this is the first permanent European colony in the North American West.

A *plateau* is a flat area, often in a high place or on top of mountains.

Santa Fe is Spanish for "holy faith."

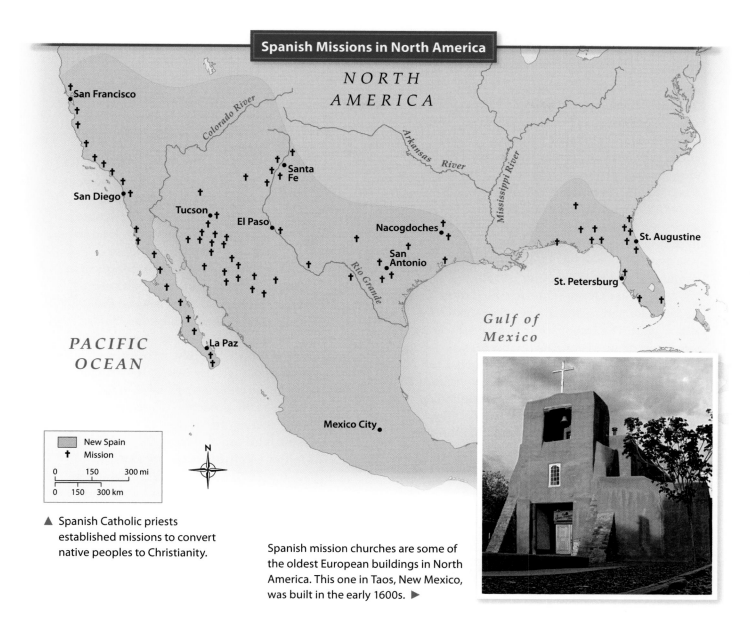

NORTH AMERICA

San Francisco

Colorado River

San Diego

Tucson

El Paso

Santa Fe

Arkansas River

Nacogdoches

San Antonio

Rio Grande

Mississippi River

St. Augustine

St. Petersburg

Gulf of Mexico

PACIFIC OCEAN

La Paz

Mexico City

New Spain

✝ Mission

0   150   300 mi

0   150   300 km

N

▲ Spanish Catholic priests established missions to convert native peoples to Christianity.

Spanish mission churches are some of the oldest European buildings in North America. This one in Taos, New Mexico, was built in the early 1600s. ▶

The gold-seekers return to Mexico; their pockets are empty. Priests and settlers take their place. By 1630 the Catholic missionaries say they have converted 60,000 Indians to Christianity. But many of these new Christians continue their traditional religious practices along with the Catholic rituals. A priest named Eusebio Francisco Kino arrives in Arizona around 1680. He will stay for 25 years, exploring and founding missions and ranches.

By this time the Indian peoples of the Southwest have been devastated. Diseases, brought from Europe and Africa, have almost wiped them out.

A *missionary* is a member of a religious group who goes out into the world to try to persuade others to *convert*—that is, to change their religion.

Las Casas Cares

In 1542 King Charles I—who was the grandson of Ferdinand and Isabella—ruled that Indians could not be made slaves. The king made his ruling because of a man named Bartolomé (bar-toh-loh-MAY) de Las Casas. Las Casas spoke out for human dignity and liberty as few people do. But that was after he turned 40. Before that he seemed to be like most other people.

In 1502 Las Casas sailed for the Indies because he had received a royal grant of New World land. The Indians who lived on the land were part of the grant. The Spaniards were conquerors (as were the English, Dutch, French, Portuguese, and Swedes later). The conquerors needed workers to make the land productive.

It may have bothered Las Casas that the Spaniards, his people, were enslaving the Native

▲ In a book called *The Tears of the Indians,* Las Casas said: "Once it happened that [the Spaniards] used 800 of the Indians instead of a team to draw their carriages, as if they had been mere beasts."

◄ The painter symbolizes the concern of Las Casas for the native people by depicting an Indian standing at the priest's shoulder.

Americans. But since everyone was doing it, he did it, too.

In 1512 Las Casas became a priest, but he was still a landowner, and he took part with other Spaniards in the bloody conquest of Cuba. He took more Indians as slaves.

About this time some priests on the Spanish islands spoke out. They said that keeping slaves was unjust. One day Las Casas read these words in his Bible: "The gifts of unjust men are not accepted [by God]." He realized he was being unjust when he enslaved others. On August 15, 1514, he preached a famous sermon announcing that he was giving up his slaves. He spoke of the injustice of slavery.

His fellow colonists were shocked and outraged. But, from that day, Las Casas never changed his ideas. He was 40 years old and lived to be 92. He spent the rest of his life traveling back and forth between Spain and the New World pleading for fairness for the Native Americans.

Some people thought Las Casas was a nuisance. Thanks to the labor of the enslaved people, gold, silver, and sugar were pouring into Spain from America. They were making the nation rich. Las Casas was spoiling things. He was like a conscience that bothers you just when you are having fun. It was greed against goodness, and goodness was losing out.

Still, Bartolomé de Las Casas was not one to give up. He kept working for fair treatment for the Native Americans. He was still writing when he was 90. The king ordered that all his writings be collected and preserved, even though most Spaniards had stopped reading his words.

France in America: Pirates and Adventurers

When you look at the big picture, what the Spaniards did is astounding. In 30 years Spain conquered more territory than the Romans had conquered in 500 years. Spanish conquistadors cut their way through steaming jungles and thick forests. They scaled mountains, crossed deserts, and defeated brave and determined Indian foes. They created new nations, a new people, and a new

▲ Spanish conquistadors conquered native civilizations and created new nations in their quest for gold, glory, and land in the New World.

▲ Spanish colonies sent home shiploads of gold and silver from the New World.

way of life. In Mexico and South America the Spanish built great cities. If they had found gold in North America, they would have built great cities here. And if they had, everyone in the United States might be speaking Spanish today.

By the middle of the 16th century everything seemed to be going right for Spain. Spanish ships were said to be the best in the world. Spanish colonies were sending shiploads of gold and silver home from Mexico and Peru. As you might guess, some of the other European nations were jealous. They didn't like Spain having all that power and wealth. There was something else that made some other European nations unhappy with Spain. That had to do with religion. Spain was a Catholic nation, but the new Protestant religions were growing in other parts of Europe.

In France, during the last half of the 16th century, the French people fought eight ferocious civil wars—and all over religion. Some French people wanted to be Catholic, some Protestant, and they couldn't seem to agree to live peacefully together. Can you understand why, during almost 40 years of war, many French men and women were eager to head for the New World?

When the French began to dream of territory and riches, they found an Italian, Giovanni da Verrazano (jo-VAH-nee dah vay-rat-ZAH-no), to sail for them. Italians were such good sailors that other nations hired them.

The king of France sent Verrazano off to find a river passage through the American continent to Asia. Everyone was sure there was one. They called it the "Northwest Passage." The nation that controlled that passageway would control the route to China and its spices and jewels.

In 1524 Verrazano sailed up the North American coast and into what would someday be New York City's harbor. No passageway was there. So he sailed on, still farther north, to Newfoundland in Canada. "My intention was to reach Cathay," he reported to the

It was an Italian, Cristoforo Colombo (Christopher Columbus), who first sailed to America for Spain. And it was an Italian, Giovanni Caboto (John Cabot), who first sailed for England.

French king, "not expecting to find such an obstacle of new land as I found; and if for some reason I expected to find it, I thought it to be not without some strait to penetrate to the Eastern Ocean."

He didn't find the passageway, or gold, because there was none to be found. Verrazano tried to tell that to King Francis I, but the king wasn't about to give up. A French privateer had captured a rich haul of Spanish treasure—a ship packed by Cortés himself—and the French king was determined to find his own treasure.

He next sent a Frenchman, Jacques Cartier (jhak kar-tee-AY), to the New World. Cartier made three voyages, explored the north country—New Brunswick and Newfoundland—and brought back samples of a stone he thought was gold. It turned out to be something called "fool's gold," or iron pyrites (puh-RY-teez). The French just weren't any good at finding real gold.

The Spaniards, on the other hand, were very good at it. They had captured the Incas' gold and silver mines and were filling ship after ship with the glittering rocks. To get that treasure to Spain, ships sailed through the Straits of Florida and then through the narrow channel between the Bahama Islands and the coast of Florida. That passageway led to favorable winds and to the best route across the Atlantic. The best route was on the Gulf Stream, which is actually a river in the ocean. Sailing on the stream is like stepping on a moving belt. Ships get a free ride on the current.

Now imagine that you are a pirate or a privateer and you want to capture a gold-filled ship. Where will you go? Certainly not to the Caribbean Sea, where you can easily be trapped and captured yourself. The coast of Florida is the perfect place. There you can seize a treasure

The entrance to New York Harbor is called the Verrazano Narrows. Today a huge suspension bridge, also named for the explorer, spans the narrows and links Staten Island and Brooklyn.

A *privateer* is a pirate ship in a nation's service. Pirate ships were sailed by outlaws. They captured, stole, and plundered other ships and split the loot among themselves. Privateers stole, too, but they were backed by a king. Privateers split their haul with the royal treasury.

French sailor and explorer Jacques Cartier ▶

A *galleon* is a big, three-masted sailing vessel. Spanish ships were spacious and seaworthy, but they weren't as fast or agile as the small pirate ships.

Pirates plied the waters along the East Coast from Florida to Virginia. ▼

ship and then head out to sea. In the 16th century, there were pirate bases on the coast from Florida to Virginia.

If France had a base on the Florida coast near the Gulf Stream, it just might be a good spot for French ships to pick off Spanish treasure galleons. So on April 30, 1562, two small ships with 150 Frenchmen aboard landed in Florida (at a site that later became a Spanish town called St. Augustine, which survived to become the first permanent European settlement on the North American continent). Their leader was a remarkable man named Jean Ribaut (jhon ree-BOW), an expert sailor, a devout Protestant, and a patriotic Frenchman. The story of his trip, *The Whole and True Discovery of the Land of Florida,* was published a year later.

In several voyages to the New World, Jacques Cartier explored the north country—New Brunswick and Newfoundland. Here he finds the St. Lawrence River. ▼

Protestants, known as Huguenots (HUE-guh-nots), were being persecuted in France because of their religion. Ribaut believed this colony would give the Huguenots a chance to prove their loyalty to their country, to be heroic, and to gain land and gold for France.

Things began well. Ribaut's group made its way north to what is now the coast of South Carolina. There they built a fort called Charlesfort. But they were soon in need of food and ammunition and farming tools. They were sailors and hadn't planned to grow crops. Ribaut decided to go back to France for supplies; 30 of his men volunteered to stay in America.

Back in Europe, things were all upset—from those religious wars—so it wasn't easy for Ribaut to return with supplies. In the meantime, the Frenchmen at Charlesfort were in trouble. They had been depending on the Indians for food, but the Indians stopped feeding them. That was because the Frenchmen had taken part in some fights between Indian tribes—and double-crossed both sides. They ended up making everyone mad at them.

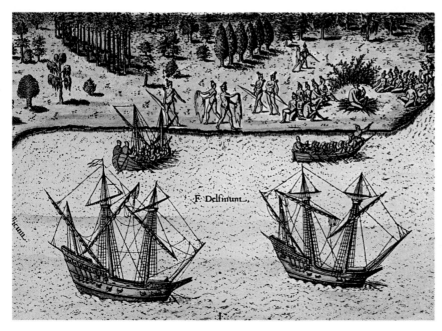

▲ Jean Ribaut and the Huguenots were greeted by friendly Indians when they arrived in Florida in 1562.

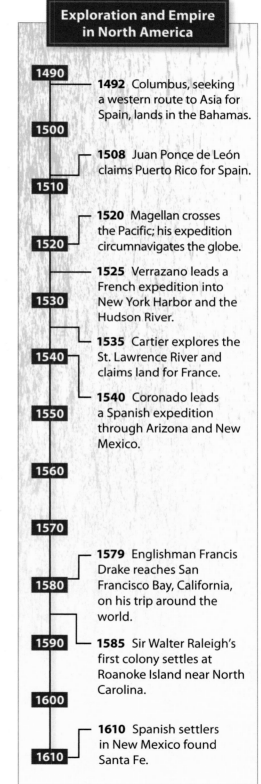

Exploration and Empire in North America

1490

1492 Columbus, seeking a western route to Asia for Spain, lands in the Bahamas.

1500

1508 Juan Ponce de León claims Puerto Rico for Spain.

1510

1520 Magellan crosses the Pacific; his expedition circumnavigates the globe.

1520

1525 Verrazano leads a French expedition into New York Harbor and the Hudson River.

1530

1535 Cartier explores the St. Lawrence River and claims land for France.

1540

1540 Coronado leads a Spanish expedition through Arizona and New Mexico.

1550

1560

1570

1579 Englishman Francis Drake reaches San Francisco Bay, California, on his trip around the world.

1580

1585 Sir Walter Raleigh's first colony settles at Roanoke Island near North Carolina.

1590

1600

1610 Spanish settlers in New Mexico found Santa Fe.

1610

▲ The French got involved in fights between Indian tribes, which only made all the tribes angry with the French.

One 16-year-old French boy at Charlesfort thought the plan to sail home was crazy. He chose to live with the Indians and was later picked up by a Spanish ship.

The situation was bleak. The Huguenots were starving, and suffering from New World germs. In addition, they were probably homesick. So they built a boat, used their shirts for sails, and set out for France. They were drifting, half-dead, when an English ship found them and took them to London.

In England everyone wanted to meet them and hear their tale, even Queen Elizabeth. The French sailors raved of the beauty and wonder of America. (When they were there, they couldn't wait to leave!) Their stories of the New World got fancier and fancier. One spoke of precious jewels that could be mined only at night because in daylight they blinded men with their dazzling reflections. All told of gold and silver, and of pearls and spices.

Ribaut, who had been fighting in France (with the Huguenots against the Catholics), turned up in England, where he also met the queen. The English were soon reading Ribaut's book. It was 1563, and the British caught New World fever. They began making their own plans for settlements.

New France

France, England, and Spain argued and fought over who had the right to settle the land that the English called Virginia, the Spaniards called Florida, and the French called New France. No one asked Native Americans what they thought.

The Spanish drove the French out of Florida. The French moved far north, to the region that is now Canada. There they stuck to fishing, fur trapping, and trading. Frenchmen had been doing that in America since the beginning of the 16th century.

The French found the waters near Newfoundland so thick with fish that boats had a hard time passing through. They came in the spring, fished all summer, salted and dried their catch, and went home for the winter.

Sometimes strange things influence history—sometimes even hats. People in France and England were crazy about beaver hats. They were the latest fashion and the American woods were full of beavers. So Frenchmen came to America to trap beavers or to trade with the Indians for beaver skins.

For trifles, as knives, bells, looking glasses, and such small merchandise which cost him four English pounds, a French trader had commodities that sold at his return for 110 pounds.
—Richard Hakluyt, 1598

The English have no sense; they give us twenty knives… for one beaver skin.
—An Algonquian Indian, 1634

▼ A beaver pelt stretched on a frame

▲ Fur trappers set beaver traps in streams.

▲ A Huron Indian encampment

Those who came usually got along with the Indians. They had to—there were too few Frenchmen to start a fight.

The French fishermen and fur traders lived much as the Indians did. They became friends with the Algonquian and Huron tribes and traded with and learned from them.

The Algonquians and Hurons were enemies of the powerful Iroquois Indians. So the French took sides with their friends against the Iroquois. A French explorer, Samuel de Champlain, joined the Algonquians and Hurons in a raid on their enemy.

The French brought their arquebuses (ARK-wuh-bus-iz), big clumsy weapons. The Indians called them "thunderhorns." Never before had the Iroquois seen guns. Three Iroquois chiefs were killed. A hundred years later the Iroquois would still hate the French because of the deaths of those chiefs.

It's too bad Champlain made that mistake, because everything else he did was outstanding. He was not only a fine sailor and leader, but also a writer, artist, and mapmaker. Writing a description of what he thought "a good captain" should be, he didn't realize he was describing himself. This is what he wrote: "An upright, God-fearing man, not dainty about food or drink, robust and alert, with good sea legs."

Robust (roe-BUST) means "strong, healthy, and sturdy."

Samuel de Champlain dreamed of a new French nation in America. He realized that if the French wanted to stay in the New World, they would need to bring their families and start colonies where French people could live.

In 1608 Champlain founded a settlement called Quebec. Today Quebec is the second-oldest continuously occupied city on the North American continent. You already know the oldest city. (If you don't remember, it's St. Augustine, founded in 1565.)

Notice those words, "continuously occupied," meaning cities that still exist. Other early settlements disappeared.

Samuel de Champlain understood that the American continent was a wonderful place to live, but few people in France agreed. Life seemed good enough in France; there was no need to leave—especially for an unknown wilderness. The French Huguenots, who were persecuted because of their Protestant religion, might have come, but their faith made them unwelcome in Catholic Canada. So New France grew, but slowly. Brave and energetic explorers helped it grow.

A French Catholic priest, Jacques Marquette (jhak mar-KET), came to Canada. In just six years he learned many Indian languages. Most people call him "Père (PEAR) Jacques." *Père* is the French word for "father"; a priest is a Catholic "father."

Marquette is a gentle, sweet man, and nothing seems to disturb him—not even the worst hazards of the wilderness. He is a Jesuit (JEZ-yoo-it), a member of a scholarly order of priests who have come to New France to teach the Indians about Christianity. Marquette goes freely among the Indians; they love him. Native Americans call the priests "black robes," because of the long, dark garments they wear.

We have come here in our time capsule. Notice: it is 1673. (Just for this chapter, we are leaping ahead to the 17th century, to give you an idea of what the French explorers will accomplish in this New World. In the next chapter we will be back in the 16th century.)

▲ Samuel de Champlain founded the settlement of Quebec in 1608.

Repeat: it is 1673. The governor of New France has ordered Father Marquette and Louis Joliet (LOO-ee joe-lee-AY) to find the Northwest Passage. For almost 200 years, Europeans have searched for that route through America. The French are determined to find it. Like Columbus, they want to sail west and reach the Far East.

Joliet is a mapmaker. He was born in New France; a priest says he has "the courage to fear nothing where all is to be feared." Perhaps this team will find the Northwest Passage. Marquette and Joliet go in birch-bark canoes with five other Frenchmen and two Indian guides.

Let's follow them. We will be gone four months and will travel 2,500 miles. Marquette and Joliet will take notes and make maps as they go. Mostly they will eat "Indian corn, with some smoked meat." (Father Marquette writes this in his journal.) We will watch as the French explorers paddle on the Wisconsin, Mississippi, Illinois, and Chicago rivers. Sometimes it will be necessary to carry the canoes overland from one river to another. This is called "portaging."

▲ Father Jacques Marquette (standing), Louis Joliet, and their companions descend the Mississippi River.

▲ Father Marquette is offered the pipe of peace by the Potawatomi Indians.

Watch out! Indians are attacking. Will we live through the raid?

Don't worry. Father Marquette will save everyone. The Indians see the peace pipe he smokes. The Illinois Indians gave it to him, and other tribes respect it—and him.

This expedition makes an important discovery. Marquette and Joliet learn that the Mississippi River empties into the Gulf of Mexico, not the Gulf of California, as had been thought. But this expedition will not get to the river mouth. The Indians tell of Spaniards with guns; it is wise to head back to Quebec. Marquette and Joliet have not found the Northwest Passage (and it will not be found until the 20th century; the passage is so far north that most of the year it is under thick ice).

Marquette and Joliet claim much land for France. That the Indians have lived here for centuries does not seem to concern France. Nor does it concern England or Spain or any of the nations that attempt to colonize America. In Paris, French leaders decide to let England have the eastern edge of North America (below Nova Scotia); France will take the rich interior lands.

If we zoom on, nine years in time, we will meet René-Robert Cavelier (ruh-NAY roe-BEAR kav-ul-YAY), a Frenchman with the title of Sieur de La Salle (syur duh la SAHL). A French *sieur* is like an English lord or knight. Robert Cavelier is Lord La Salle. He has received a grant of New World land from the king; he will sell it to pay for this expedition. That is how important it is to him to be able to explore.

▲ The expedition of René-Robert Cavelier de La Salle in the territory he named Louisiana

La Salle claimed Louisiana for France. ▼

La Salle is fearless and stubborn. He will travel even farther and faster than Marquette and Joliet. He is told the Mississippi is "guarded by monsters...and barbarous nations who eat their enemies." He believes that may be true. Besides, he knows that Spaniards are in the Gulf of Mexico, and they are as dangerous to him as any monster.

But La Salle isn't the kind to be stopped by a few monsters—or Spaniards. He hikes and canoes from Canada down the Mississippi to its mouth at the Gulf of Mexico, and then claims the river and everything west of it for France and the French king, Louis XIV. La Salle names the territory Louisiana in honor of the king.

After that he heads for France to tell King Louis of his adventures. But La Salle hasn't finished exploring. He sails back from France to the Gulf of Mexico. He is trying to find the Mississippi River by coming from the other direction. He can't find it. He goes too far, lands in Texas, and marches his men so hard and fast that most of them die. Finally, those who

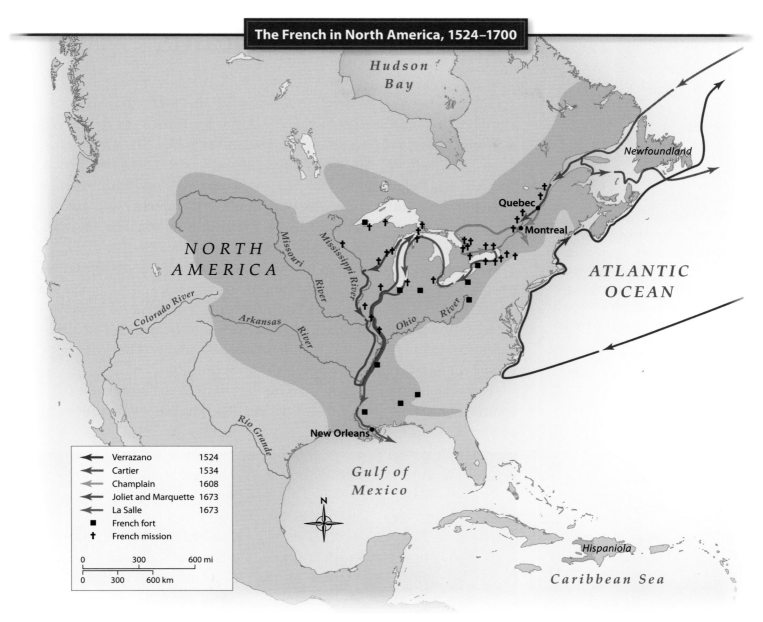

The French in North America, 1524–1700

Hudson Bay

Newfoundland

NORTH AMERICA

Quebec †
† Montreal

ATLANTIC OCEAN

Missouri River

Mississippi River

Colorado River

Arkansas River

Ohio River

Rio Grande

New Orleans

Gulf of Mexico

	Verrazano	1524
	Cartier	1534
	Champlain	1608
	Joliet and Marquette	1673
	La Salle	1673
■	French fort	
†	French mission	

0	300	600 mi
0	300	600 km

Hispaniola

Caribbean Sea

▲ The French claimed a vast territory in North America.

are left can take no more. They murder La Salle and leave his body 350 miles from the Mississippi.

Because of those French explorers, France claims all of Canada and all the land west of the Mississippi. It is a vast territory—the French have no idea of its actual size. They hope it contains riches. They are eager to find wealth on this great continent, to "civilize" its peoples, and to bring them Christianity.

Elizabeth and Friends

And now, back to the late 16th century—to the Elizabethan Age. Elizabeth became queen of England in 1558. She turned out to be amazing, perhaps the best monarch England ever had. She was smart, tough, and energetic. She was a musician and a poet. She spoke French, Spanish, and Italian, and could read and write Greek and Latin. She filled her court with people who were intelligent and witty and got things done. The Elizabethan Age was the greatest of times in England.

It was then that Shakespeare wrote his plays and English developed into a language of richness and beauty. It was an age when people wanted to act like knights and be chivalrous.

In the Elizabethan Age, the English people also began to create a great empire that would one day stretch around the world. The queen seemed to infect the nation with her taste and energy. That energy would change America, but not in the 16th century.

It was Spain that England had on her mind in the 16th century. Spain was a greater power than England. The English wanted their

The word *court* has many different meanings. There is a basketball court, a law court, and a royal court. A royal court usually consists of a king or queen and his or her advisers and servants. It can also be the king and queen's home.

England's remarkable Queen Elizabeth, who once said: "I count the glory of my crown that I have reigned with your loves…and though you have had, and may have, many mightier and wiser princes sitting in this seat, yet you never had nor shall have, any that will love you better." ▶

nation to be the world's greatest. The French and the Dutch wanted the same thing for their nations. Spain would fight to hold on to her exalted position. That duel for first place between the great European powers seemed much more important to most people than anything that might develop in the wilds of a distant continent.

England did try to plant colonies in the New World during Elizabeth's reign. She just didn't seem to have much luck.

From the beginning, the Europeans who came to America had two dreams:

There was *the dream of riches*, of America as a land of gold where one could become wealthy.

And there was *the dream of a new world,* of an ideal place where the mistakes of Europe could be avoided, where people could pursue happiness. Sometimes those dreams pulled in opposite directions; sometimes they worked in harmony.

Sir Humphrey Gilbert may have held both dreams. He was the first Englishman to hold a royal charter to "have, hold, occupy and enjoy…remote heathen and barbarous lands." Those barbarous lands were America; Sir Humphrey meant to settle English people here. His charter said that all settlers should "enjoy all the privileges of free…persons native of England" and that all laws should be as close to English law as possible.

Now that was unusual. English men and women would lose no rights when they moved to the new land. They would be entitled to trial by jury and other English rights. The head of the colony (sometimes called the *proprietor,* which means "owner") could not be a dictator.

Sir Humphrey Gilbert never got a chance to use his charter: he was lost at sea. His small ship, the *Squirrel,* was swallowed by a huge wave. Just before he went under, Gilbert was seen reading a book called *Utopia*, written by Sir Thomas More.

Utopia was about an imaginary island. (The word *utopia* came from Greek and meant "no place.") Sir Thomas described its people, its government, and its way of life as being close to perfect.

We think Sir Humphrey Gilbert hoped to set up a utopia in America—a close-to-perfect place to live—and perhaps find gold, too.

When "Sir" appears before a man's name it tells you he was knighted by an English king or queen.

Barbarous (BAR-ba-russ) means "wild," "primitive," "harsh," or "cruel."

▲ This map of More's Utopia was drawn to illustrate his book in 1518, when people were fascinated by reports of the New World.

Remember those two dreams: gold and a good society—that was what many Englishmen hoped for in America, especially Sir Walter Raleigh.

Sir Walter was Sir Humphrey's half brother. After Sir Humphrey Gilbert drowned, Sir Walter Raleigh decided to take over his charter and dream. The queen was happy to have him do it. Raleigh was not only chivalrous, he was handsome, and Queen Elizabeth liked him—a lot.

Sir Walter Raleigh sent three expeditions to the New World.

The first one went to look the place over and pick out a good spot for a colony. The ships' captains came back with a report of a wonderful land and of Indians who were "most gentle, loving and faithful…and live after the manner of the golden age." The captains were describing the coastal area that would someday become North Carolina. Raleigh named the whole land Virginia, after Elizabeth, who was called the Virgin Queen. (Queen Elizabeth never married, and an unmarried woman is sometimes called a virgin. That's how the name Virginia came about.)

Sir Walter Raleigh wrote poetry, fought pirates, and had adventures. One day, while Queen Elizabeth was out walking, she came to a huge puddle (or so they say). There was no way around it. Sir Walter saw she would dirty her feet, so he whipped off his cloak, spread it out over the mud, and let her walk across it. That was chivalry! (Even if it wasn't true.)

▲ Queen Elizabeth and Sir Walter Raleigh

▲ Sir Walter Raleigh and the Indians of the land he named Virginia

Raleigh's second expedition was a big one: in 1585 seven ships sailed with 100 men. They planned to start a colony. The men included John White, an artist; Thomas Harriot, a famous mathematician, poet, and astronomer; Thomas Cavendish, a navigator who later became the third man to sail a ship around the world; and a Jewish mineral expert from Bohemia (now part of the Czech Republic) named Joachim Ganz, who was to search for gold and silver.

Ganz found copper but no precious minerals; White drew pictures; and Harriot wrote a story of their adventure. We have the story and pictures today.

The men found that colonizing was a lot harder than they had expected. They were homesick and hungry when an English ship commanded by Sir Francis Drake came by to check on them. All climbed aboard and went home.

Raleigh tried once more. In 1587 he sent out a new colony. Its mission was to establish the city of Raleigh in Virginia.

This time he sent families. He finally realized that you can't have a real colony without women and children.

But the settlers didn't know how to survive in the wilderness.

Giving Away America

Queen Elizabeth gave Sir Walter Raleigh a *grant* to start a colony in North America. A grant is a "deed of land." Kings and queens were giving away America. What made them think they had a right to that land?

Unfortunately, it had something to do with European arrogance. *Arrogance* is a strong word. The dictionary says that someone who is arrogant overestimates his importance. Many Europeans in the 16th and 17th centuries saw themselves as civilized and important. They saw the Indians as savage and unimportant. To the Europeans, America was empty. It was as if the Indians didn't exist. Since the country was empty—in their eyes—it was available to anyone who could grab it. And so they raced for it; Spain, England, France, Portugal, the Netherlands, and Sweden all claimed parts of the land.

The first three permanent colonies in the lands that would become the United States and Canada were St. Augustine (founded in 1565), Quebec (founded in 1608), and Santa Fe (founded in 1610).

They spent too much time thinking about Spaniards and not enough time looking for food or building shelters. Some of them hoped to turn their settlement into a base for raiding Spanish ships. Most hoped to find gold. They built a fort to protect themselves from Spanish attack.

The colonists landed on Roanoke Island late in the spring of 1587—too late to plant crops. The artist John White was back, this time as leader of the group. He brought his sketch pad and paints. White's daughter, Eleanor Dare, came with him. White soon realized they would need more food; he decided to go back to England for supplies. Just before he left, Eleanor Dare gave birth to a baby. The baby, John White's granddaughter, was named Virginia. Virginia Dare was the first English baby born in the New World.

When White returned to England, he found the country was fighting Spain. The queen would not give him a ship to go to America because she needed all her ships in England. One thing after another happened, and it took three years before

English settlers land at Roanoke Island. ▶

▲ The baptism of Virginia Dare, the first English baby born in the New World

John White was able to return to Roanoke Island. When he got there, the colonists had vanished. The letters "C R O" were carved on a tree. John White knew that Croatan was the name of a nearby island (and also the name of an Indian tribe). Had the colonists gone to Croatan Island? Had Indians attacked?

White was desperate. He wanted to find his daughter, his granddaughter, and the other colonists. But a treacherous storm was on the horizon. The captain and crew decided to sail away. Naturally, John White was very, very upset. So were other people in England. They began talking of the "Lost Colony."

No one has ever solved the mystery of the Lost Colony. Some Indians in North Carolina say they are descended from people with gray eyes. Indians usually have brown eyes. Could Virginia Dare have become a gray-eyed Indian?

A few years later England tried another settlement, this time at a place we know as Maine. But freezing weather got to the settlers (as well as a lack of supplies), so they sailed back to England.

If it wasn't poor planning, then it was the weather or the Spanish or the Indians. England just couldn't seem to get herself planted in American soil.

In 1992, archaeologists digging on Roanoke discovered something momentous: a 16th-century metallurgical laboratory. Bits of Bohemian glass, a ceramic heating pot, and pieces of copper—found in an earthen fort—were clues that led them to conclude that this was where Joachim Ganz conducted experiments.

And, in 1998, climatologists studying ancient tree rings found that the settlers on Roanoke Island had terrible luck. They arrived during the worst drought that part of the country had seen in 800 years. Even Native Americans must have seen their crops shrivel and their livestock die. The newcomers hardly had a chance to survive.

Treacherous (TRETCH-ur-uss) means "very dangerous."

The *horizon* (hur-IZE-un) is the farthest point of the earth that a person can see. On the ocean, it is the line where the sea and the sky seem to meet.

A "Master-Thief" and a Mighty Armada

Eฬngland wanted some of that Spanish gold, and she got it the only way she could: by stealing it. Some Englishmen said that since the Spaniards had stolen the gold from the Indians, they had a right to steal it from the Spaniards. What do you think of that argument?

An Englishman named Francis Drake went after Spanish treasure. Drake was a daring and fearless seaman. He hated the Spaniards, and they didn't like him either. Queen Elizabeth gave him a privateering commission, and he used it to raid Spanish ports, sink Spanish ships, and burn Spanish towns.

In 1577 Drake sailed through the Straits of Magellan and into the Pacific Ocean. His ship, the *Golden Hind,* was the first English vessel to reach the western side of America. Spanish ships were unguarded on

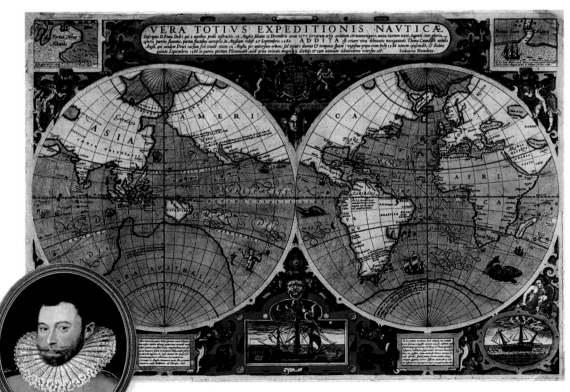

◀ Francis Drake went after Spanish treasure.

▲ This world map, made around 1595, shows the voyages of Francis Drake. Drake sailed through the Straits of Magellan and into the Pacific Ocean.

▲ Drake's ship, the *Golden Hind*, was the first English vessel to reach the western side of America.

▲ Queen Elizabeth makes Drake a knight on the deck of the *Golden Hind*.

that western coast because they thought they were safe from privateers. Then along came Drake. Near the coast of Peru he captured a huge treasure ship full of gold. The *Golden Hind* became so heavy with gold it began to ride low in the water. That didn't stop Drake. He sailed on—to California and even farther north—trying to find the Northwest Passage from the West Coast. When he couldn't find it, he headed west, to China, picked up spices, and brought everything home to the queen. It was quite a haul for Drake, England, and the queen.

The English people were proud: Drake was the first sea captain to take a ship around the world. (Remember, Magellan hadn't lived to finish his voyage.) The queen made Drake a knight: he was now Sir Francis Drake.

In England he was a national hero, as famous as anyone in his time. But to the Spanish ambassador he was "the master-thief of the unknown world." That should tell you something about history. One nation's hero is often another's villain.

While the Spanish were preparing the Armada, Drake made a sneak attack. He took 24 ships right into the Spanish harbor of Cadiz, where the warships were at anchor, and captured or destroyed 37 of them. He returned to England and declared he had "singed the king of Spain's beard."

The Spanish Armada
* met its fate*
In fifteen hundred
* and eighty-eight.*

Even though some of her treasure ships were being captured, Spain was still the greatest power in the world—at least that is what everyone in Europe thought. In 1588, the Spaniards sent a great fleet of ships—called an *armada*—to fight against England.

It was easy to predict who would win this fight. But when the mighty Spanish armada faced the smaller English navy, some astonishing things happened. The big Spanish galleons weren't prepared for the small, fast English ships. Besides, the Spaniards expected to fight in the traditional way—by boarding enemy ships and fighting hand-to-hand. But the English set old ships on fire and sent them into the crowded armada. (That was Drake's idea.) The winds were fierce, the ships were wooden—and you can guess what happened. The underdog England won. Spain lost 63 ships and about 20,000 men. England did not lose a single ship, except those that were purposely set on fire. Only 100 Englishmen died.

After that, power began to shift. France and England became the nations to watch, especially in North America.

▲ The sea battle between the Spanish Armada and English naval forces, in which Spain lost 63 ships and 20,000 men

PART 2

MAKING
13 COLONIES

The First Virginians

In 1607 Europe was changing. In the great Catholic nation of Spain, the government was bankrupt. Although nobody knew it, Spain's glory days were over. Would that arrogant little Protestant island—that England—become Europe's new leader? Now that England's magnificent Queen Elizabeth was dead, no one knew where England was heading.

The world was in for astonishing changes in 1607. Would they be changes for the better? Not for those people called Indians, who would soon meet the pale-skinned English.

When English parents told stories to their children, they often spoke of monsters, trolls, wild beasts, and witches. But they also told tales of splendor and goodness. Every child heard the Bible's first story, which is of a Garden of Eden. Eden was a place of great beauty, a paradise. Many of the goodness stories were about sweet, simple people who lived in harmony with nature. And those stories seemed real, too, because there was much goodness in the world.

So when English men and women learned of a land of great beauty, where people lived close to nature, many of the English

Jamestown Island in Virginia ▼

thought of that land as paradise. They called the natives "savages." It was a patronizing use of the word, but not meant unkindly. The first English visitors to the New World described the Indians as "courteous" and "gentle" and "great."

But, later, when others met those great savages, they found they didn't always act as people do in storybooks. Soon some were calling them worse names than "savages." They called them "beasts." Some said they were servants of the devil. Others said they were part animal and part human.

But those people—the Indians—were just real people, like the English. They lived in families, in towns, governed by leaders. They farmed, hunted, played games, and fashioned beautiful objects. Some of them were wise and some were foolish. Some were kind and some were mean. But most were a bit of all those things.

One of the most interesting Indians the English would meet was the Powhatan, the ruler or emperor of eastern Virginia. His real name was Wahunsonacock, and he had inherited an empire of five tribes. Through daring, strength, and leadership, Powhatan soon held sway over dozens of villages and thousands of Indians. The English would call the Indians of his empire Powhatan Indians.

They were Woodland Indians, who spoke Algonquian (al-GON-kwee-un) dialects and hunted, fished, and farmed in a region of great abundance. The area surrounded the Chesapeake Bay and went west to mountain foothills and south to what would someday be North Carolina's border. It was

◀ The Powhatan had about 9,000 subjects; his land stretched from what is now Washington, D.C., to northern North Carolina. Powhatan was said to have 100 wives. One-third of his 9,000 subjects were warriors.

Patronizing means condescending. It means thinking you are better than someone else.

Earthly Paradise
Letters like this one, written by Ralph Lane in 1585, made people want to go to the New World. Lane was a member of Raleigh's Roanoke Colony.

We have discovered…the goodliest soil under the cope of heaven, so abounding with sweet trees, that bring such sundry rich and pleasant gums, grapes of such greatness, as France, Spain, nor Italy have no greater…. The continent is of huge and unknown greatness, and very well peopled and towned, though savagely, and the climate so wholesome, that we had not one sick since we landed here.

▲ Powhatan men hunted for small game and deer.

▲ Powhatan women grew corn and other vegetables.

An *estuary* (ESS-tew-air-ee) is the body of water where the mouth of a river meets the sea.

a land of rivers, bays, and estuaries; of ducks, geese, wild turkeys, and deer; of fertile soil, fish, and shellfish; of wild berries, nuts, and grapes.

Powhatan's people raised vegetables—corn, beans, squash, and pumpkins—which was more than half the food they ate. Because they farmed, they lived in settled villages. Corn was their most important food. They ground it and made it into flat pancakes that served as bread or rice does in many other cultures. Aside from corn, the food they ate changed with the seasons: fresh vegetables in summer and fall; game in winter; and fish, stored nuts, and berries in the spring. (Spring was when corn supplies ran low and they sometimes went hungry.)

There was much small game in the region: raccoon, opossum, squirrel, turkey, and rabbit. But it was deer these Indians relied on most for food and clothing. Unfortunately, like people elsewhere, they overhunted; deer became scarce. And they knew if they roamed outside the Powhatan's territory—looking for better hunting grounds—they risked war with other tribes.

It was the men who hunted, fished, and fought. Women farmed. Men and women had set roles in this society and rarely changed them. Children helped their parents, played, and didn't go to work until they were young adults.

The boys often played in scarecrow houses that stood in the middle of the fields. From there they threw stones at rabbits or other animals that might nibble on the crops. It trained their throwing arms, and that helped when they became hunters. Little girls played with clay, made pots, and helped their mothers plant and cook. Boys and girls played running games. There were no horses (they hadn't arrived in this part of the New World yet), so fast runners were prized. Sometimes they would dress up like their parents—painting their bodies and wearing necklaces and bracelets of shells and beads and animal bones.

Men and women tattooed beautiful designs all over their bodies. Men sometimes hung animal claws, birds' wings, bats, even live green snakes around their necks. They rubbed themselves with bear grease—it repelled mosquitoes, kept them warm, and made their skin glisten

Remember, horses first came to America with the Spanish conquistadors. Even 100 years later they were still a rarity.

The bear grease that the Indians rubbed on their bodies made their brown skin shine with a reddish glow. Europeans thought it really was red, and that was how the name "redskin," which many Europeans once used for Native Americans, came to be. It's based on a *misperception*, which is an error in the way things are seen.

This etching of Virginia Indians is based on a drawing by John Smith. ▼

The Chesapeakes lived on land that is now included in the cities of Virginia Beach, Norfolk, Portsmouth, and Chesapeake.

Werowance is a Delaware Indian word that means, literally, "he is rich."

▼ A deerskin mantle that belonged to Powhatan

in the sunshine. Most of the year these Indians needed little clothing, although in winter they wore deerskin garments and, sometimes, cloaks of feathers or fur.

The great Powhatan had a beautiful deerskin sewed with designs in lustrous pearls. Powhatan had stacks of deerskins and a storehouse of corn, and he had copper and pearls. The tribes brought all this and more to him. It was tribute given to a ruler.

Each tribe had its own leader, called a werowance (WEER-ah-wunts), and also priests and healers and others with power. But the Powhatan was special. All those who met him noted it. He knew how to command, when to be stern and unforgiving and when to be understanding. The story was told of the time he visited the Potomacs (puh-TOW-mucks), who were under his rule. The young Potomac warriors came before him, and each told of awesome deeds of valor against fierce enemies or wild beasts of the forest.

Finally one young man stood before Powhatan and said, "I, my lord, went this morning into the woods and valiantly killed six muskrats. While that may be no more than boys do, it is true, while much you have heard is fable." When Powhatan heard that, he broke into laughter and gave a reward to the truth teller.

Powhatan's priests had foretold that his mighty empire would one day be destroyed by men from the east. The Chesapeakes, who lived by the ocean, were the easternmost of his tribes. Perhaps that is why, just before the 16th century turned into the 17th (in the European method of reckoning), Powhatan fought the mighty Chesapeake Indians and left them weak and powerless.

Powhatan didn't yet know that three small ships were heading for his realm. They were coming across the ocean from an island far to the east.

English Settlers Come to Stay

In December 1606, three ships set sail from the docks on the river Thames (temz), near London. About 144 men were on board. Some were sailors. A little more than a hundred were voyagers in search of adventure and riches. Of these, more than half listed themselves as "gentlemen." In England, gentlemen were not expected or trained to work. They lived on family money. Most brought their best clothes for the trip: their puffed knee pants, their silk stockings, their feathered hats, their gaudy blouses.

The voyagers were sent from England by a business corporation called the London Company. They had been told to look for gold and a river or passage that would go through the country to China and Japan. They were also to see if there were other ways to make money on this unknown continent.

In April of 1607, three small ships—the *Susan Constant*, the *Discovery*, and the *Godspeed*—landed at the mouth of the Chesapeake Bay. In Virginia, April is a sweet month. Strawberries and white dogwoods blossom below the green of tall pines. Redbuds are emerging, and so are grape leaves, honeysuckle, and wild roses.

The three ships anchored near an elbow of beach they named Cape Henry (in honor of young Henry, the king's oldest son). Some of the mariners rowed to shore and set out exploring. "We could find nothing worth the speaking of, but fair meadows and goodly tall trees, with such fresh waters running through the woods, as I was almost ravished at the first

A reconstruction of the *Susan Constant,* one of three ships that brought English settlers to Jamestown ▶

Christopher Newport was one of England's finest sailors. As a privateer, he had sailed the New World's seas. (A *privateer* was a pirate with a government license. Privateers split their loot with the king or queen.) Queen Elizabeth had encouraged English captains to prey on Spanish ships. And Newport had led an expedition that destroyed or captured 20 Spanish vessels and sacked four towns in the West Indies and Florida. He was an English hero. What the Spaniards thought of him is something else.

A *yeoman* was a small farmer who cultivated his own land (it was the area of land that was small, not necessarily the farmer).

sight thereof," wrote George Percy, who was one of the gentlemen adventurers.

On their way back to the ship the Englishmen were attacked by Indians, who came "creeping upon all fours…like bears, with their bows in their mouths," but when "they felt the sharpness of our shot, they retired into the woods with a great noise."

The local Indians knew about white men, and they didn't want them around. Spain—England's old enemy—had tried to start two colonies in the Chesapeake Bay area. An Indian prince from the region had been taken to Spain, baptized a Christian, educated, and returned to his people. That prince had far more schooling than most of the Englishmen who now wished to invade his land. The Englishmen didn't seem to know any of that. They thought of the Indians as savages.

The Englishmen spent a few weeks exploring the bay area. They feasted on strawberries ("four times bigger and better than ours in England"), ate oysters ("which were very large and delicate in taste"), and noticed grapevines ("in bigness as a man's thigh"). The oysters and mussels "lay on the ground as thick as stones; we opened some, and found in many of them pearls…. As for sturgeon [there were so many of these fish] all the world cannot be compared to it."

They planted a cross at Cape Henry, thanked God for their safe voyage, and watched as Captain Christopher Newport opened a sealed metal box. The box had been entrusted to him by the London Company. (Newport would soon sail back to England.) He opened the box and read six names and his own. They were to be members of a council and elect a president. One of the names was a surprise. It was John Smith; he was locked up in the ship's belly.

Smith was of yeoman (YO-mun) stock—and feisty; he was not one of the gentlemen. He had angered some of those gentlemen and they had put him in chains. They were planning to send him back to England. Now they would have to work with him.

The instructions in the box said they were to go inland, up a river, and find a suitable place for their colony. So they left the mouth of the Chesapeake Bay and sailed up a river they called the James, to a site they named Jamestown.

Several men, including John Smith and Christopher Newport, went on, up the James River, in search of a passage to China. They

▲ The Virginia Company settlers established their colony at Jamestown in 1607.

had no idea of the size of the country. When they saw breaking waves, they were sure they had found the western coast and the Pacific Ocean. John Smith wrote in his log of the "ocean ahead."

They soon discovered that the waves were caused by water tumbling over rapids in the river. They were at a site that would someday be the city of Richmond. The river would not let them go farther.

All those Jameses—the James River and Jamestown—were named to honor the new king, James I. When Queen Elizabeth died in 1603, still unmarried and childless, her cousin James was brought from Scotland to become king of the United Kingdom of Scotland and England.

▲ Jamestown, as it looked in 1607; the settlement is protected by a ditch and palisade (a high fence made of stakes). A baking oven is outside the wall (why outside?). In the center is a church. Most of the houses have thatched roofs made from river grass or reeds, but some are covered with tree bark (an idea borrowed from the Indians). Today the place where Jamestown once stood is an active archaeological site. Archaeologists have located evidence of all three sides of the fort. You can also visit a reconstructed Jamestown nearby.

▲ The settlers built small houses of wattle and daub—sticks and clay.

King James had worked out a kind of deal with the Spaniards. It went like this: we English will stop raiding your ships if you Spaniards will promise not to attack our settlers. So the new settlers weren't as worried about Spanish attackers as they might have been in the 16th century. As it turned out, there may have been Spanish spies among them.

But it was gold that was on their mind when they reached Jamestown, and they soon began searching for it. They also built rough huts for shelter and a triangular fort for protection.

Jamestown was almost an island, with a narrow sandbar link to the mainland. It would be easy to defend against Indian raids or against ships, just in case the Spaniards did decide to come up the river. Besides, deep water touched the land. They could sail right up to the site and tie their ships to trees.

As it turned out, they couldn't have picked a worse spot. The land was swampy, the drinking water was bad; it was hot in summer and bone-chilling in winter. The mosquitoes drove the settlers crazy and carried malaria germs.

They might have handled all that if they had been a decent bunch. But, for the most part, they were lazy and vain and fought among themselves. And their first two leaders were incompetent—which means they made a mess of the job.

All were men; they brought no women. Remember, most were gentlemen, with no training or taste for hard work. To be fair, they had been misled about the New World. They expected to find gold at their feet, and they wasted valuable time looking for it. And there wasn't a farmer among them.

To make things worse, the London Company, which had paid for the voyage, showed poor sense. It gave all the colonists salaries and did not allow them to own property. No one had a reason to work hard, because the hard workers got the same pay as those who did nothing.

Besides all that, they had bad luck—lots of bad luck. The worst may have been that they brought some English germs across the sea. One was a typhoid fever germ that killed many of them. Tidewater Virginia had other germs (especially dysentery germs) that made some sicken and die. The Indians killed still others.

Yet the news wasn't all bad. This was the first English colony that survived in the New World. A few things had to go right to make that happen. One man, more than any other, helped make things go right. He was short, scrappy, red-bearded John Smith—who had come to Virginia in chains. He was Jamestown's third president and a born leader, even though many of the voyagers didn't like him.

When Christopher Newport sailed back to England, the adventurers were on their own in America. Newport thought he had gold when he took a barrel of shiny earth back to England. It turned out to be "fool's gold" (iron pyrites).

John Smith's portrait labels him "Admiral of New England." Even if this wasn't an official title bestowed by the king, Smith deserved it. He not only explored and mapped Virginia but charted the New England coast from Cape Cod to Maine. ▼

John Smith

The Jamestown colony might not have survived without Captain John Smith. He was a tough, no-nonsense man who worked hard and expected everyone else to do the same. Some people admired him; others hated him.

Pocahontas admired him and saved his life—twice. She was a bright-eyed Indian princess who was about 12 years old when the settlers first came to Virginia. The pale-skinned men and their strange ways intrigued her and she came to visit them often. Sometimes she just turned cartwheels in the middle of the Jamestown settlement; sometimes she brought food. It was John Smith who seemed to interest her most. In him she recognized a person whose intelligence and curiosity matched her own. Like her father, the great Powhatan, Smith seemed fearless.

Many of the settlers hated Smith, but they recognized that he was a leader. When he went back to England, even his enemies missed him. They said he was a braggart and that he couldn't possibly have done all the things he said he had done. He might have exaggerated a bit, but he really did do those things—like selling his schoolbooks and running away to sea. Or going off to Hungary to fight the Turks. There, on one bloody afternoon, Smith beheaded three Turks. A grateful Hungarian prince granted him a coat of arms with three Turks' heads emblazoned on it.

That first summer in Jamestown the settlers barely made it. "Our drink was water, our lodging, castles in the air," they reported. "With this lodging and diet, our extreme toil in bearing and planting palisades strained and bruised us.… From May to September those that escaped lived upon sturgeon and sea crabs. Fifty in this time were buried." (A *palisade* is a fence of pointed wooden stakes set firmly in the ground, built for defense.)

▲ "…nor fed more plenty…."

But those early days weren't all misery. After their first Christmas in Virginia, Captain Smith wrote, "We were never more merry, nor fed more plenty of good oysters, fish, flesh, wild fowl and good bread, nor never had better fires in England than in the dry smoky houses of Kecoughtan."

▲ John Smith trading with Indians

He wasn't a Hungarian hero for long; he was captured and sent as a slave to Constantinople, where a Turkish woman bought him. But her relatives didn't think much of him, and he was sold again. This time he killed his master, escaped, got thrown into the Mediterranean Sea, wandered through Russia, Poland, and Germany doing heroic things, and ended up in North Africa fighting pirates.

Naturally someone who liked adventure the way John Smith did would be attracted to the adventure of a new world. Besides, like Sir Walter Raleigh, he had an idea that America could someday be an English land. He understood that there was more to be gained in the New World than gold. He realized that there were great opportunities for men and women with energy and courage.

John Smith was 28 when he took over the leadership of the Jamestown colony, and things were in a bad way. This was his motto: "If any would not work, neither should he eat." There were some grumblers, but everyone wanted to eat. So everyone worked.

Smith went and got food from the Indians. He learned their language and he learned the ways they hunted and fished. He had been a soldier and he was tough, but he was also fair and honest; the Powhatans soon understood that. They respected him and he respected them. They called him "werowance," or chief, of Jamestown. And that was what he was.

The Native Americans seemed undecided about how to act toward these strangers on their land. What would you have done if you were a Powhatan? How would you have treated the English leader John Smith?

He had goods they wanted—axes and shovels and blankets—so they traded with him. He was a natural trader. He took his English goods to their villages and he came back to Jamestown with boatloads of corn. They told him of the prediction: that men from the east would destroy their villages. He told them he came in peace. Still, the Indians couldn't seem to make up their minds.

Sometimes they entertained Smith with dances and feasting. Other times they tried to kill him. Once he was brought before an Indian werowance and he expected to die. He pulled out his compass, showed how it worked, talked about the heavens and the earth, and soon had a tribe of friends. Another time he was taken to the great Powhatan, who seemed to have several Indian warriors ready to beat his brains out. But Pocahontas, who was the Powhatan's favorite daughter, came to his rescue. She put her head on Smith's, and Powhatan let him live. Was it a prearranged ceremony, or did Pocahontas actually save his life? No one knows for sure, but the Indians ended up adopting Smith into their tribe and making him an honorary chief. Now he was a member of Pocahontas's family.

When some other Indians tried to ambush Smith, Pocahontas warned him of the trap. Cats are supposed to have nine lives. John Smith had even more. While exploring the Chesapeake Bay, he was stung by a deadly stingray and was in such agony that he had his grave dug. He recovered—and ate the stingray. (The place where this happened, near the mouth of the Rappahannock River in Virginia, is now called Stingray Point.)

Pocahontas, the Powhatan's favorite daughter ▼

▲ John Smith lies captive before the Powhatan while Pocahontas pleads for his life to be spared.

John Smith was asleep in his boat when some gunpowder exploded. It "tore the flesh from his body and thighs nine to ten inches square....To quench the tormenting fire, frying him in his clothes, he leaped over board in the deep river, where...he was near drowned." Smith was so badly wounded that he had to return to England. Pocahontas was told he was dead.

John Smith never got back to Virginia. But he did get to New England, which he named, and he mapped its coast as he had mapped much of Virginia. He wrote many books and became famous because of them. "I am no compiler by hearsay, but have been a real actor," he said. And so he was. We still read his books today, because they are so interesting.

What Happened to Pocahontas?

Pocahontas had two names. Her real name was Matoax. It means "little snow feather." Pocahontas, her nickname, means "playful."

Once when Pocahontas was visiting some Potomac Indians, an Englishman lured her onto his ship and wouldn't let her off. He took Pocahontas as a hostage to Henrico, held her there, taught her the Christian religion, and gave her a new name, Rebecca.

A young Englishman named John Rolfe had a plantation nearby. He fell in love with the beautiful Indian princess and she fell in love with him.

Rolfe married Pocahontas. It was a fine wedding, and it took place in the church at Jamestown. The Powhatan wouldn't come.

◀ A portrait of Pocahontas in European dress

Perhaps he feared a trap, or perhaps he was sad to see his daughter leave the Indian world. Pocahontas's marriage helped bring peace between Indians and colonists.

Soon Pocahontas had a baby and John Rolfe was so proud he took his family to England. There Pocahontas charmed everyone—even King James. (And King James didn't charm easily; he was a bit of a grouch.) The English people called her Lady Rebecca and treated her as the princess that she was. But she must have longed for a familiar face, someone she could talk to in her native language.

Perhaps Pocahontas, wearing a long dress like a proper Englishwoman, didn't know in which world she belonged.

When John Rolfe decided to go back to Virginia, she didn't want to go. She didn't feel at all well when they boarded a ship and sailed down the Thames River. Before they reached the open sea, she was so sick that her husband took her off the ship. It was smallpox. Pocahontas died, and was buried in the churchyard at Gravesend, a town that is now part of London, but in those days was in the country. She was 22.

When the Powhatan learned of his beloved daughter's death, the peace between Indians and settlers ended.

▼ An artist's interpretation of the baptism of Pocahontas, an event that is believed to have taken place in Virginia before her marriage to John Rolfe

The Starving Time

Before John Smith left for England, he counted the food in the storehouses at Jamestown. "Ten weeks' provisions in the stores," he wrote. It was October of 1609. Was there enough food to get through the winter? Smith seemed to think so. He expected the Indians to supply corn, as they had before. Besides, the settlers had hens, chickens, and goats—and so many pigs that a nearby island was called Hog Island. In addition to all that, the woods abounded with deer, rabbit, and squirrel; the river was thick with fish, frogs, and oysters.

There were new people in Jamestown, brought from England by Captain Newport. Two were women: Mrs. Thomas Forrest, the wife of a settler, and her maid, Anne Burras. Anne Burras's arrival led to a happy event. The serving-maid married a laborer, John Laydon. The Laydons soon had a baby. Can you guess what they named her? (They named their baby *Virginia*.)

Still more colonists arrived. Now there were many mouths to feed, but most people were optimistic. Everyone thought Jamestown had seen the worst of its troubles.

Everyone was wrong. That winter of 1609–1610 was as awful a time as any in American history. It was called the Starving Time.

New clues tell us that nature wasn't on the side of the English settlers. Rainfall records from 1587 to 1589 (the time of the Lost Colony) and from 1606 to 1612 (early Jamestown) show the two worst droughts in an 800-year period in that part of the country. How do we know that? Archaeologists and climatologists, working together at the William and Mary Center for Archaeological Research, studied the rings inside ancient cypress trees near the coasts of Virginia and North Carolina. Trees grow more slowly during times of drought, and the tree rings from those years are very close together. Droughts kill crops, animals, and people.

Nearly 90 percent of Jamestown's settlers had died by the spring of 1610. ▼

Captain George Percy, who was now governor of the Jamestown colony, said the settlers felt the "sharp prick of hunger which no man can truly describe but he who hath tasted the bitterness thereof." They ate "dogs, cats, rats and mice," said Percy, as well as "serpents and snakes" and even boots and shoes.

There were never Englishmen left in a foreign country in such misery...Our food was but a small can of barley, sod in water, to five men a day...our men night and day groaning in every corner of the fort most pitiful to hear...some departing out of the world, many times three or four in a night; in the morning their bodies trailed out of their cabins like dogs to be buried.

What happened? Some historians say the Starving Time was an Indian war against the English invaders. The Powhatan may have decided to get rid of the settlers by starving them. He wouldn't trade with them. He laid siege to Jamestown. That means armed Indians wouldn't let anyone in or out. The settlers couldn't hunt or fish. They could hardly get to their chickens and pigs. The gentlemen ate the animals that were inside the stockade—without much sharing. That made the others angry. Soon there was nothing for anyone to eat.

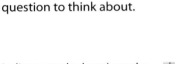

Would Powhatan have behaved differently if John Smith had been around? This is a historical question to think about.

Indians attacked settlers who left the Jamestown fort. ▶

▲ Artisans and laborers arriving in Jamestown brought needed skills. Here, workers shape and dry bricks.

A few escaped. "Many of our men this Starving Time did run away unto the savages, whom we never heard of after," Percy wrote.

In London the Spanish ambassador learned of the misery in Virginia. (Some said there was a Spanish spy at Jamestown, but a spy wasn't needed; the disaster was common news in London.) The ambassador urged the Spanish king to send a ship and finish off the English colony. The Spaniards could have done it easily. So could the Indians, who never went that far. (What do you think American history might have been like if either of those things had happened?)

Finally, in May 1610, two English ships tied up at Jamestown's docks. Of the 500 people who were in Jamestown in October, when John Smith left for London, only 60 were still alive.

In the spring of 1610, the remaining colonists set to work. They cleaned, fixed, and built. The Indians continued to make their lives miserable, but now the settlers fought back. Then a few Indians and a few colonists began to trade. Some Englishmen began going up the rivers to trade with distant tribes.

More ships came. Artisans and laborers arrived, together with "gentlemen of quality" and more livestock.

And still many died, not from starvation but from the diseases that abounded in the damp atmosphere at Jamestown.

The colonists needed a healthier settlement. So one was built at a great bend of the James River, near the falls that John Smith had mistaken for the Pacific Ocean. The new settlement was named Henrico, for Henry, the king's oldest son.

Of the first 10,000 settlers who landed in Virginia, only 2,000 survived. (What percentage is that?) They died of disease, Indian attack, and hunger.

Jamestown Makes It

More English ships sail for Jamestown…and more settlers…and more again.

It seems as if everyone in England wants to be part of the American adventure. And everyone can be part of it by giving money to the Virginia Company, the outfit that is paying for all the exploration. The Virginia Company is a stock company, just like stock companies today. You can buy shares in the company; your money helps pay the company's expenses; if there are profits you will get your share of them.

Some of those people expect to make money from the gold that they are sure will be found. Many just want to take part in a great national venture. Some want to save the North American Indians from the Spaniards. In England people have read stories about the way some Spaniards treat the Indians: how they make them dig for gold, how they starve them, how they make slaves of them. Good people are horrified.

They don't realize that English men and women are just like Spanish men and women. Some are good, some are not so good.

With help from the local Algonquian Indians, the Powhatans, Captain John Smith made this map of Virginia. ▶

At last the settlers found gold. Gold in the form of a leaf. A leaf that dried to a golden brown and could be put in a pipe and smoked. That tobacco leaf made people rich; it made the Virginia colony prosperous.

King James hated tobacco. He thought it unhealthy and he was right. But there is a limit to what even kings can do when money is involved. Growing tobacco was very profitable, especially after John Rolfe, Pocahontas's husband, developed a sweet variety that was all the rage in England.

But there was a problem. It takes hard fieldwork to grow tobacco, and Englishmen were not anxious to work in the fields. Besides that, even the best farmers could tend only a limited number of tobacco plants. So if you wanted to get rich by growing tobacco, you had to have people working for you. The more people you had, the more tobacco you could grow. The more tobacco you sold, the richer you would get. That made servants and other workers very valuable in Virginia.

In the words of the king of England himself, James I: "Smoking is a custom loathsome to the eye, hateful to the nose, harmful to the brain, [and] dangerous to the lungs."

So the Virginians did everything they could think of to get people to come to America. But since most of the settlers were dying, it wasn't easy. Most of those who came were poor or in trouble with the law.

The colonists were so eager to have workers that they were willing to pay for them. Sometimes they paid so much money that ship's captains would kidnap people from the streets of London.

Many of those who came to Virginia started out as indentured servants, and usually they were very poor. Some of them were criminals who were let out of jail if they would agree to come to the colony. You can understand that most people didn't want to go to a land where so many people were dying. The indentured servants didn't have enough money to pay their boat fare to the New World. They had to work for the person

Class System

To some extent, the English will bring their class society to Virginia. An upper class of landowning aristocrats will be the leaders. There will be a middle class of yeomen owning small farms. The lower class will be made up of indentured servants and slaves. The Virginia aristocracy will differ from the English aristocracy in an important way: the idea that gentlemen should not work will be rejected in the New World.

who paid the fare. They worked from four to seven years before they were free. That was their time of indenture. Some indentured servants were treated just like slaves.

What about slaves? Were there slaves in Jamestown? Yes, there were. Slavery in the English colonies began without much thought, which is the way bad things often begin.

In 1619 a Dutch ship brought a boatload of Africans to Jamestown. These people had been kidnapped from their homes by African traders and sold to the ship's captain. He in turn sold them to the Virginia settlers. Those first African Virginians were treated like indentured servants. After a few years of working for someone else, they became free. Soon there were Africans who had land of their own—and servants, too. But some colonists got the idea of making black people into slaves. That way they wouldn't have to keep buying workers on the docks. It must have seemed a good idea to people who were desperate for workers. Tobacco agriculture demanded much labor as well as a lot of land. There was an abundance of land in America, but few people willing to do hard work in the fields.

Captive Africans first arrived in Virginia in 1619. ▼

When Indians were enslaved, they ran away. It was difficult for the blacks to run away. Where would they go? Everything was new and strange to them. Gradually laws were passed to trap black people in slavery. It was the beginning of a way of life that would bring misery to many, many innocent African Americans.

◀ Slave shackles

1619—A Big Year

The English found those first years in America really hard. Remember, four out of five of the first 10,000 settlers died soon after they arrived in Virginia. Most people would have given up—but not the English. The harder the challenge, the more determined they became.

If the colony was to survive, it had to grow. That meant sending women as well as men.

The year 1619 was a turning point. After 1619 you could tell the English were in America to stay. It was a year of many firsts in Virginia:

- first boatload of Africans
- first boatload of women
- first labor strike
- first time English settlers are allowed to own land
- first elected lawmakers.

That is a lot for any year. You already know about that boatload of Africans. Now, about those women. They, too, were sold on the docks.

"Do you want a wife?"

"It will cost you 120 pounds of tobacco."

Those are the terms when a shipload of women arrives in Jamestown in 1619. These are poor women who are unable to pay the

The first African Americans, mostly from Angola, were urban people who spoke Bantu languages and had had previous contacts with Europeans. Many had been baptized Christians. Many were literate.

◄ Women first came to Jamestown in 1619. Their arrival signaled that the English were planning to settle down and make their homes in America.

cost of their Atlantic journey. They want a new life in this new land. The lonely men want wives. There will be instant romances on the docks. What do you think of these women? Do you think they are scared? Courageous? Crazy?

A few white women have already been to Jamestown, but sending an entire boatload of them to be wives means that the English plan to stay and make homes in America. The French, who are settling in the North, are less likely to send women. Still, in 1619, the men in Jamestown outnumber the women by eight to one.

In 1619 the Virginia Company lets the settlers have land of their own. That gives them a reason to work hard.

The first workers' strike in British America happens in 1619. Polish workers at Jamestown, who are glassmakers, demand the same rights as Englishmen. They get those rights and go back to work. There are Poles, Dutch, Germans, and Italians at Jamestown. Do you think it strange that they all want English rights? What about their own rights?

> After seven years' work, those who wanted were given their own land. Captain Smith said, "When our people were fed out of the common store, and laboured jointly together, glad was he who could slip from his labour, or slumber over his tasks, he cared not how; nay, the most honest among them would hardly take so much true paines in a week, as now for themselves they will do in a day."

▲ Polish, Dutch, German, and Italian workers settled in Jamestown. Here, a glassmaker and an indentured servant make glass bottles.

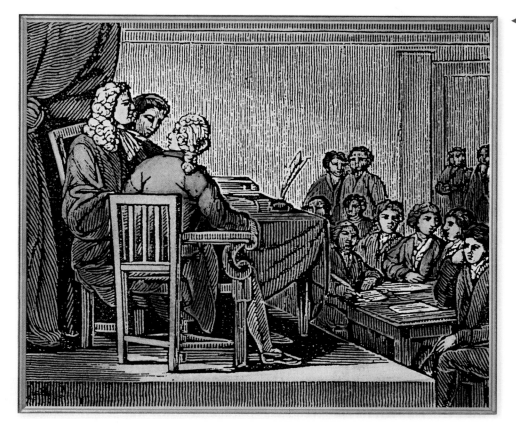

Virginia's House of Burgesses was the first representative assembly in the European colonies.

The answer to that is very simple. English men and women have more rights and freedom than people do in other European nations. They expect those same rights in America and so do people from other nations who come to the English colonies.

John Smith said no one would come to the New World "to have less freedom." The Charter of the Virginia Company said, "all and every of the persons...which shall dwell and inhabit within every or any of the said several colonies and plantations, and every of their children...shall have and enjoy all liberties...as if they had been abiding and born, within this our realm of England." That means that nobody will lose freedom if he moves from England to America.

In 1619, a group of lawmakers—known as "burgesses"—is elected to make laws. They form an assembly called the House of Burgesses. In England laws are made by Parliament. The House of Burgesses gives the Virginians their own form of Parliament. That has never happened in a colony before.

Abiding means permanent or lasting.

A *realm* is the kingdom or country where a ruler holds sway.

A *colony* is land controlled by a distant, or foreign, nation.

In the 17th century many European nations have colonies in America as well as in other parts of the world. Those colonies are not all alike. In the Spanish colonies no Europeans except Spaniards are allowed to settle. France admits only Catholics. The English colonies have open doors.

Think about that for a minute. That decision, way back in the 1600s, to let all kinds of people settle in the English colonies, made a big difference to our country. We would become a pluralistic society. (What does that mean?)

Now that you know about colonies, let's get back to the House of Burgesses. In the 17th century, laws for colonies were made in the home country, or by appointed governors and their councils. The House of Burgesses changed that.

England was letting colonists make laws for themselves. That was a big first in history. (An English governor did have *veto power* over the burgesses. What is a veto? Okay, you can do some work. Go to the dictionary and look that word up. The governor didn't use the veto very often.)

This is something you should remember: the House of Burgesses, formed in 1619, gave America its first representative government. It was the beginning of self-government in America.

Whoops! Hold on, that isn't quite true. Some Indian tribes had representative government. The House of Burgesses was the first representative assembly in the European colonies.

It was only a dozen years since those three small ships were tied to the trees at Jamestown and the English colonists were doing something very unusual. They were making laws for themselves.

The House of Burgesses was made up of Anglican landowners elected for two-year terms. (You had to own land and be a member of the Church of England to vote. The Church of England is also called the Anglican Church.) The burgesses levied taxes. Collecting taxes, rather than having them controlled by the royal governor, gave the burgesses power—power they would not want.

Some of the early laws passed by the burgesses of Virginia forbade pastimes that were thought immoral, like playing cards or dice. If you got caught not going to church, you were fined 50 pounds of tobacco—about a week's wages. It was against the law to swear, too.

Indians vs. Colonists

From the time of Columbus the pattern was the same. The newcomers and the Indians would meet as friends and trade with each other. Then something would happen. Often an Indian was killed or sold into slavery, and the Indians would strike back. Sometimes they showed remarkable patience. Sometimes they were just waiting for the right moment. For the Native Americans were much like the New Americans: good and bad, fierce and gentle. Warriors on both sides went too far. The massacres were horrible.

At first the Indian leaders tried to live in peace with the settlers. But some of them realized that it would not work, that it would be the end of Indian ways. The Europeans used up land. They cut the forests and filled the land with people. Indians were hunters. To keep their way of life, the woods had to be protected. Wild animals need woods to live in, and hunters need wild animals.

Most Europeans understood that, too. One Virginia governor said, "Either we must clear the Indians out of the country, or they must clear us out." The members of the House of Burgesses ordered three expeditions to drive out the Indians "in order that they have no chance to harvest their crops or rebuild their wigwams."

There was another problem: arrogance (which means thinking you are better than others). In the 17th century arrogance was often tied to religion.

Many Christians believed that anyone who was not Christian must be inferior. (The Aztecs believed those who weren't Aztec wereinferior.)

Before long, that arrogance would become racism. Some whites believed themselves better than all Indians. Some believed themselves better than all blacks. History shows that racists are troublemakers and often the worst of their own race. There were bigots and racists in early America and they made trouble. Some of them wanted to kill all the Indians. (And some Indians wanted to kill all whites.)

However, the real problem was the fight for control of land. Even when Indians and settlers were friendly, it usually didn't last long. The newcomers wanted Indian land, and naturally the Indians didn't want to give it up. Some fair-minded white leaders respected the Indians and wanted to share the land, but they were never able to control the land-hungry settlers.

European settlers cleared forestland for lumber to build houses, barns, and fences. ▶

Massacre in Virginia, Poverty in England

Just when things seemed to be going well for the colonists, Pocahontas's uncle, the sachem Opechancanough, decided to try to get rid of them all. Some historians think that Opechancanough was the Indian prince who had been taken to Spain by Spanish priests, educated, and returned to his people. Whether he was or not, everyone agrees that he was intelligent and crafty, and that he hated the white men who were stealing his land.

> Opechancanough never gave up. In 1644 his warriors attacked Jamestown again. He was so old and feeble he had to be carried about on a bed. Attendants held his eyelids open so he could see. But his mind had not lost its power.

In 1622 Opechancanough was an old man. Perhaps he thought it was his last chance to save his people. So he planned a great massacre. Indians knocked on the colonists' doors—pretending to be friendly—and then they murdered and scalped them. They might have killed everyone if an Indian boy, Chanco, hadn't warned the men and women at Jamestown. Chanco had been treated kindly by the settlers and had become a Christian. The settlements outside Jamestown didn't get warned. Hundreds of English men, women, and children were killed in the Great Massacre of 1622.

> To *massacre* (MASS-uh-ker) means to "kill brutally" and often in large numbers.

After the Jamestown Massacre the English had an excuse for killing Indians, and the bloodshed became intense. Killings were followed by revenge raids, more killings, and more revenge—on both sides.

King James was upset; there were too many deaths in Virginia. He set up a government investigation, and then he closed down the Virginia Company. The stockholders were wiped out; their stock was now worthless. King James took Virginia; it became a royal colony. Actually, the king didn't spend much time thinking about the Virginia colony; it was too far away. And he had problems, big problems, at home.

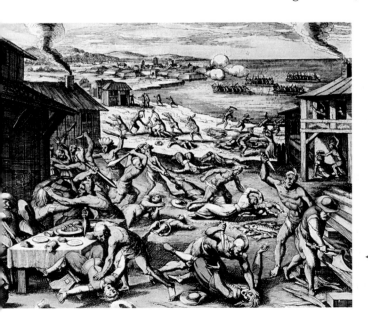

◄ Opechancanough and his warriors attacked Jamestown on March 22, 1622. They killed nearly a third of the town's 1,200 inhabitants. Afterward, the settlers destroyed many of the Indians' villages, and their crops, too.

James believed that God had given him the right to rule—he called it "divine right." He thought that divine right meant he could do almost anything he wanted to. Parliament didn't agree, and Parliament controlled most of the money in England. Parliament wouldn't give James the cash he wanted. Things got edgy.

James was a thoughtful man who might have made a fine professor. While he was on the throne the Bible was translated into English. That translation is called the "King James Bible." It was read in most Protestant churches in America until the 20th century. Many people think it the most beautiful translation ever.

But what England needed was a strong political leader, not a professor.

Let's get into a time capsule and take a look at King James's realm. Things are not going well at all. Farmers, who rent land from the rich landowning lords, are being thrown off their farms. The landlords want the land because of the new craze for sheep raising.

For some reason no one quite understands, the population is growing faster than it has ever done before. Jobs are hard to find. London and the countryside are full of beggars and starving people. Some of them climb on ships and pray for luck and a better life in the New World. Boatloads of people begin crossing the ocean.

Many of those who sail are convicts let out of jail if they will make the voyage. Englishmen write of America as a place to send their poor and troubled.

Some of the settlers are orphans. Many are very young. Heat and germs and Indians will kill most of them, yet they keep coming. Some prosper.

By midcentury (which century?) there are brick houses at Jamestown, a brick church, a fine State House, and plenty of food. For the European settlers, the American Dream has begun. Those who are tough and work hard will find in America a land of opportunity, like no land before it.

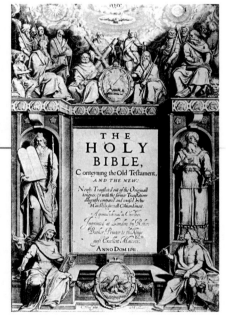

▲ An early edition of the King James Bible

Bibles and Books

The King James Bible is made up of two parts: the Old Testament and the New Testament. These books, or parts of them, have other names, too. The Old Testament is also the *Hebrew Bible;* and the first five books (do you know their names?) in the Old Testament make up the Jewish *Torah.* The Greek name for the first five books is the *Pentateuch* (PEN-tuh-tewk). The first four books of the New Testament are the *Gospels.* Another name for the King James Bible is the "Authorized Version"—because its publication was authorized by the king himself.

America, Land of the Free

From its beginnings, America was a land of freedom and opportunity for all. True or false?

The answer is FALSE.

For many of us, America was a land of humiliation and enslavement.

Africans came to the New World not because they wanted to but because they were taken from their homes by men with powerful weapons. When they protested, they were beaten and killed.

There was big money in it for those who stole them. There was big money in it for those who transported them. There were profits and an easy life for those who bought them.

Slavery was as old as history's records. Probably older. When Moses led the Israelites out of Egypt, they were escaping slavery. The ancient Greeks and Romans kept slaves. But in olden days, slaves were usually the booty of war. If you were captured in battle, you might end up a slave of the enemy. Slavery had nothing to do with skin color. Slaves were sometimes allowed to buy their freedom. Children of slaves were not always enslaved.

It was a Portuguese prince who got the African slave trade started in Europe. Remember Prince Henry the Navigator? In 1442 one of

Men, women, and children kidnapped by slave traders in Africa are marched to ports where they will be loaded onto slave ships for transport to the Americas. ▼

▲ Members of a family are separated at a slave
market on the coast of West Africa.

his ships arrived in Portugal with 10 captured Africans. The Portuguese were looking for ways to make money. Africans were good workers. Selling them as slaves would be a profitable business. Prince Henry gave those 10 black Africans as a gift to the Roman Catholic pope. The pope gave Portugal the right to trade in Africa. But by 1455 the slave trade had become so abusive that Prince Henry tried to stop it. It was too late.

When the New World was discovered, workers were needed to mine its resources and to work its fields. Europeans didn't want those jobs; slaves had no choice.

Slavery in America developed into a terrible and degrading system. To justify that terrible system, a myth arose that blacks were inferior, that they weren't capable people.

Of course, that was just a myth. Africa had produced great cities and beautiful arts. In the 11th century the great African empire of Ghana was flourishing, with "fine houses and solid buildings," and a royal pavilion where pages held gold-tipped swords, horses gleamed in cloths of gold, and princes were "splendidly

clad and with gold plaited into their hair." Slaves, in the ancient African kingdoms, were a sign of wealth. It was the way of the world. To be a slave was considered bad luck, not a wrong. The slave trade with other lands thrived—especially with Arabia, Persia, India, even China. Then the Portuguese arrived.

In America an entire way of life depended on the labor of black people. Despite harsh treatment, blacks produced writers, scientists, political leaders, musicians, and many others who enriched our nation.

A famous philosopher—named George Santayana—said, "Those who cannot remember the past are condemned to repeat it." What do you think he meant? Do you think he was talking of nations, or people, or both?

American slavery was a horror. We should never pretend it was anything else. But the American system of government lets us correct mistakes. When you study history you see we usually do. Of that we can be proud.

CHAPTER 31

The *Mayflower*: Saints and Strangers

The times were religious—and angry. To understand them we need to review some English history. Remember King Henry VIII? He was the father of Queen Elizabeth. King Henry tossed the Catholic Church out of England long before Jamestown got started. Why Henry did that is an interesting story, but you'll have to look up the details yourself. It had something to do with King Henry's wanting to get married again, and again, and again, and—whew—he had a lot of energy.

The head of the Catholic Church, the Pope, didn't approve of all that marrying. So King Henry founded the Church of England (which is sometimes called the Anglican Church) and made himself its leader.

By the 17th century most English men and women belonged to that church. (As they still do.) It was called the "established church" because it was linked to the government. Since he was king, James was head of the Church of England. The man who actually ran the church was called the Archbishop of Canterbury, and he was appointed by the king.

By the 17th century, most English men and women belonged to the Church of England. (Shown here is Christ Church Cathedral in Oxford, England.) ▶

The Pope lived in Rome in a great palace called the Vatican. The Vatican was, and is, the control center for the entire Roman Catholic Church. The Pope is elected by bishops of the Catholic Church.

Except for that matter of control and leadership, the Anglicans and Catholics were much alike, although they didn't think so and often hated and persecuted each other. As I said, the times were not only religious, but also intolerant. People took their differences very seriously. Wars were fought over them.

Some Englishmen wanted the differences between Catholics and Protestants to be greater. They felt that King Henry VIII didn't go far enough when he outlawed the Catholic Church. They didn't want the Anglican church service to be at all like the Catholic service. They said they wanted to "purify" the Church of England, so they were called Puritans.

Others wanted to go even further. They believed people could speak directly to God without a priest or bishop at all. They wanted to separate themselves from the Church of England and form congregations of their own. They called themselves "Saints." Other people called them "Separatists." Some people called them troublemakers.

King James would not let the Separatists practice their religion. They had to go to the Church of England or go to jail. Their religion was more important to them than their homes—and sometimes than life itself. Some of the Separatists, especially a group from a village in northeast England called Scrooby, decided to move to Holland, where they were promised religious freedom.

And they got religious freedom in Holland—but they didn't feel at home with the Dutch. They were English, and they liked their own customs and language and villages. When their children started speaking Dutch and forgetting English ways, the people from Scrooby decided it was time to move again. They read John Smith's book, *Description of New England,* and they said, "This time to America."

▲ Statues of the popes at the Vatican in Rome

John Smith offered to hire himself out to the Pilgrims as their guide. They told him his book was "better cheap" than he was.

The Pilgrims board the *Mayflower* to begin their journey to North America. ▶

Anyone who takes a trip for religious purposes is a *pilgrim*. So now these Scrooby people who were called Separatists or Saints had a new name: Pilgrims. They were the first of many, many boatloads of pilgrims who would come to America to be free to believe whatever they wanted to believe. They, however, were pilgrims with a capital P: *the* Pilgrims.

The year is 1620. The boat they take is named the *Mayflower*. Of the 102 on board, only about half are Saints; the Scrooby people call the others "Strangers." The Strangers are leaving England for adventure, or because they are unhappy or in trouble. Saints and Strangers have many things in common. Most are from the lower classes; most have a trade; they expect to work hard; they are ambitious; and they can't stand the new ideas that are changing England. All want a better life, but the Saints hope to build a society more perfect than any on earth.

Among the Strangers are 10 indentured servants, a professional soldier, a barrelmaker, four orphans indentured, or "bound," to work without pay until they are 21, and a man soon to be convicted of murder.

Among the Saints is William Bradford, who will be elected as the colony's second governor and will write their story.

It is a terrible voyage, taking 66 days. The ship is small, wet, and foul. The smells are horrid. There is no place to change or wash clothes. Each adult is assigned a space below deck measuring seven by two and a half feet. Children get even less room. None of the

The word *indentured* originally came from the paper that the contract between master and servant was written on. After they signed it, the paper was torn in half, so that each piece had an *indentation* that fitted into the other piece. The master kept one piece and the servant kept the other. That was the proof of their agreement.

passengers is allowed on deck; there is little fresh air below and many are sick. Fresh food soon runs out and then there is hard bread and dried meat that is wet and moldy. But the Pilgrims have onions, lemon juice, and beer to keep them from getting the dreaded scurvy. Amazingly, only one person dies. He is replaced on the roster by a baby born at sea, Oceanus (oh-shee-ANN-us) Hopkins. Another child, Peregrine White, is born just before they dock.

Scurvy is a disease resulting from lack of vitamin C. It makes people bleed easily and causes their teeth to fall out.

When they first sight American land, it is at Cape Cod. They planned to go to Virginia, but they are exhausted. Bradford describes Cape Cod as a "hideous and desolate wilderness, full of wild beasts and men." They sail around the cape to a place they see on Smith's map. He has called it Plymouth, after a town in England.

Before they get off the ship, there are matters to attend to. There has been trouble between Saints and Strangers, and it needs to be settled. They must live together peacefully. They need rules and laws and leaders. So they draw up a plan of government, the Mayflower Compact, which establishes a governing body:

> *To enact, constitute, and frame such just and equal laws, ordinances, acts, constitutions, offices…for the general good of the Colony; unto which, we promise all due submission and obedience.*

The Mayflower Compact ▼

◀ Before going ashore, the men on board the *Mayflower* drew up an agreement on how they would govern themselves. The Mayflower Compact is one of the great founding documents of American history.

That Mayflower Compact is one of the great documents of American history. Here is a group of settlers able to govern themselves; reasonable people who agree to live together under a government of laws. The king doesn't realize what is in the future. This breed of people will not allow others to rule them for long.

Then, wrote Bradford, "being thus arrived in a good harbor, and brought safe to land, they fell upon their knees and blessed the God of Heaven who had brought them over the vast and furious ocean."

When they land, they find empty fields cleared for planting. They will learn that smallpox, caught from white fishermen, has wiped out many of New England's Indians. The Pilgrims believe that God has made the land theirs for the taking.

But it is December—too late to plant crops. Many will hunger and die before spring comes. Fewer than half of the 102 who land will survive the first winter. But no one wants to return to England. These are sturdy folk who intend to start a nation. William Bradford writes of the colony "as one small candle may light a thousand, so the light here kindled hath shone unto many, yea in some sort to our whole nation."

The Pilgrims about to land at Plymouth ▶

Pilgrims, Indians, and Puritans

Like the Jamestown colonists, the Pilgrims have picked a poor site. The New England coast is cold and wind-whipped; the land is rocky, the soil is thin. But these industrious people will use the sea and the forest to sustain themselves. Soon they will be shipping fish, furs, and lumber back to England.

Without the Indians they might not have survived. Picture this scene: Pilgrims are struggling to find ways to live in this difficult region, when out of the woods strides a tall man in deerskin clothes. They are astounded when he greets them. "Welcome, Englishmen," he says. His name is Samoset, and he has learned some English from fishermen and traders.

▲ In the cold of winter, the Pilgrims struggle to build a settlement. Fewer than half survived the first winter.

Squanto's real name is Tisquantum. These Native Americans are Algonquians of the *Wampanoag* tribe, who live in what is now Rhode Island. Wampanoag means "eastern people." They hunt, fish, dig for clams, and gather berries and nuts. They are good cooks; they make venison (deer) steak, fish chowders, succotash, cornbread, and maple sugar.

One of America's first folk songs praised the humble but essential pumpkin.

For pottage and puddings and custards and pies

Our pumpkins and parsnips are common supplies.

We have pumpkin at morning and pumpkin at noon,

If it were not for pumpkin, we should be undone.

Samoset returns with 60 Indians, a chieftain named Massasoit, and an Indian whom the settlers name Squanto. Squanto speaks English well. He had been kidnapped by sailors, taken to London, befriended by a London merchant, and then returned to his native land.

Trumpet and drums are played as the Pilgrims' governor, John Carver, leads Massasoit to his house, kisses his hand (as is proper to a king), offers refreshments, and writes a treaty of peace between the Indians and the English. While Massasoit is alive, the peace will be kept.

Squanto stays with the settlers. To the Pilgrims he was "a special instrument sent of God for their good beyond their expectation…He directed them how to set [plant] their corn, where to take [catch] fish, and to procure other commodities, and was also their pilot to bring them to unknown places."

In 1621, after the first harvest, the Pilgrims invite their Indian friends to a three-day feast of Thanksgiving. In one year they have accomplished much.

The Pilgrims are frugal, but the celebration is unusually generous. They will need their food to get through the winter and to help feed the new colonists who are beginning to arrive.

William Bradford, who is elected governor when John Carver dies suddenly, keeps a record of the arrivals. When the ship *Fortune* docks he writes, "there was not so much as biscuit-cake, neither had they any bedding… nor pot, or pan."

▲ Squanto

The Wampanoag chieftain, Massasoit ▶

Abraham Pearce, a black indentured servant, is one of those who comes in 1623. A few years later he will own land, vote, and be a respected member of the community.

The new arrivals bring reports from England that are not good. Now the Puritans are in trouble. The Puritans are also called Saints, but they are more moderate than the Pilgrims. Remember, Puritans don't want to separate themselves from the Church of England, they want to purify the church. What they really want is to control the Church of England; of course, King James and those in charge don't want that at all.

The Puritans can't stand King James and he doesn't like them either. Of the Puritans he says, "I will make them conform themselves, or else I will harry [harass] them out of the land." The Puritans can see that King James isn't good for England's economy. First there is inflation and then a depression. James has brought his big-spending friends to England from Scotland, where he is also king. They are getting special favors. The Puritans are not.

And so a group of Puritans gathers at Cambridge University, where most of them have gone to college, and makes plans to sail to America. The Puritans are better educated than the Pilgrims—and richer, too. John Winthrop, their leader, is a lawyer, born on a manor, with servants and tenants.

When King James dies, in 1625, and Charles I becomes king, things get even worse for the Puritans.

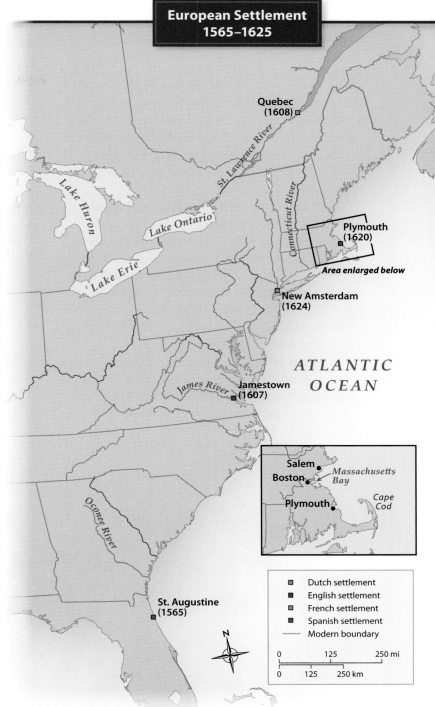

▲ By 1625, England and other European nations established settlements on the eastern edge of North America.

Giving Thanks

The story that the first American Thanksgiving was held at Plymouth Colony is a real turkey. In 1540, long before the Pilgrims sat down to their big dinner, Francisco Vasquez de Coronado and his men conducted a thanksgiving service in their camp at Palo Duro Canyon in what is now known as the Texas Panhandle.

Half a century before the Pilgrims landed, French Huguenots settled near today's Jacksonville, Florida. They "sang a psalm of Thanksgiving unto God, beseeching Him…to continue his accustomed goodness toward us." Unfortunately for the French, the goodness did not continue. Their colony was wiped out by Spanish raiders. Still, some Floridians claim that as the first American Thanksgiving.

A group of English Catholics arrived in Maine in 1605, said prayers of thanks, faced a year of Maine weather, changed their minds about living in America, and sailed back to England. But some Mainiacs (yes, that's what they are called) say their state had the first Thanksgiving.

Two years before the feast in Massachusetts, the settlers at Berkeley Hundred, on the James River in Virginia, decreed that the day of their landing, December 4, 1619, "shall be yearly and perpetually kept holy as a day of Thanksgiving." Did they have a feast? It depends on whom you ask at Berkeley Plantation. (There is no documented record of one.)

Now, to give the Pilgrims their due: they did eat a big meal, and one of them—Edward Winslow—wrote six sentences about it. None of the other claimants can say that.

Those Pilgrims needed a good meal. Fewer than half of the 102 passengers who came on the *Mayflower* in 1620 survived their first American winter. The local Indians weren't in good shape either. They had been hit—hard hit—by diseases brought by French fishermen, who had made contact four years earlier.

The English colonists wouldn't have survived at all—and they

◀ After their first harvest, the Pilgrims invited their Indian friends to a three-day feast of Thanksgiving.

knew it—if it hadn't been for corn and other help from the Indians. And Massasoit was forever grateful to Winslow, who made a nourishing broth that helped him recover from a serious illness. Good will, necessity, and plain good sense seem to have made them all good neighbors.

So when harvest time arrived in 1621, the Pilgrims had much to be thankful for. They had made a start at the beaver trade, they lived in peace with the Native Americans, 11 houses had been built, and, thanks to Squanto, the corn harvest was good. They had celebrated harvest time in Holland; they wished to continue that tradition.

They invited Massasoit to join them. He came with 90 hungry Indians. They might have wiped out the larder, but the Indians "went and killed five deer, which they brought to the plantation and bestowed on our governor," Winslow writes.

We don't know exactly what the Pilgrims cooked, but ducks, geese, turkeys, clams, eels, lobsters, squash, wild grapes, dried fruit, and cornbread are all good guesses, along with watercress and other "sallet herbes." Winslow says, "Our governor sent four men on fowling, that so we might after a special manner rejoice together after we had gathered the fruit of our labors. They four in one day killed as much fowl as, with a little help beside, served the company almost a week." That's as detailed as he gets, with this addition: "for three days we entertained and feasted."

That's all we know? That's it. Except for a brief word from Governor William Bradford, who doesn't write specifically about a feast with the Indians, but does say that "they began now to gather in the small harvest they had....

All summer there was no want; and now began to come in store of fowl, as winter approached, of which this place did abound....And besides waterfowl there was great store of wild turkeys, of which they took many, besides venison, etc. Besides, they had about a peck of meal a week to a person, or now since harvest, Indian corn in that proportion."

Did they eat cranberries, which were thick in the nearby bogs? Or pumpkin pie? Not likely. You need sugar for those dishes, and they didn't have any.

As devout Christians, the Pilgrims gave thanks before each meal. But this was a harvest festival, not, primarily, a celebration of thanks to God. And it probably came at the end of September. Still, all in all, the spirit was the same as at today's November festival where we give thanks, we remember, we enjoy—and we eat!

The first national Thanksgiving was actually proclaimed by George Washington in 1789. But Thanksgiving was not celebrated officially again until Abraham Lincoln (urged on by a magazine editor, Sarah J. Hale) decreed a national holiday in 1863. Since then it's been turkey all the way.

◀ Pumpkins and turkeys are native to North America. It is likely the Pilgrims ate them along with other native plants and animals.

Puritans, Puritans, and More Puritans

In 1630, the first Puritan ship, the *Arbella,* sets out for the New World. By summer's end 1,000 Puritans have landed in New England. They bring a charter from the king: the Charter of the Company of the Massachusetts Bay in New England. King Charles is happy to see the Puritans leave England.

The charter is a document written by lawyers, setting the rules that tell how the colony will be run. It allows the colonists to govern themselves. It is important to remember that, from the beginning, English settlers expected to govern themselves. It is important to remember that each colony had a charter: a written set of rules. Those charters would evolve into constitutions.

Massachusetts is an Algonquian word that means "at the big hill." The Puritans called their new home the Massachusetts Bay Colony.

An English settlement in New England ▶

Can you guess what might happen in a community without a charter or constitution? Would you like to live in a country without laws? Would you want to write your own laws or have someone write them for you?

You can think about those questions and then get back to the Puritans, who are beginning to pour out of England. Most of them go to the Caribbean islands, where sugar is creating great fortunes. But, between 1630 and 1640, 20,000 Puritans sail for New England. Think about all those people risking their lives to cross the ocean and settle in an unknown land. It is almost as if tens of thousands of people today decided to live in outer space.

Why did they come? Many came because they really cared about their religion and wanted to practice it in peace. They wanted to build a holy community, where people would live by the rules of the Bible. Puritans believed the Bible was the whole word of God. They tried to follow its every direction, which means they tried to live very good lives.

Although the Puritans tried hard to be good, things didn't work out as they wished. They expected their colony to be an example for all the world. John Winthrop, who was chosen as governor, said, "We must consider that we shall be as a city upon a hill. The eyes of all people are upon us."

One thing they didn't understand at all was the idea of *toleration*. Puritans came to America to find religious freedom—but only for themselves. They didn't believe in the kind of religious freedom we have today. But don't be too hard on them. Almost no one else believed in it either. And how many people do you know who are willing to devote their lives to an idea they believe to be right?

In those days each nation had its own church, and everyone was expected to pay taxes for its support. Suppose you didn't believe in the ideas of that religion. Too bad. You had to keep quiet, leave the country, go to jail, or maybe get hanged.

▲ John Winthrop served as governor of the Massachusetts Bay Colony for 12 years.

At first, the name *Quaker* was used to make fun of people; so, too, was the word *Puritan*. Then both groups decided to be proud of those words and use them themselves.

Pretend you are a Puritan. You think that yours is the only true religion, so you believe the Reverend John Cotton when he says toleration is "liberty…to tell lies in the name of the Lord."

Since you are convinced that only you Puritans are right, you think it is wrong to let anyone practice another religion. You believe that is helping the devil. You especially dislike Quakers. Your leaders call them a "cursed sect." You use the name *Quaker* to describe religious people who call themselves "Friends." Friends believe that each person has an inner light that leads him to God. People with an inner light do not have to rely on a minister to tell them what is godly. The inner light is available to everyone. This is a highly democratic idea, and most Europeans thought it very dangerous. They were used to kings and priests and ministers. It seemed reasonable to them to persecute Quakers. When Quakers came to New England or Virginia, they were whipped, sent away, and even hanged.

Remember, you are a Puritan and you've left your home and everything you know and love. You've crossed a fierce ocean to live as you wish. You don't want people with strange ideas bothering you. Democracy is another strange idea. "If the people be governors, who shall be governed?" the Reverend Cotton asks. John Winthrop, the beloved Puritan governor, who always tries to do what is best, calls democracy the "meanest [lowest] and worst" form of government.

And yet the Puritans do practice a kind of democracy—but only for male church members. Once a year they form a General Court and vote to elect the governor and council. The General Court is a lot like the House of Burgesses, or Parliament, or Congress.

Some people call the Massachusetts Bay Colony a "theocracy" (thee-OCK-ruh-see), government by church officials in the name of God. But they are wrong. It is not a theocracy. The ministers are the most important people in the colony, but they are not allowed to hold political office. They do not govern. It is a small step toward the idea of the separation of church and state. Someday that idea will be a foundation of American liberty.

At a Quaker meeting, as shown here, men and women sat together, which differed from Puritan services, in which women sat upstairs or at the back. ▼

Of Towns and Schools and Sermons

At first the New England settlers built their homes behind high fences called "stockades." They were fearful of the unknown—of Indians and animals.

Soon they began spreading out, beyond the fences, into small towns with names like Greenfield, Springfield, and Longmeadow. The names described the land. Many of those early settlements were just a row of houses strung alongside abandoned Indian fields that the English settlers found and took. Sometimes they lived with Indians as neighbors, although their domesticated animals made that difficult.

▲ Early settlers often built stockades around their homes for protection.

The Native Americans hunted animals; they had no horses, cows, sheep, or hogs. The Indians soon discovered that those English grazing animals could destroy their cornfields. In 1653 the people of the town of New Haven agreed to work for 60 days to build fences around fields planted by neighboring Indians. New England's courts ordered colonists to pay the Indians for damage done to their fields by wandering animals.

As the colonists began to prosper, they built towns in America that were something like the villages they left behind in Europe. They were compact, easy

People in New England villages were usually friendly and neighborly to each other. They had to be. A family needed the neighbors' help to clear rocks out of a field or raise a barn roof. Usually one cowman looked after everybody's cows. But if a stranger came hanging around with no invitation from a local family, he was chased out of town.

The community comes together to build a house. ▶

Puritans liked to give their children names that were reminders of goodness and holiness. Some we still find occasionally, like Constance, Faith, or Hope; and some seem strange: Joy-from-Above, Kill-sin, Fear, Patience, Wrestling-with-the-Devil.

to defend, and friendly. Castles and manor houses dominated European towns; in New England's villages it was the meetinghouse that stood out. The meetinghouse was used as a church, a town hall, and a social center. It was usually placed at one end of a big field that was called a common, because everyone used it in common. Sometimes, where sheep chewed the field's grass and kept it short and green, the common was called a green. Houses were built around the green. The houses nearest the meetinghouse belonged to the most important people in town: the minister and the church leaders.

Many villages had a stream. The tumbling water of the stream turned a big wheel, and that provided power for the mills where wood was sawed and wheat ground into flour.

As the town grew other buildings were added: a general store, a blacksmith's shop, a furniture maker's shop, a candle maker's.

If the town was large enough, there might be an inn. Almost always there was a school.

The Puritans cared about schooling. By 1636 they had founded Harvard College. It was amazing that they had a college so soon after they arrived, although Harvard did get off to a rocky start. The first teacher beat his students, fed them spoiled meat, and ran off with college money.

◀ Flowing water turned the wheel that provided power for the mill.

Then they got a college president, Henry Dunster. He was so good that students began coming to study with him from Virginia and Bermuda and even England itself. Of course, they were all Puritans.

Because of their religion, Puritans weren't allowed to attend college in England. That was one reason it was so important to have Harvard succeed. To do that it had to have a supply of students. So, in 1642, the Massachusetts Bay Colony passed a law saying that parents must teach their children to read.

The Puritans wanted everyone to be able to read the Bible, even those who weren't going to Harvard. So the next thing they did was pass a law that said:

A young Puritan woman reads while spinning at her wheel. All Puritan children, both boys and girls, were taught to read so they could read the Bible. ▼

> *It is therefore ordered, that every township in this jurisdiction, after the Lord has increased its number to 50 householders, shall then forthwith appoint one within their town to teach all such children as shall resort to him to write and read, whose wages shall be paid either by the parents or masters of such children, or by the inhabitants in general.*

Harvard College was founded in 1636. For many years the college had a very English class consciousness. Until 1769 the roster of students was not listed in alphabetical order but according to social status—which meant that if you were from an important family, you were listed ahead of somebody of low rank. ▼

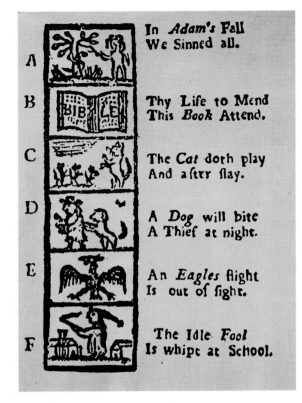

▲ Several generations learned their ABCs from the New England Primer (above), which used rhymes to help children remember letters.

In plain English, that means that every town with 50 or more families must have a schoolteacher.

Do you see something unusual in that law? Read that bit at the end, "shall be paid…by the inhabitants in general." Do you know what that means? It means that everyone in the town has to pay for the education of the children. Not just the parents. That is what public education is all about. It guarantees that every child, not just those with wealthy parents, can go to school. In America, it all began with that school law in 1647.

I know what you're thinking. Why did they have to go and do it? Who needs school anyway? But you don't really mean it. It isn't fun to be ignorant.

In the 17th century much teaching was done by parents, or in church, or, if you were an apprentice, by your master. But the Puritans could see that sometimes that wasn't enough. Some parents just weren't good teachers, even though many Puritans were highly educated themselves. The Puritans thought it important that everyone read the Bible. In Boston and the larger towns some children were actually taught to read the Bible in its original languages. So little Puritan boys and girls of six and seven learned to read Latin and Greek, and a few learned Hebrew, too. That sounds hard, and it was, but learning languages is good training for the mind. Many of this nation's greatest thinkers came from Puritan stock.

Blowing Thy Nose

Many little Puritan boys and girls had to study a book called *The School of Good Manners*. It reminded them to "stand not wriggling with thy body hither and thither, but steady and upright," or that "when thou blowest thy nose, let thy handkerchief be used." Naughty children were whipped with a birch stick or cane. "Spare the rod and spoil the child" was a firm belief even of kind parents and teachers.

An early New England school room ▶

▲ Puritans on their way to worship

Puritans used time in the stocks as a punishment for many offenses. ▼

Try and take yourself back to Puritan times, and see what you think of Sunday churchgoing. Those Puritan ministers gave sermons that lasted for hours and hours. Sometimes there was an intermission for lunch, and then everyone went back to hear more. There was no heat in the meetinghouse, and New England can get very cold. People brought warming boxes with hot coals in them to keep their feet from freezing. Sometimes they brought their dogs to church for the same reason.

A church official held a tickling rod to wake up anyone who looked as if he might be falling asleep. The dog whipper took out dogs who barked. If you were a troublemaker and wiggled and made noise you could get locked up in the town stocks. You'd have to sit there with your hands and feet stuck into a wooden contraption and everyone would make fun of you.

We know you wouldn't like that kind of life, but maybe things weren't so bad for the Puritan boys and girls. Maybe some of them even looked forward to the sermons. Remember, in Puritan Massachusetts there were no movies and no TVs. At first, there were no newspapers, no magazines, and only a few books. The Puritans were intelligent people who could read and think well. Maybe that will help you understand why everyone tried to listen to the weekly sermon and why Puritans sometimes spent all week talking about it.

Feeling Blue

Rules banning work, trade, and playing on Sundays—the Sabbath—are still called "blue laws," because the Puritans wrote the laws in books bound in blue paper. You could be fined or punished for doing these things on Sunday: running, cooking, making a bed, or shaving. A man was whipped for saying that the minister's sermon was boring. Another was put in the stocks after kissing his wife on his return home from three years at sea. And celebrating Christmas was forbidden. It was considered "popish"—something that Roman Catholics did. Most Puritans worked on Christmas—unless, of course, it happened to fall on a Sunday.

Roger Williams

The Puritans, who were victims of intolerance in England, were not tolerant themselves. Although they preached the Golden Rule—do unto others as you would have them do unto you—most never understood that they were breaking that rule. Roger Williams did.

Williams was a Puritan minister who came to Massachusetts seeking a "pure" religious community. Like the other Puritans, he was a serious Christian. Like the others, he disapproved of Catholic and Quaker ideas. Like the others, he thought the Indian religions were pagan.

But that's where "like the others" stops.

He didn't believe in forcing anyone to believe as he did. He believed that killing or punishing in the name of Christianity was sinful. He thought that church members—not general taxes—should pay the bills at each church. He respected the beliefs of others. Those were strange ideas in 17th-century Massachusetts.

The Puritans didn't know what to do with Roger Williams. He was a Puritan, he was brilliant, he was a minister, and he was so nice that even his opponents had a hard time disliking him.

But what an ungrateful young man he seemed! The Puritans had offered him good jobs, as teacher and minister, and he thanked them by criticizing their practices.

Governor Winthrop was shocked. So was John Cotton, the minister who took a job that Williams refused. They were especially shocked when Williams wrote a book saying it was wrong to persecute people for their beliefs. Williams called his book *The Bloody Tenet*. (The blood was from those killed because of their religious ideas.) John Cotton wrote his own book. He called it

Catholics, Quakers, and Puritans were all Christians, but they each interpreted Christianity in a different way. To the Puritans—and to most Christians—pagan religions were not "real" religions, as Christianity was.

A *tenet* (TEN-it) is a basic idea, a fundamental concept.

▲ This statue of Roger Williams stands in the U.S. Capitol.

The Bloody Tenet Washed and Made White.
Of course that didn't end it. Williams's next
book was *The Bloody Tenet Made Yet More
Bloody by Mr. Cotton's Endeavor to Wash It
White in the Blood of the Lamb.*

When Roger Williams started preaching
that land shouldn't be taken from the
Indians—that the king had no right to charter
land that didn't belong to him—that was too
much. The officers of the Massachusetts Bay
Colony made arrangements to ship Williams
back to England. They sent armed men to put
him on a boat.

Roger Williams's wife heard the verdict of the court—that he
was to be arrested and banished—and began to cry. Williams told
her, "Fifty good men did what they thought was just." Roger
Williams didn't hold grudges.

But he wasn't about to let himself get shipped back to
England, and so he fled from Massachusetts. It was January 1636,
he was sick, and the weather was freezing. Later, when he was an old
man, Roger Williams would still remember that terrible winter. He was
always thankful to the Narraganset Indians, who helped him survive
the cold. He learned to love them as they loved him.

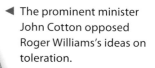

◀ The prominent minister
John Cotton opposed
Roger Williams's ideas on
toleration.

▲ In *The Bloody Tenet* (which
can also be spelled *Tenent*),
Roger Williams opposed
the persecution of people
for their beliefs.

◀ When Roger Williams fled
New England, the Narraganset
Indians helped him survive
the winter.

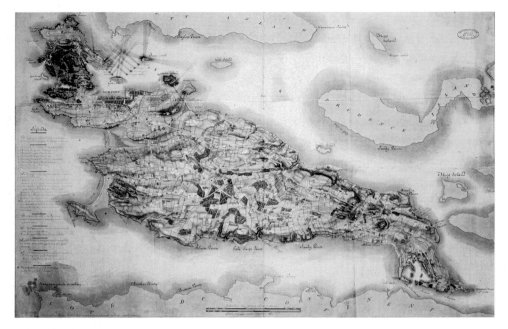

▲ Rhode Island

He bought land from the Indians and started a colony called Providence. It became the capital of Rhode Island and soon attracted many of those who were not wanted elsewhere. Someone described Providence as the place where "all the cranks of New England" go.

There were plenty of cranks in Providence. But there were also many who were searching for what Williams called "freedom of conscience."

When Roger Williams said *freedom of conscience,* he meant the freedom of each person to follow his own mind and heart and choose his own religion. That was to become an important right in America.

Roger Williams welcomed everyone who wished to come to Rhode Island, including Quakers and Catholics. And, while he continued to disagree with those religions, he never let that stop him from liking some of the people who practiced them. Jews, who were often persecuted elsewhere, were welcome in Rhode Island. Atheists were welcome, too.

Atheists believe there is no God.

Williams believed that state governments should not have any connection with a church. We call that separation of church and state. It was a very new idea at the time.

He knew that people could be forced to go to church, but that no one's mind could be forced to believe. "Forced worship stinks in God's nostrils," said Roger Williams.

He learned the language of the Narraganset Indians and wrote a book so that others could learn it, too. When the great Narraganset chief Canonicus (kuh-NON-ih-kuss) was dying, he called for Roger Williams to be with him. White men had destroyed the Indian chief's kingdom, and he hated most of them. But Williams and Canonicus had something in common. Each was able to judge people by their character, not by their skin color or religion. They loved and respected each other.

Edmund S. Morgan, a historian who wrote a book about Roger Williams, said "We may praise him…for his defense of religious liberty and the separation of church and state.…His greatness was simpler. He dared to think."

▲ In 1763, thanks to the atmosphere of tolerance that Roger Williams fostered, Rhode Island became the home of the first permanent Jewish house of worship in America, the Touro Synagogue.

Church and State

The Puritans forced some Indians to become Christians. Roger Williams wrote a letter to the Massachusetts governor. "Are not the English of this land generally a persecuted people from their native land?" he asked. How could those who had been persecuted persecute others, he wondered? He said that the Indians should "not be forced from their religions."

Roger Williams didn't think anyone should be compelled to follow a religion. Besides, he knew it never works to try that. You can make people do things, but you can't make them believe what they don't want to believe.

Williams said that it was "against the testimony of Christ Jesus for the civil state to impose [force] upon the souls of the people a religion."

Most Puritans didn't agree with Roger Williams. They thought it was the job of the government leaders to tell people what to believe.

But Roger Williams's ideas won out. They helped bring about the separation of church and state that is one of the most important of all of America's governing ideas. In Europe and the rest of the world, millions of people have died in wars over religion, but that has not happened in this country.

Roger Williams, a devout Puritan, wrote, "Jesus never called for the sword of steel to help the sword of spirit."

"Woman, Hold Your Tongue"

Anne Hutchinson was another troublemaker. At least that is what some Puritans thought. Here was a woman with 14 children who was interpreting the Bible. No one objected to that, until she began to question some of the ministers' beliefs. Soon she was trying to reach everyone with her ideas about God. Governor Winthrop was outraged. Didn't Mistress Hutchinson have enough to do, with all those babies to feed?

What was worse, in Winthrop's view, was that people were listening to her. Even men were listening. There was a reason: Anne Hutchinson had a fine mind, and she loved God. Besides, what she was saying made sense. Winthrop admitted that she was "a woman with a ready wit and bold spirit." Before long, Massachusetts was split between people who believed what Anne Hutchinson said and those who believed the ministers. She claimed God was guiding her; the ministers said they were doing God's work on earth.

Anne Hutchinson on trial in Boston in 1637 ▼

Finally, the Puritans held a trial. You can read the court records for yourself. You may agree that Mrs. Hutchinson was smarter than her accusers, but that didn't help her a bit. She was kicked out of Massachusetts and out of the Puritan church, too. She moved to Rhode Island. Later Anne Hutchinson moved to New York and was killed by Indians. Governor Winthrop saw it as the judgment of God.

In those days, women, like children, were expected to be seen but not heard. They belonged to their husbands. The word for them was *chattel*. That means a "piece of property." A husband could sell his wife's labor and keep the wages. If she ran away, she was accused of stealing herself and her clothing. Her husband even owned her clothes.

From a Massachusetts Court Record, 1637

ANNE HUTCHINSON: Therefore take heed how you proceed against me, for I know that for this you go about to do me, God will ruin you and your posterity, and this whole state.

MR. NOWELL: How do you know that it was God that did reveal these things to you, and not Satan?

MRS. HUTCHINSON: How did Abraham know that it was God that bid him offer [sacrifice] his son, being a breach of the sixth commandment?

DEPUTY-GOVERNOR DUDLEY: By an immediate voice.

MRS. HUTCHINSON: So to me by an immediate revelation.

DEPUTY-GOVERNOR: How! an immediate revelation?

MRS. HUTCHINSON: By the voice of his own spirit to my soul.

GOVERNOR JOHN WINTHROP: Daniel was delivered by miracle; do you think to be delivered so too?

MRS. HUTCHINSON: I do here speak it before the Court. I look that the Lord should deliver me by his providence....

GOVERNOR WINTHROP: The Court hath already declared themselves satisfied concerning the things you hear, and concerning the troublesomeness of her spirit, and the danger of her course amongst us, which is not to be suffered. Therefore, if it be the mind of the Court that Mrs. Hutchinson, for these things that appear before us, is unfit for our society, and if it be the mind of the Court that she shall be banished out of our liberties, and imprisoned till she be sent away, let them hold up their hands.

All but three held up their hands.

GOVERNOR WINTHROP: Those that are contrary minded, hold up yours.

Mr. Coddington and Mr. Colburn only.

MR. JENNISON: I cannot hold up my hand one way or the other, and I shall give my reason if the Court require it.

GOVERNOR WINTHROP: Mrs. Hutchinson, you hear the sentence of the Court. It is that you are banished from out our jurisdiction as being a woman not fit for our society. And you are to be imprisoned till the Court send you away.

MRS. HUTCHINSON: I desire to know wherefore [why] I am banished.

GOVERNOR WINTHROP: Say no more. The Court knows wherefore, and is satisfied.

▲ A Quaker meeting

Anne Hutchinson wasn't the only strong woman to trouble John Winthrop and the Massachusetts Bay Puritans. Her best friend was a problem, too.

Mary Dyer followed the ways of Anne Hutchinson. When Anne Hutchinson was cast out of Massachusetts, Mary Dyer and her husband, William, and other believers went with her.

Later, Mary Dyer took a trip back to England and found other truths for herself. She became a member of the Society of Friends, the people who were known as Quakers. Quakers call their church services "meetings." In a Quaker meeting everyone is equal, anyone may speak out, and there are no ministers. Now, in the 17th century equality was not fashionable. Besides, Quakers refuse to swear oaths of allegiance to anyone but God. But oaths of loyalty to king and country were expected in England and everywhere in the 17th century.

At Quaker meetings, the congregation sits and meditates in silence. Sometimes a member feels that God is communicating with him or her directly. The Friend might start talking aloud about this "inward light," or might shake and tremble—which was how the Quakers got their name.

You need to understand that the church and the government were all part of one package in the Old World. It was the church that gave the king his right to govern. It was called the "divine right of kings." It was the government that gave the church support and lands. That was the way it had always been. It seemed as if people like the Quakers wanted to mess things up. The Quakers believed in toleration, and they believed each person could think for himself. What happens if you let people think for themselves? Why, the next step might be for them to say that the king's church and the king's priests weren't needed. And Quakers did say something like that when they sat in their meetings without ministers.

So maybe you can see why Quakers were hated and persecuted by the authorities in England. They weren't liked any better in the colonies. The magistrates of the Massachusetts Bay Colony passed harsh laws to keep them away, but that didn't stop them. Some Quakers seemed determined to be martyrs, and Mary Dyer was one of them. She came to Boston and was sent away. She came back. This time she was tried, with two Quaker men, and all three were led to the gallows.

The men were hanged, but at the last minute Dyer was sent off to Rhode Island. She came back again. The Puritans tried Mary Dyer again. This time they offered her her life if she would leave Massachusetts forever. She refused. Mary Dyer was hanged, on June 1, 1660, on the Boston Common in front of where the State House stands today. Her death was too much for some Puritans. In 1661 the law was changed. Today, statues of Mary Dyer and Anne Hutchinson can be seen on the Common.

▲ Mary Dyer going to the scaffold

A *martyr* (MAR-tur) is someone who would rather die than give up his or her belief.

A *gallows* was the two standing poles and crosspiece from which people were hanged.

Of Witches and Dinosaurs

How many Puritans do you know? Don't think too hard. The answer is zero. Puritans are like dinosaurs: they are extinct.

I'll tell you what happened to them in just a minute, but don't worry, things worked out well. Many of their descendants turned into New England Yankees. Others are spread all across the nation. Many go to the Congregational church. In some ways, however, we are all descendants of the Puritans.

If you are an American, you are a descendant of the Puritans—at least a little bit—because many American laws and ideas come from Puritan laws and ideas, and they are some of the best we have.

You see, the Puritans hoped to build a place on earth where people could live as the Bible says they should, a place where people would be truly good. Governor Winthrop called Puritan Massachusetts "a city upon a hill." He expected it to stand tall as a symbol to the rest of the world. "The eyes of all people are upon us," he said.

That phrase, *city upon a hill,* is one to put in your head and remember. You'll hear it again and again when you read American history.

▼ In Puritan times, almost everyone believed in witches. Here, a suspected witch is under examination.

▲ In Puritan New England and elsewhere, people viewed each other with suspicion.

The Puritans came to the New World to try and build a godly community where they could live close to perfect lives. No human beings have ever been able to do that, but the Puritans tried.

To make their community pure, the Puritans expected everyone to act like a spy and report any neighbor who did or said anything wrong. Self-righteous people are apt to judge other people. Sometimes the Puritans were like that. They spent time judging their neighbors.

The Puritans believed that God saves only a very few people and that the rest go to a terrible hell filled with fires. They thought that God decided when a child was born if he was saved or not. They used the word "elected" instead of "saved," and they thought they were God's elect. Because of that, they thought they should act like God's elect and lead good lives.

Puritan ministers said that people were naturally sinful, but if they sinned they would go to that terrible hell. That kept everyone under constant pressure to be close to perfect. No one could relax. And that may be what caused the nightmare of the witches.

Almost everyone believed in witches—there was nothing new about that. People thought that if you wanted to make a bargain with the devil you could do it, and then torment people and fly through the air on a broomstick, or become invisible and squeeze through keyholes. Everyone *knew* that witches could create thunder, sink ships, kill sheep, and make tables and chairs rattle.

Back in the days of Christopher Columbus, all over Europe hundreds of people were condemned as witches and burned at the stake.

It wasn't only people from European cultures who feared witches or killed people suspected of witchcraft. Some Native Americans did the same thing. It happened among people who—like the Puritans—were very religious, and wanted an answer to an overwhelming question: If God is good, how do you explain evil?

Suppose you can't explain a sudden earthquake that destroys your town, or a blight that settles on the corn crop and destroys your winter food supply. Witchcraft is the easy answer.

Many people in Salem believed that Tituba, a woman from the West Indies, was bewitching young girls. ▼

In the colonies some men and women were hanged or drowned for witchery, but what happened in Salem, Massachusetts, was different from the usual story.

It all began with some little girls and their servant, Tituba, a poor woman from the West Indies who told stories of the devil and witches and voodoo. The girls were nine-year-old Elizabeth Parris, eleven-year-old Abigail Williams, and their friends. Tituba's stories must have been scary, especially around the fire at night. But when Tituba taught the girls to bark like dogs and mew like cats and grunt like hogs, that might have been fun. Although Elizabeth's father, the Reverend Samuel Parris, didn't think it was fun at all. When he saw the children grunting and mewing and sometimes acting as if they were having fits, he remembered reading books from England about spells laid on people by witches. He became alarmed.

And then, to everyone's astonishment, on Sunday the girls spoke out during church meeting and said silly things. "There is a yellow bird on the minister's head," cried Anne Putnam. No one would interrupt a church service except the devil! So when the girls said Sarah Good, Sarah Osburn, and Tituba were bewitching them, everyone believed them. The two Sarahs denied the charge. But they were old and poor and no one listened to them, especially after Tituba said that she did indeed fly through the air on a broomstick.

The little girls might have been pretending when they started, but soon they were telling of torture and witchery, and perhaps they convinced themselves. (Or maybe, now, they were afraid to tell the truth.) Their stories grew longer and their screeches louder. Suddenly, anything that went wrong in that little town was the fault of a witch. Salem was mad with witch fever. Five-year-old Dorcas Good was taken to jail and chained to her mother when the girls said she was tormenting them. Then other people began talking of witches and pointing at their neighbors. A court was called to hear the evidence.

The judges were scared, like everyone else. The leaders of the community, who might have done some thinking, didn't. More than 100 people were tried as witches; 20 people and two dogs were put to death. Then the Reverend Hale's wife was accused. But there was no one in Massachusetts more beloved and godly than she! Could it be that the girls were wrong? Everyone had believed them; no one had believed the victims. Were those people who had been killed innocent? Yes, an awful tragedy had occurred.

The witch trials were a shameful chapter in American history.

▲ In Salem, Massachusetts, more than 100 people were tried as witches.

Connecticut, New Hampshire, and Maine

No one is ever all bad or all good. The witch trials may have been a low point for the Puritans, but mostly these were good, strong, intelligent people. If they hadn't been, they never would have crossed the ocean; they would have stayed in England, as most English people did—even when they didn't like the way they were ruled.

Because the Puritans were independent thinkers they sometimes disagreed with each other. When they did, there was plenty of room in America. They could just start a new settlement.

Thomas Hooker was minister in a little town near Boston when, in 1636, he decided to move west; 100 of his followers went with him. He went to the beautiful valley of the Connecticut River. Today, no one is quite sure if he moved because of religious disagreements, or because the valley was fertile and farming was easier than in rocky Massachusetts. He found good farmland and he was free to preach as he wished.

> The name Connecticut comes from a Mohican word, *quinnitukqut*, meaning "at the long tidal river."

Thomas Hooker and his followers moved from Massachusetts to Connecticut in 1636. ▼

Hooker had no charter when he arrived in Connecticut. The king hadn't given him permission to be there. He moved in anyway. He had no legal right to the land in the eyes of the English (and certainly none in the eyes of the Native Americans), so the Connecticut settlers sent their governor, John Winthrop II, to England to get a charter.

When he went to see King Charles II, Winthrop wore a handsome ring that had belonged to Anne of Denmark, who happened to be Charles's grandmother. Winthrop gave the ring to Charles. The king, naturally, was delighted to have his grandmother's ring.

Connecticut got a charter. The land it granted stretched as far west as the Pacific Ocean (although no one knew how far that was)!

Soon Puritans were heading straight for Connecticut. Massachusetts was getting crowded and the land in Connecticut was inviting. A group settled at New Haven in 1638 and another at New London in 1646. Each town had its own minister. The New Haven colonists published a list of laws that said how you were to behave. One law said "Every male shall have his hair cut round." Another said, "Married persons must live together, or be imprisoned."

In 1639, the settlers in the Connecticut River colony had an open meeting in which they drafted a groundbreaking document known as the Fundamental Orders. It was a constitution establishing a democratic state controlled by "substantial" citizens.

While all this was going on, some people were moving north. The king had given a big piece of northern land to two friends: John Mason and Ferdinano Gorges. They divided that land, Gorges taking what became Maine, and Mason taking New Hampshire.

The New England Colonies

Area enlarged below

Quebec

St. Lawrence River

Montreal

Lake Champlain

MAINE
(part of Massachusetts)

Connecticut River

NEW HAMPSHIRE

ATLANTIC OCEAN

Boston • Salem
MASSACHUSETTS
Providence • Plymouth

CONNECTICUT
New Haven
New London
RHODE ISLAND

New York City

N

Modern boundaries

0   50   100 mi
0 50 100 km

▲ The settlement of Dover, New Hampshire, in 1623

▲ The four New England colonies shared a cold climate and limited farmland. Most settlers in New England were Puritans who built towns near rivers or the sea.

John Mason named New Hampshire after the county of Hampshire, which is on England's south coast.

Mason and Gorges advertised for settlers in England, and people came.

At first, New Hampshire was part of Massachusetts, with John Mason as its proprietor. Then it became a separate colony; finally the king took it back and held it himself as a royal colony.

Maine was never a separate colony; it was part of Massachusetts until 1820, when it became the 23rd state.

As soon as colonies were established, they began competing for good land and good people. The more people who came, the more land they needed.

The big losers in this contest were the Indians. Serious colonization could not take place until the Indians had been pushed off the land. And pushed off they would be.

Land Greed

In Europe only the really wealthy—the aristocrats—could own land. Ordinary people didn't even dream of their own land. In America the land was so vast it would take the Europeans more than 200 years just to know how much there was. For a very long time, almost every free person who came to America could afford land.

Almost as soon as the European Americans got land, they became greedy for more. And they wanted to change the land, as Europe's land had been changed.

They looked at the beautiful forests and saw an enemy that needed conquering. They cut down trees, leveled hills, filled in swamps, and killed animals and birds. They didn't understand how to work with nature, as the Indians often did. They forced nature to conform to their ways and wants.

It turned out that the land wasn't endless, as they seemed to think at first. One day it would almost all be tamed. Then they would wish for some of those thick forests, some of those songbirds, some of the native animals. There would be few of them left.

The Indians didn't accept the European idea of landownership. Their religions taught them that the land and waters and animals belonged to God. They thought land could only be shared, not owned. So at first, when they signed treaties selling land, they thought they were selling the right to share it. They didn't expect to be ordered off the land.

Their beliefs told them to live in harmony with nature. Land was to be used by a tribe as a whole, not owned by individuals. It was a way of looking at the land that did away with most greed, but not all greed. Tribes often fought each other for control of the use of land.

Of course, if large numbers of people were to live on the land it had to be changed. Millions and millions of people can't live in a forest. Cities were needed for all the people who would come to live on this bountiful land. And so we built cities and suburbs and in the process often polluted and burned and destroyed. Did we have to do that? Can we have cities and also sheltering woodlands and clean rivers and abundant wildlife? Yes, but it isn't easy. We have to care about our environment. We have to respect the natural world.

Europeans and Native Americans looked at the land in very different ways. ▼

King Philip's War

Massasoit was a friend of the English colonists. The first New England settlers might not have survived without his help, and they knew it. Once, when he seemed near death, a group of settlers came from Plymouth with goose soup and a broth made from the root of the sassafras tree. Massasoit got better.

Massasoit's people, the Wampanoags, were hunters and fishermen and farmers whose lives turned with the cycle of the seasons. They were peaceful people and good neighbors. When some Pilgrims visited his village, Massasoit honored them by letting them spend the night on a plank bed with himself, his wife, and two of his chiefs.

Massasoit, a chieftain of the Wampanoag, is welcomed with honor by the Pilgrims. ▼

A year after the Pilgrims arrived, Massasoit signed a treaty of peace with them. For more than 50 years, while he lived, there was peace in Massachusetts. But, even before he died, there were some—Indians and English—who saw trouble ahead. Mostly it was because there were so many English men and women. At first there had been only a few of these newcomers, but soon they were pushing the natives off the land.

▲ The Pilgrims sign a peace treaty with Massasoit.

Massasoit's two sons were troubled. Their generation was different from that of their father. They were not awed by the English, as their father sometimes seemed. The two boys were Wamsutta and Metacom, but Massasoit had asked the General Court in Plymouth to give them English names. So they were named for ancient kings of Greece: Alexander and Philip.

When his father died, Wamsutta-Alexander became ruler. Some Englishmen feared him. They sent troops, dragged him to Plymouth, threatened him, and acted haughty and superior.

Alexander became ill and died on his way home. Metacom-Philip was now leader of his people. He believed the English had killed his brother, and he wanted revenge.

Besides, Metacom saw that the new people were destroying his land. (The English now called him King Philip. Some meant it respectfully, but others were mocking when they used the title.) And so Metacom began visiting other Indian leaders trying to convince them to join him to fight the English and drive them from America. That wasn't easy. There was no history of Indian unity. The Indian peoples were as different from each other as Swedes are from Spaniards, or Chinese from Pakistanis. They were descended from different peoples who came in different waves of immigration over the Bering Strait.

Metacom wasn't ready when war began. As with many wars, it was really an accident that started things. A Christian Indian named John Sassamon was killed. Sassamon had been to Harvard and was a friend of the Plymouth colonists. Today, no one is sure who killed him, but the English executed three members of Metacom's tribe for the murder. Metacom was furious. He attacked for revenge.

As the Indians' land shrank, King Philip told a friend, "I am resolved not to see the day when I have no country." ▼

Tomahawk comes from an Algonquian word for a war club, *tamahakan.*

Many settlers survived King Philip's War only to die of starvation because the fields were trampled or never got planted. The Massachusetts Bay Colony almost went bankrupt, and 12 towns vanished.

King Philip's War had begun. It was fought, off and on, for two years, 1675 and 1676, and it was horrible. If you have read about Indian wars—with scalpings, torched villages, tomahawks, and war whoops—you may have been reading about this war. Both sides were incredibly brutal.

Six hundred colonists lost their lives in King Philip's War; 3,000 Indians lost theirs. Fifty of 90 English villages were attacked; many were burned to the ground. The peaceful Narraganset Indians, who had nothing to do with the war, were massacred on their own land in Rhode Island because some of the settlers now feared all Indians. Many innocent white people were killed in Indian raids of revenge.

Indian disunity hurt their cause. Some tribes helped the English. In addition, Indian warriors weren't used to long wars. They knew how to attack and destroy in quick raids. When the war went on and on, many Indians got tired of it. They wanted to plant their crops and get back to normal activities. They deserted their leader. Finally Metacom was trapped in a swamp, where he was killed by an Indian who was loyal to the colonists. Metacom's head was chopped off and hung on the fort at Plymouth; there it stayed for 25 years. His wife, children, and other captured Indians were sold in the West Indies as slaves.

It was a pattern that was repeated over and over again until the Indians could fight no more.

The Pequot War

The Pequots were Indians who lived in New England near Narragansett Bay. Settlers moved into their territory until the Pequots controlled less and less of it. The Indians got angry about this and killed some settlers and traders. In 1636 the colonists retaliated (fought back) by destroying a Pequot village. The next year war broke out. Captain John Mason (who founded New Hampshire) and his allies from the Mohican and Narraganset tribes attacked the Pequots' fort, near what is now West Mystic, Connecticut. The Indians inside were burned alive. Those who didn't die were sold into slavery. The Pequots were almost wiped out. It was a taste of what was to come in King Philip's War.

A Pequot village burned by New England colonists ▶

Civilizations in Conflict

At the very time that Metacom was fighting to free his land from the English invaders, thousands of miles across the continent, in a place the Spaniards called New Mexico, the Pueblo Indians were preparing for the same kind of fight.

The people of the pueblos have seen their land invaded by Spanish men and women. The Spanish live in missions. The missions are small farms built around a church. Sometimes soldiers live nearby in forts called "presidios." Sometimes the mission and the presidio are combined.

Indians live in the missions and do most of the farming and building. The Indians are forced to grow crops for the Spaniards, to pay them taxes, to clean their houses, to do their heavy work.

The Spaniards consider it their duty to convert Indians to Christianity. They call the Indian religion evil. The Spanish priests are determined to destroy the old Indian ways. The Pueblo Indians pretend to do as the Spaniards wish, but, secretly they keep to the old ways. When the Spanish find out, they round up the Indian religious leaders. Four are hanged in the big plaza in the town called Santa Fe, and the others are whipped and thrown in a dungeon.

An Indian leader and medicine man named Popé (poe-PAY) carefully plans how to drive the

▲ The Pueblo people united to drive the Spanish out of their land in 1680, but the clash of cultures continued.

enemy from his country. He unites the various pueblo peoples. He even gets the Apache, his people's ancient enemy, to agree to help.

In August 1680, the Indians attack—burning, killing, and destroying. By nightfall only two Spanish communities are left: Santa Fe and Isleta.

Popé gives the Spanish governor a choice: he can stay in Santa Fe and starve, or he can leave the land and take his people with him.

The Spaniards leave—all of them. They march away, back to Mexico. But the leaders in Spain and Mexico don't give up easily. They will be back. The Spaniards and the Pueblo Indians will do the same things that Englishmen and East Coast Indians are doing: they will fight, steal, trade, make peace, and misunderstand each other. These are civilizations in conflict.

▲ Spanish missionaries sought to convert the Indians to Christianity.

Silvernails and Big Tub

England had 13 American colonies. Remember, a colony is a place that belongs to another country. You'll be reading about all 13 of the English colonies, because they turned into the United States. We're going to divide the colonies into three groups, north, middle, and south: the New England colonies, the Middle Atlantic colonies, and the Southern colonies.

- The New England colonies are Massachusetts, New Hampshire, Rhode Island, and Connecticut.

- The Middle Atlantic colonies are New York, New Jersey, Delaware, and Pennsylvania.

- The Southern colonies are Virginia, Maryland, North Carolina, South Carolina, and Georgia. (Some people call Maryland a middle colony.)

Don't confuse states with colonies. The 13 colonies will turn into states later when the Constitution is written and our nation—the United States—is formed.

Let's turn to one of the middle colonies, New York, where the Dutch are in control. (It wasn't called New York at first, as you'll see.)

The Dutch had colonies all over the world. It's hard for us to realize now that tiny Holland was once a great power. A business firm, the Dutch West India Company, owned most of the colonies, just as the Virginia and Plymouth companies owned English colonies.

Back in 1609, Henry Hudson, an Englishman sailing for the Netherlands, had gone up the river that is now called the Hudson. He was looking for the Northwest Passage and the river seemed likely, but he was stopped by rapids in the river near Albany. Because of Hudson's voyage, Holland claimed a large hunk of American land. It was land wedged between the stern Puritans in the North and the Anglican tobacco planters in the South; the Dutch called it New Netherland. Today we know it as New York and New Jersey.

The Dutch had a great piece of property, but they didn't seem to realize that. They just kind of fooled around on the North American continent. They were more serious in other parts of the globe. (For example, the Dutch thought India—with its silks and spices— was much more important than America.)

In case you're confused: Holland, the Netherlands, and the land of the Dutch are all the same place. Why don't you find it on a map? And, while you're looking, can you find England? Can you see why both nations became sea powers?

▲ Henry Hudson

In 1626 the Dutch West India Company made what may be the most famous real-estate deal in history. It bought Manhattan Island (now the center of New York City) and Long Island from the Indians who lived there for some beads and goods said to be worth $24. Since the Indians didn't think people could own land, they may have thought they were outsmarting the white men.

By this time, the Dutch had decided that American furs might be almost as good as American gold, so they set up some trading posts. People in Europe were eager to buy American furs. Beaver, bear, fox, and other fur pelts could be made into sumptuous hats, coats, and blankets. The Dutch merchants hoped to get rich in the New World.

On Manhattan Island the people from Holland built a town called New Amsterdam. At one end they put a wall because they feared wolves and because cities in Europe had walls. Today that wall is the site of a famous street. Can you guess what it is called? (You guessed it—Wall Street!) Outside the wall were farms, which the Dutch called *bouweries*. Today a street in New York is called "the Bowery." (It doesn't look much like a farm now.)

Manhattan is an island 12 1/2 miles from end to end. Broadway, its longest street, runs the length of the island.

Indians bring furs to Dutch traders. ▼

' Fort nieuw Amsterdam op de Manhatans

▲ The settlement of New Amsterdam in about 1628

▲ New Amsterdam, with an excellent natural harbor, was a center of barter, banking, and shipping.

▲ In 1709, a market was set up on the corner of Wall and Water streets. It was a slave market, a place where men, women, and children were bought and sold. New York paved its streets with money raised by a tax on each slave brought into its port. By the middle of the 18th century, one in every 10 New Yorkers was black. Most of them were slaves, but some were free; a few owned indentured white servants—"bound" men, women, girls, and boys.

Because of its great harbor, New Amsterdam was soon a sailor's town, bustling with people who arrived on ships from faraway places. It was said that you could hear 18 different languages being spoken in the city of New Amsterdam. Right away, in 1626, the Dutch brought slaves to New Amsterdam. You could buy a slave for about the same amount it would cost to pay a worker one year's salary. So some people thought it made good sense to own slaves. It was an economic, or money, decision.

When it came to colonial leaders, the Dutch came up with some strange men, such as "Old Silvernails"—that's what they called him, because the stick of wood that stood in place of his right leg was decorated with silver nails. He had lost the leg in a battle in the West Indies. His real name was Peter Stuyvesant (STY-viss-unt), and he was a Dutch governor and a hard-swearing, tough man. Maybe the Dutch thought Silvernails Stuyvesant was the right kind of person to run a colony in America. Maybe they didn't have any other volunteers.

Grouchy Old Silvernails was in charge of all of New Netherland. He was pretty good at running things, but he would stomp his wooden leg and swear at anyone who disagreed with him. When the Dutchmen who had been elected councilors objected to something he said, he called them "ignorant subjects." Another time he said he would ship them back to Holland—in pieces—if they gave him trouble.

But if you were going to run a swearing contest, Stuyvesant might lose. Johan Printz (YO-han PRINCE) had a mouth that was even more foul. He was governor of New Sweden, on the Delaware Bay, not far from New Netherland.

Printz was a whale of a man. The Indians called him Big Tub, and he may have been the biggest man on the continent. He was seven feet tall and weighed 400 pounds. Big Tub was an autocrat—an absolute ruler—and he liked to hang people who opposed him. But he did hold his colony together for 10 years, with very little help from the Swedes at home. And he introduced a new style of architecture, the log cabin, that became popular in frontier settlements.

Finally, Johan Printz got tired of trying to run things himself and went back to Sweden. The new Swedish governor decided to get tough and capture a Dutch fort, but he didn't realize what Old Silvernails was like. Stuyvesant sent seven ships, and that wiped out the Swedish colony.

That made Stuyvesant popular in New Amsterdam—but not for long. Nine years later, in 1664, the English decided to do to the Dutch what the Dutch had done to the Swedes. Old Silvernails stomped on his wooden leg, but nobody came to his rescue. The British took New Amsterdam without firing a shot. They renamed it New York.

▲ Peter Stuyvesant

One day a ship sailed into New Amsterdam's harbor with a group of Jews aboard. Peter Stuyvesant didn't want them to land. He was a bigot and didn't believe in religious freedom. Stuyvesant was a member of the Dutch Reformed Church and saw no reason to tolerate others. But the Dutch West India Company said the Jews could stay, so there was nothing Stuyvesant could do. After a while, Jews in New Amsterdam were allowed to trade and own houses. But they were not allowed to build a synagogue until 1730, so they had to hold services in their homes.

◀ The Dutch, under Governor Peter Stuyvesant, surrendered New Amsterdam to the British in 1664.

West to Jersey

The Netherlands pulled down its flag and left America. It was 1664, and the Dutch had been here for 50 years. During those years they had gone up the Hudson River, built a town at Fort Orange (Albany), and established big plantations along the river. The Dutch farm owners were called "patroons." People came from Holland to work the patroons' farms. They brought their tulips, their hardworking habits, their neatness, and their storytelling ways with them. (Their children's favorite story was about a fellow named Santa Claus, who visited just before Christmas, on December 6.)

Actually, most of the Dutch people didn't leave, and the British even let Peter Stuyvesant stay. They let the Dutch have religious freedom. The Netherlanders just weren't in charge anymore. It was the Duke of York who owned the place now.

The Duke of York was named James, and his brother was the king of England. York (that is what some people called James) was one of the owners of the Royal African Company, which controlled the British slave trade. It seems to have occurred to the duke that if he encouraged the use of slaves in the New World, he would make lots of money. And that is just what happened.

York must have been conceited and vain, because you can see what he named his land. Well, that isn't quite true. It wasn't all called New York. Some of it became New Jersey. The Duke of York gave a big chunk of land to two of his friends. One of them, Sir George Carteret, came from the island of Jersey, which explains why it was "New" Jersey. The duke's other friend was Lord John Berkeley. Berkeley's brother was governor of Virginia.

◀ James, Duke of York, later became King James II of England.

▲ Sir George Carteret arriving in New Jersey

Those two owners were called "proprietors." They expected the people who lived on their land to pay them a tax called a "quit rent." That didn't make them very popular.

But they had good qualities all the same. They wrote a plan of government, a charter, that was the best any English colony had. It set up an assembly that represented the settlers. (Assemblies, parliaments, and congresses are all similar organizations.) The charter provided for freedom of religion. You could be a Quaker or a Puritan or an Anglican in New Jersey, and, as long as you were a man, you had the right to vote. You didn't have that freedom in Massachusetts or Virginia or most of the other colonies.

Soon people were pouring into New Jersey from all over: Finns, Swedes, Germans, English, and others. In New Jersey everybody lived together in harmony.

At first New Jersey was divided into East Jersey and West Jersey. Then the king bought out the proprietors, united New Jersey, and made it a royal colony. That meant the king was now the owner of New Jersey. He sent a royal governor to take charge and collect his rents. The king allowed the colonists to keep making their own laws through the elected assembly.

For a while, New Jersey was part of the western frontier of the country. The frontier was land that was on the edge of what Europeans considered civilization. If you look at a map, you can see where the frontier of European civilization was in 1700.

Is there a frontier today? Where might it be? Clue: look up.

A Civil War in England

Even though this is a book about US, you need to keep up with events in England, because what was going on there was very important to the colonists in America. A civil war was being fought in England. The war was between King Charles I and the Puritans. The king lost the war. Then the Puritans executed him. In the colonies, Virginians were on the side of the king; people on that side were called "Cavaliers." (They got that name because the king's soldiers fought mostly on horseback, and soldiers on horseback are called "cavalry.")

The New Englanders, naturally, were for the Puritans, who were sometimes called "Roundheads" (because when they needed a haircut, Puritan men would put a bowl on their heads and cut around the bowl).

The revolution in 1649—and it really was a revolution—was called the English Civil War. I'll say it again, because it is so important: in 1649 the Puritans won the English Civil War, and Charles I lost his head. The English Civil War made an important point: people can change their government if they want to badly enough.

After the execution of King Charles I, the Puritan leader, Oliver Cromwell, took charge of the government. I would like to tell you that Cromwell did a splendid job as ruler, but he didn't. He acted like a tyrant.

When Cromwell died (in 1658), the English people, who were tired of the stern Puritans, put the old king's son on the throne. He ruled as Charles II. The time in which he ruled is called the "Restoration" (because a king was *restored* to power). Under Charles II, things got so bad for the Puritans that many left England and came to America.

As king, Charles II rewarded friends who had stayed loyal to his family while Cromwell was running things. He gave them gifts of land in America. As you know, he gave his brother, the Duke of York, the gift of New Netherland. (Then he sent an army to take it from the Dutch.)

He gave the Carolinas to eight of his favorite lords. He gave Pennsylvania to a young man whose religion made it dangerous for him to live in England. (You'll meet him soon.)

◀ King Charles addresses the crowd before being beheaded.

William the Wise

William Penn was born with a silver spoon in his mouth and servants at his feet. His father was an important admiral: rich, Anglican, and a friend of King Charles II.

What did William Penn do when he grew up? He became a member of a radical, hated, outcast sect, the Society of Friends, also known as the Quakers.

What did being a Quaker do for William Penn? It got him kicked out of college when he refused to attend Anglican prayers. It got him a beating from his father, who wanted him to belong to the Church of England. It led him to jail for his beliefs—more than once. It gave him a faith that he carried through his life. And it also gave him a reason for founding an American colony.

King Charles II liked William Penn in spite of his religion. Everyone, it seems, was charmed by his sweet ways. But when Penn came before the king and refused to take off his hat—Quakers defer only to God—some people gasped and wondered if Penn's head, along with his hat, might be removed. But Charles, the "merry monarch," must have been in a good mood. As the story goes, he laughed and doffed his own hat, saying, "Only one head can be covered in the presence of a king."

Now King Charles had borrowed money from Admiral Penn, and a goodly sum it must have been, because, after the admiral

▲ William Penn said, "I have led the greatest colony into America that ever any man did upon a private credit."

You've probably noticed that the spelling of the documents quoted in this book isn't always the same as the spelling you've learned. Until Noah Webster wrote a speller (in 1783) and an American dictionary (in 1828), there was no standard spelling. People just wrote words the way that seemed right to them. Sometimes the same word could be spelled two different ways in a single sentence.

Gabriel Thomas, one of the earliest settlers in Pennsylvania (which he spelled *Pensilvania*), wrote a pamphlet in praise of its charms. ▶

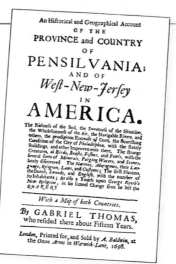

An Historical and Geographical Account
OF THE
PROVINCE and COUNTRY
OF
PENSILVANIA;
AND OF
West-New-Jersey
IN
AMERICA.

The Richness of the Soil, the Sweetness of the Situation, the Wholesomeness of the Air, the Navigable Rivers, and others, the prodigious Encrease of Corn, the flourishing Condition of the City of *Philadelphia*, with the stately Buildings, and other Improvements there. The strange Creatures, as Birds, Beasts, Fishes, and Fowls, with the several sorts of Minerals, Purging Waters, and Stones, lately discovered. The Natives, Aborgines, their Language, Religion, Laws, and Customs; The first Planters, the *Dutch*, *Sweeds*, and *English*, with the number of its Inhabitants; As also a Touch upon George Keith's New Religion, in his second Change since he left the QUAKERS

With a Map of both Countries.

By GABRIEL THOMAS,
who resided there about Fifteen Years.

London, Printed for, and Sold by *A. Baldwin*, at the *Oxon Arms* in *Warwick-Lane*, 1698.

▲ Charles II of England grants William Penn the charter of Pennsylvania in 1681.

died, when William asked that the debt be paid with land in America, he was given a tract of land larger than all of England. King Charles named it Pennsylvania, which means "Penn's woods."

Pennsylvania was situated midway between the pious Puritans in New England and the agreeable Anglicans in the South. Quakers weren't wanted in either region.

Thanks to William Penn, Quakers now had their own colony. But he made it different from most of the other colonies. Penn really believed in brotherly love. He said that Pennsylvania was not just for Quakers but for everyone.

The king had picked a good man to lead a colony—perhaps the best of all who tried it. Penn was an educated man, a philosopher, a town planner, and a lawyer. He wanted Pennsylvania to be a colony where Quaker ideas about peace and goodness would prevail.

In England, Quakers seemed a threat to everyone who felt comfortable with the old, established ways of thinking. The country had beheaded a king, and that didn't work out. New ideas seemed dangerous, as they often do. Quakers had notions that would change Old England. Wealthy citizens didn't want things to change, so it was poor people, mostly, who were Quakers.

In Penn's day, some people—ministers, kings, lords, and dukes—were considered superior to the average person. They expected others to bow to them, but Quakers wouldn't. They wouldn't bow to anyone. They even refused to pay taxes to support the Church of England. Can you see a problem? The Anglicans did.

England had lords and ladies in the rich upper class, merchants and farmers in the middle class, and peasants and poor people in the lower class. It was almost impossible to rise from the lower class to the upper. The upper-class lords and earls often acted as if they were better than anyone else. It was that class system that made many ambitious people come to the New World. In America, with hard work, many poor people would rise to the top.

Because the Bible says, "Thou shalt not kill," Quakers believe all war is wrong. They won't fight even when drafted into the army. They are called "conscientious objectors," because their conscience tells them not to fight.

And they won't swear allegiance to a king or government or flag or anyone but God. That was another real problem in England, where people were expected to swear their loyalty to the king.

William Penn wanted to practice Quaker ideas in America. That meant treating all people as equals and respecting all religions. Those new ideas of "toleration" and "natural rights" were confusing. It was difficult for good people to know what was right.

Do you understand the difference between toleration and equality? Some colonies offered freedom of religion but not equality. You could practice any religion but you couldn't vote or hold office (be a mayor or sheriff) unless you belonged to the majority's church. That wasn't true in Penn's colony. While he was in charge, all religions were equal.

Your *conscience* is your sense of right and wrong. It's something that tells you when you're doing right and warns you when you're doing wrong. *Conscientious* means being careful to do what you know is right.

William Penn signs a treaty with the Native Americans of Pennsylvania. ▼

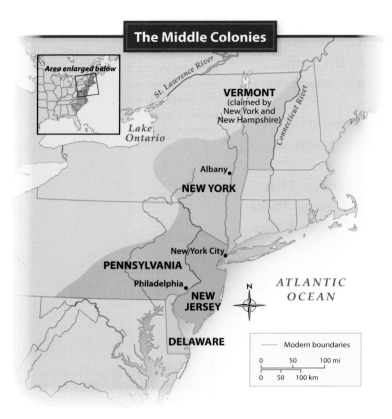

The Middle Colonies

Area enlarged below

St. Lawrence River

Lake Ontario

VERMONT
(claimed by New York and New Hampshire)

Connecticut River

Albany

NEW YORK

New York City

PENNSYLVANIA

Philadelphia

NEW JERSEY

ATLANTIC OCEAN

DELAWARE

N

Modern boundaries

0   50   100 mi
0   50 100 km

▲ People from many countries settled in the four Middle Colonies, which had natural harbors and good land for farming. Philadelphia became the largest, most prosperous city in the colonies.

Today the capital of Pennsylvania is Harrisburg.

When Penn said all people, he meant *all* people. Quakers were among the first to object to slavery and to treat the Indians as equals. In 1681, William Penn wrote a letter to the Native Americans of Pennsylvania. He said:

May [we] always live together as neighbors and friends, else what would the great God say to us, who hath made us not to devour and destroy one another, but live soberly and kindly together in the world?

Penn proposed a "firm league of peace." He continued:

I am very sensible of the unkindness and injustice that hath been too much exercised toward you by the people of these parts of the world…but I am not such a man…I desire to win and gain your love and friendship by a kind, just, and peaceable life.

Penn was generous as well as fair. He offered land on easy terms to those who came to his colony.

On his first visit to America, he sailed up the Delaware River and picked the site of Pennsylvania's first capital, Philadelphia. Then he helped plan the city by using a pattern of crossing streets, called a "grid," that would be copied throughout the new land. He gave numbers to all the streets that went in one direction; the streets that went the other way he gave tree names, like Pine and Chestnut and Walnut. Philadelphia is still thought of as a fine example of town planning.

Penn wrote a Charter of Liberties for Pennsylvania. Penn said the charter set up a government "free to the people under it, where the laws rule, and the people are a party to those laws."

The southeastern part of Pennsylvania was called the "Three Lower Counties." In 1704 those counties asked for their own assembly and William Penn gave it to them. In 1776 they became an independent state named Delaware.

William Penn didn't stay in America for long. He had business to attend to in England, and so he chose rulers for Pennsylvania. Since he owned the place, he had a right to do that.

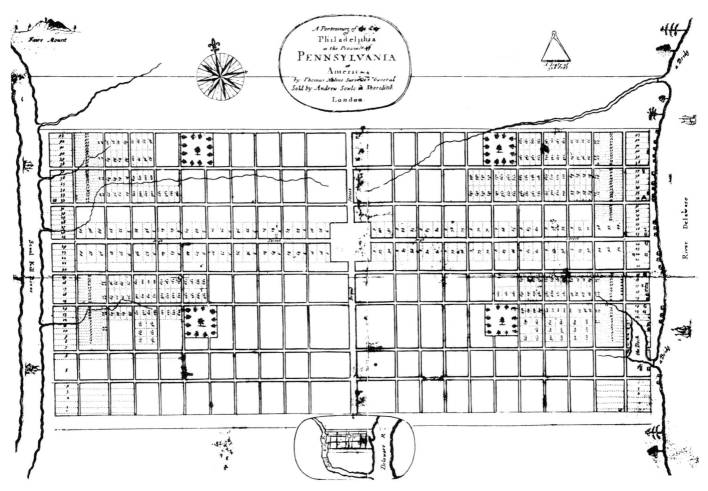

▲ An engraving of William Penn's plan for the city of Philadelphia

Penn did not believe in democracy. (Hardly anyone did at the beginning of the 18th century.) He was an aristocrat. In those days, ordinary people were not thought to be capable of picking their own leaders. William Penn thought he was choosing good people to lead his colony. But, as it turned out, he was too trusting.

The men he picked to run his colony fought among themselves and cheated him. (He would have been better off if he had believed in democracy.) William Penn lost most of his fortune developing Pennsylvania.

But Penn did prove that freedom and fairness work. Philadelphia was soon the largest, most prosperous city in the colonies. People came from Germany, France, Scotland, and Wales—as well as England—looking for religious freedom and a good place to live. One, a boy named Benjamin Franklin, came from Boston.

Ben Franklin

Some people had problems with Benjamin Franklin. They accused him of not having any gravity. Now that doesn't mean he floated around like a weightless space voyager. *Gravity* has another meaning, as in "grave." No, not a place where you get buried, but you are getting closer. Someone who is grave is very serious, maybe a bit dull, and certainly not much fun. Ben Franklin did have a problem. He just couldn't stay serious or dull. He was always playing jokes or having fun.

The French had no trouble with Ben. They loved his jokes and admired his good mind. They were amazed by all the things he had done. He was a scientist, an inventor, a writer, and a great patriotic American.

His mind never seemed to stop for rest. Daylight saving time was his idea; and he invented bifocal glasses, the lightning rod, the one-arm desk chair, and an efficient stove. He founded the first public library, the first city hospital, and the University of Pennsylvania. He was the most famous journalist of his time, and the first editor to use cartoons as illustrations. He made electricity into a science. And that is only part of what he did.

Benjamin Franklin helped with the ideas that made this country special, and he got the French to help pay for the revolution that made us free.

But, as I said, some people had problems with Franklin. The English people didn't much like him. Well, that's not quite true. It was English politicians who didn't like him, especially when the colonies began to object to the way England was treating them.

When Ben was sent to London to represent the Americans, one Englishman wrote, "I look upon him as a dangerous engine." And Lord Sandwich (that really was his name) called him one of the "most mischievous enemies" that England ever knew. (By the way, sandwiches were named for Lord Sandwich, whose real name was John Montagu. He liked his servants to fix him a snack—meat between bread—when he played cards.)

▲ Benjamin Franklin

▲ Benjamin Franklin is credited with inventing bifocal glasses.

◄ Franklin, who became the most famous journalist of his time, was an innovator in printing newspapers, an almanac, illustrated stories, and political cartoons.

Some Americans accused Franklin of liking the English too much; the English, of course, said he didn't like them at all. What Ben was doing was trying to be fair and also trying to prevent war. He said, "There never was a good war or a bad peace."

I think you would have liked him. And if you want to have a real hero, someone to use as a guide for ordering your life, you can't do better than Benjamin Franklin. He had what has been called a "happy balance of earnestness and humor." He made the most of what he had.

One of his biographers wrote, "He had a talent for happiness." Another said, "He hated solemn pompous people.... He gave away much of his money...he set about improving himself."

But you need to know something of his life, so you can judge the man yourself.

Franklin was born in Boston on January 17, 1706, and died on April 17, 1790. His life spanned the 18th century.

Benjamin Franklin was the 15th child in a family with 17 children. He was the youngest son of the youngest son of the youngest son— back to his great-great-grandfather. His father was a hardworking candlemaker descended from Puritan stock. Young Franklin went to school for three years, and then his parents could afford no more. It was enough to get him started; he loved books and reading, and he educated himself.

One thing he didn't like was candlemaking. So his father signed him as an apprentice to Ben's older half-brother, James, who was a printer. In return for room and board (food) and training, an apprentice had to work for a certain number of years. He was not free to quit. It was something like being an indentured servant. Ben was 12 years old, and his father signed him for nine years.

He didn't get along with his brother, and what he really wanted to do was to go to sea. But he made the best of a bad situation. The print shop was a good place to learn. There were stacks of books—he read them all—and interesting people dropped by. Some wrote for the newspaper James printed and owned.

Ben wanted to write for the paper, but he knew James wouldn't publish his work. So he wrote letters to the editor and signed them with the made-up name of a woman; he called her "Silence Dogood."

The letters were a big hit. Silence wrote that she was "naturally very jealous for the rights and liberties of my country: and the least appearance of an incroachment on those invaluable privileges, is apt to make my blood boil exceedingly."

Incroachment (which we spell encroachment) means "taking another's possessions gradually or slyly." Usually the word is used to describe the illegal taking of land: "He encroached on his neighbor's property."

▲ Franklin learned to be a printer as an apprentice to his brother, a printer in Boston.

When Dogood wrote a description of herself, it could have been a description of Franklin: "I never intend to wrap my talent in a napkin," she wrote. "To be brief; I am courteous and affable, good-humoured (unless I am first provoked), handsome, and sometimes witty."

Everyone wanted to know who Silence Dogood was. When Ben's brother found out, he stopped printing the letters.

Ben wasn't happy, but he didn't sit around and mope. One thing Benjamin Franklin did all his life was to try and find ways to improve himself. Maybe it was his Puritan background that made him industrious.

He decided he wanted to be a writer. Ben had learned to spell at the printing house, but his father told him that the style of his writing was not good. So he found a friend and they wrote letters back and forth. Then he worked out exercises to improve his writing style. Sometimes he turned stories into poems, then back again into prose. It was a fine way to learn to work with words.

When Ben was 16, he read about a vegetable diet. He became a vegetarian and bought books with the money he saved by not eating meat. Soon he could talk about books with anyone. He was becoming very well educated.

But he still had problems with his brother. "Perhaps I was too saucy and provoking," said Ben. "My brother was passionate, and had often beaten me, which I took extremely amiss." Finally, at 17, Ben ran away from Boston. He sold his books and used the money to get to Philadelphia. In his *Autobiography,* Franklin described his arrival in that city:

> I was dirty from my journey; my pockets were stuffed out with shirts and stockings; I knew no soul nor where to look for lodging. I was fatigued with traveling, rowing, and want of rest; I was very hungry; and my whole stock of cash consisted of a Dutch dollar and about a shilling in copper.

◄ Franklin left Boston at 17 and made his way to Philadelphia.

Prose is plain language not arranged as verse.

Saucy means "fresh."

A *shilling* was an English silver coin, worth one-twentieth of a pound.

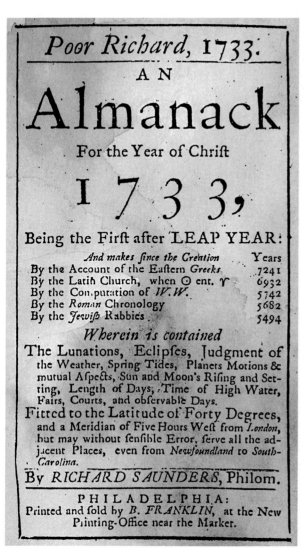

▲ The title page from the first edition of *Poor Richard's Almanack*

If you would not be forgotten,
As soon as you are dead and rotten,
Either write things worth reading,
Or do things worth the writing.

—Benjamin Franklin

Ben Franklin soon had a job working for a printer. Then he got a chance to go to London, where he learned a lot. When he returned to Philadelphia, he opened a print shop. Soon he began publishing his own newspaper. He became the best printer in Philadelphia. Because he was so good, he printed all the official papers for the colony of Pennsylvania.

Then he decided to publish an almanac. In the 17th century, almost every colonial home had two books: one was a Bible, the other was an almanac. The almanac was very useful. It had a calendar; it predicted the weather; it told when the moon would be full and when it would be a sliver; it told about the ocean's tides; and it was filled with odds and ends of information. Ben Franklin, with his curiosity, had a head filled with interesting information. His almanac, called *Poor Richard's Almanack*, became very popular. Poor Richard was always giving advice. He said things like:

Early to bed and early to rise, makes a man healthy, wealthy and wise.

God helps them who help themselves.

Three may keep a secret, if two of them are dead.

The almanac made Benjamin Franklin rich. He decided to retire, at age 42, and spend the rest of his life doing all the things he wanted to do. He studied electricity, invented things, became a politician, and was soon Philadelphia's most famous citizen. He would help found a new nation. By his example he showed that in America a poor boy could become the equal of anyone in the world.

Maryland's Form of Toleration

Back in the time when King Charles I ruled England, Sir George Calvert was an English lord and a real gentleman. That means he acted like one. He was not a poor boy who had to do everything for himself; he was wealthy, very wealthy. He was also energetic and daring.

Sir George made things hard for himself by becoming a Catholic. The English didn't like Catholics.

But, remember, the Spaniards, French, and Portuguese didn't like Protestants. This may seem a bit tiresome, but it was serious business back in the 17th century. You could get your head cut off if you practiced the wrong religion.

Sir George didn't get his head cut off, but he was forced to resign from his important government position. Since everyone liked him (he was a real gentleman), things worked out. The Irish—who were Catholic—were happy when the king gave him land in Ireland and named him Baron of Baltimore. Then King Charles I, who really liked Sir George, gave him a colony in America.

They named it Maryland. That was said to be in honor of the king's Catholic wife, Queen Henrietta Maria, although some say Calvert really meant to honor Mary, the mother of Jesus Christ.

Sir George dreamed of a colony "founded on religious freedom, where there would not only be a good life, but also a prosperous one, for those bold enough to take the risk." It was George Calvert's son, Cecil (SESS-ul), who actually founded the colony. He thought English Catholics could live in harmony there with Protestants.

Many Catholics did go to Maryland, but not as many as expected. Even Cecil, the new Lord Baltimore, didn't go. Cecil just stayed home and took the money that came from his colony.

He sent his younger brother, Leonard, to be the first governor. He told him to be "very

▲ George Calvert, Baron of Baltimore

Maryland is sometimes called a Southern colony and sometimes a middle colony.

Colonial governor Leonard Calvert meets the Indians of Maryland. ▼

201

careful to preserve unity and peace...and treat the Protestants with as much mildness and favor as justice will permit."

The Calverts ruled well. They saw that there was representative government and that people were treated fairly. In 1649, the Calverts urged the Maryland Assembly to pass a Toleration Act. The Assembly did—it was a landmark act. Religious freedom was a new idea that was being talked about by European philosophers, and practiced by Quakers (who still seemed peculiar to most people). But now a conservative American colony was trying out that freedom with an official act.

The Calverts were being practical. They meant to protect the Catholic minority and encourage settlement. This first-step act allowed for freedom of religion—but *only for Christians.*

Anyone who did not believe in Christ was to be hanged. That meant Jews or atheists or even some Christians who asked too many questions. Those people had to keep quiet or leave Maryland.

It was also a hanging offense to curse God. If you made fun of Christian doctrine, the law said you were to be whipped in public.

That sounds harsh—and it was—but remember the times. In the colonies controlled by France, Spain, and Portugal no Protestants, Jews, or atheists were allowed at all.

Bound Out

A big problem for early colonists in America was the shortage of labor. There weren't enough people to farm and do all the other work. One way of dealing with this was slavery—and Maryland imported many slaves. Another was by bringing over servants and apprentices who were "bound out" to an employer for a certain number of years—four or five at least, and, if you were a boy or girl, often until you were 21. The employer fed, housed, and clothed you. In return, you had to work unpaid, usually learning a trade. If you had a good employer it probably wasn't a bad life; but if your employer was stingy or cruel, or just indifferent, it could be miserable. The newspapers were always full of wanted notices from employers whose bound men or apprentices had run away.

In Maryland, if you stuck the job out, the law said that when your term of service was up you were to be given 50 acres of land, a suit of clothes, an ax, two hoes, and three barrels of corn. Then, if you were a Christian white man, you could vote and be elected to the assembly.

▲ Indentured servants work making pottery.

Carry Me Back to Ole Virginny

Life in 18th-century Virginia was certainly different from life in Pennsylvania or Massachusetts.

Most people in Virginia weren't Puritans or Quakers. They were Anglicans: members of the Church of England. But they were more relaxed about their religion than the Puritans. In the New England colonies the ministers were the most important people in the community; in the South, the wealthy landowners were more important.

The Virginians didn't live in towns, as people did in Massachusetts. They lived along the rivers on small farms, or on very large farms called "plantations." Living on the river made shipping easy, and that was important.

What Virginians were shipping was tobacco—to England. While a few other crops were grown, the main moneymaker was tobacco.

▲ Virginia's most profitable crop, tobacco

Workers roll barrels of tobacco onto a ship bound for England. ▼

A TOBACCO PLANTATION

▲ Slaves on a tobacco plantation plant and pick and dry and cure the tobacco. The slaves do all the physical labor—here they're making the barrels to ship the tobacco, and packing them, too.

There was little industry, and most goods came from England. In this land of magnificent forests, even fine furniture and other wood products were shipped from the "mother country."

After a few years, nothing grows well on land that has been planted with tobacco. To succeed in a tobacco economy, you need to rest the land every few years. That means you need to own a lot of land. You also need many workers.

So tobacco growers in colonial Virginia began to buy land and workers. As you know, at first they bought indentured servants. Then they bought Africans and made them slaves. By 1750 there were more Africans in Virginia than any other single group of people. More Virginians had come from Africa than from England or Scotland.

It was a few rich white planters who held power in the colony. Most whites were small farmers, and there were thousands of them. Some owned a slave or two—or hoped to—and that made them go along with the big slave owners. Virginia was not the only place where this happened. A society built on slavery stretched from Maryland to Georgia.

By the 18th century, plantation owners live a privileged, lordly life. But it isn't as easy as some people think. To run a plantation well, you need to be intelligent and industrious. (In England, aristocrats often don't work—or want to work; that isn't true in America.)

Each plantation is like a small village owned by one family. That family lives in a great house with many rooms and many servants. The house is usually built of brick and has a long lawn that leads to the river. The kitchen is a separate small building. So is the laundry, the carpenter's shop, the spinning and weaving shed, the blacksmith's shed, and the plantation office.

The plantation's business is farming, which means stables and barns and a smokehouse are needed. The smokehouse is for smoking meats. (Smoking preserves meat; there are no refrigerators.) There is a dock where ships load and unload. And a shed where the cooper makes barrels. (Tobacco is packed into barrels, called "hogsheads.") The plantation even has a kiln, where bricks are baked.

▲ A plantation is self-sufficient; it grows its own fruit and vegetables and raises its own cows and chickens and pigs. The money from tobacco or cotton pays for the owners' imported clothes and college educations.

A Paradox

By the 18th century most slave owners were beginning to realize that slavery was wrong. Many spoke out against it. (They also made excuses and tried to justify enslaving others. They knew that almost every ancient society had included slaves.) Many white people realized they were trapped in a bad system; they didn't know how to get out. George Washington, Thomas Jefferson, and many others wrote that slavery was evil—but they owned slaves.

There is a paradox connected with slavery. A *paradox* is a "puzzle." Something very puzzling happened in Colonial Virginia.

When it came time to write a constitution for our nation, it was the slave-owning Virginians who thought and wrote most about freedom. That is the paradox. Why do you think it was so?

Slaves live in cabins built near the fields. The big plantations sometimes have 200 or more slaves. A man known as "King" Carter, the wealthiest Virginian, owns 10 plantations. Some other Virginians own two or three. All the people who live on a plantation have to eat. So they grow vegetables, corn, and wheat, and raise animals, too. Can you see why it is hard work to run a plantation well?

A plantation owner is like a business executive. He runs the plantation and sees that it makes a profit. He is responsible for the work and the workers (that means food, clothing, housing, and health care). He is probably a member of the House of Burgesses, and that means that he attends assembly sessions at the capital twice a year.

He may also be a court officer, called on to decide court cases. Besides, he and his wife give parties and entertain visitors, who sometimes stay for days and days or even weeks at a time. It is a busy life.

Plantation children don't live at all the way you do. Some of the ways they live are nice, but some you wouldn't like.

If you are a very rich planter's son you have to wear velvet pants and ruffled shirts and high-heeled shoes when company comes, just like your dad. That must be uncomfortable.

A portrait of a wealthy planter and his family ▶

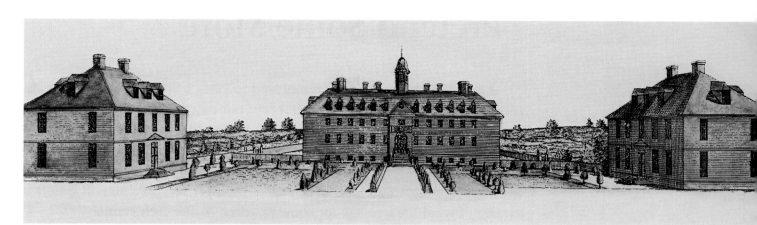

▲ The College of William and Mary in Williamsburg was named for England's king and queen and was the second college in the colonies.

How do you like shaving your head so you can wear a powdered wig? Or wearing an embroidered cap when you play? (Only the very rich go in for head shaving.)

If you are a planter's daughter, you wear satin gowns with stiff petticoats. Now that is fun, because those are party dresses. Everyday clothing for boys and girls is more comfortable than these garments, but not like the jeans and shorts that your great (lots of "greats" here!) grandchildren will wear.

One thing you do like is horseback riding. Everyone rides horses, and everyone learns to dance, too.

If you are the child of plantation owners, you have your own schoolteacher who lives with you. Life is good to you. You study and play and go to parties. You eat big meals of meats and pies and vegetables, all home cooked. Slaves pick up after you. How do you treat them? Some boys and girls are considerate; some are not.

If you are smart and study hard, you will be taught to read the Bible in the languages in which it was written. You will learn about ancient Rome and its gladiators, poets, and politicians. You will play a musical instrument. Many Americans born after you will not have as rigorous an education.

It is a patrician life, full of special privileges. If you are a boy you may finish your schooling at Virginia's College of William and Mary or perhaps at college in England. Someday you will be expected to serve as a representative of your neighbors in the House of Burgesses. Your parents and teachers are training you to be a leader.

Rigorous means "tough" or "demanding."

A *patrician* is an aristocrat, someone of high social rank. "Patrician" can be a noun or an adjective.

Pretend Some More

You are 10 years old and indentured to Patrick Beech, a silversmith in the town of Williamsburg. (You'll find out more about Williamsburg in the next chapter.) Beech was a real silversmith, we know that, but we don't know much about his servants and apprentices. We do know about the jobs they would have done and the way they might have lived. So you can pretend to be one of them. If you do, you will get an idea of what life was like for some children in the 18th century.

You have been in Virginia just a year. Your parents died of influenza in London. Since you had nowhere to go and no money, the Lord Mayor sent you and some other orphans to Virginia. Sometimes you are homesick for your friends in London, but you are beginning to like it in America. Life isn't easy, but it is better than it was in London.

Beech keeps you working from before the sun comes up until dark. Your first job in the morning is to light a fire to warm the house and another to heat the forge where silver is melted and formed. Then you clean the kitchen, run errands, and sometimes do odd jobs in the silver shop. You don't get time to play, and lately you have begun to hate Mr. Beech. He never seems to smile.

Mrs. Beech has taught you to read. She takes you to church and whips you when you are bad. She does the same with her children. She is fair but very busy. You miss your own mother.

A silversmith at work ▼

This is a pewter and silversmith workshop. Pewter, which is a mixture of tin, lead, and copper or bismuth, was for people who couldn't afford silver. The apprentice is turning the wheel that drives the bellows to keep the furnace hot. If the 'prentice got fed up and ran away, his master would offer a reward for bringing him back. In the colonies, even unskilled laborers were hard to find.

But you do have a friend in the silver shop. His name is Tom, and he was apprenticed to a watchmaker in London before he came to the colonies. Tom says Beech is not a bad man, just worried. There isn't enough work in Williamsburg. There are too many silversmiths, and the rich planters buy their good silver in England. So Beech must make silver teeth and set them in people's mouths. He repairs watches and makes clocks, and sometimes silver cups and trays and jewelry. He has a big family to feed, along with his servants. There is enough food, but nothing extra.

Neither you nor Tom is free. The law says you must stay with Patrick Beech until you are 21. Tom is also an indentured servant. Beech paid for his passage from London: he must work for him for five years. Then, Tom tells you, he will go to Charles Town and open his own shop. He has heard the planters in South Carolina are very rich.

More than anything, you want to hunt and fish and learn to use a rifle. You have seen enough of the silversmith's work—fires and forges, pouring liquid metal, hammering silver into shape, putting teeth into the jaws of people who scream in pain. You need to be patient. Someday you will have everything you wish for—and more.

▲ A watchmaker at work

▲ If you had lived in colonial Virginia, your house might have been like this, with one big room and a sleeping loft above.

Now, pretend again. This time you are the child of a Virginia farmer. You live in a small wooden house with a big fireplace at one end. The house has only one big room with a sleeping loft. At night your parents sleep in front of the fire with the baby, and you and your brothers climb a ladder to the loft. You all sleep on straw mattresses.

The only clothes you have are those you wear, and a Sunday shirt. Tobacco and corn grow poorly on your land, because it is worn out. You have enough food, but you don't eat a balanced diet. You are sometimes sick, and you will die when you are 40.

Still, you are luckier than many children. You have had a year of schooling, and you know how to read. Your parents hope your life will be better than theirs. And it will be. At 15 you will head out to the western frontier, where you will find land and opportunity. Your schooling will help you succeed. You will marry, have 10 children, and own land enough for all of them to farm.

Most poor white boys and girls don't get to school. And there are no schools for black children. Many 18th-century Southern children never learn to read or write. It is difficult to have schools when people live so far apart on farms. It is difficult to have churches, too. Some ministers ride

Unliberated

Were women treated equally in the colonies? See what you think. A woman sent this poem to the *Virginia Gazette*. It was published in October 1736.

Custom alas! doth partial prove,
Nor give us equal Measure;
A Pain for us it is to love,
But is to Men a Pleasure.
They plainly can their thoughts disclose,
While ours must burn within;
We have got Tongues, and Eyes, in Vain,
And Truth from us is Sin.
Then Equal Laws let Custom find,
And neither Sex oppress,
More Freedom give to Womankind,
Or give to Mankind less.

▲ "More Freedom give to Womankind…."

horseback from one church to another. The law says you must go to the Anglican church every Sunday.

Your parents hate that law, and another law that makes them pay taxes to help support the Anglican Church. They say the Anglican Church is for rich folks. They would like to join the Baptist church, but they can get in trouble if they do that. A law says their children could be taken from them if they join a free-thinking church. Since you are one of their children you agree that is a terrible law. Actually, it isn't enforced very often. Perhaps the law is meant to scare people away from new churches, like those of the Baptists and Methodists and New Light Presbyterians.

Belonging to that Anglican Church of England, as most Virginians do, makes you different from people in Massachusetts. Virginians love England and English clothing, paintings, furnishings, and ideas. They feel closer to people in England than they do to those in New England.

Now pretend that you are a slave. You don't want to? You are right. No one wants to be a slave. Some slaves, especially those who work in the fields on some big plantations, live in small huts and sleep on old blankets piled on the dirt floor. They don't eat well and they work almost all the time. Other slaves, especially those who are house servants, live in small wooden houses with beds and tables and furnishings that come from the plantation

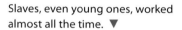
Slaves, even young ones, worked almost all the time. ▼

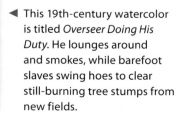
◀ This 19th-century watercolor is titled *Overseer Doing His Duty*. He lounges around and smokes, while barefoot slaves swing hoes to clear still-burning tree stumps from new fields.

No one knows who painted this picture, but it may have been done in South Carolina. The slaves may be celebrating a wedding by "jumping the broomstick." Some of their clothes look like those worn in Yoruba, which is in Nigeria in Africa. Their instruments also resemble African instruments. ▶

workshop or, sometimes, from the big house. Visitors from Europe will say they live better than most peasants in the Old World. (Which is probably why so many European peasants want to come to America.)

Your name is Sarah, and you live on a farm in North Carolina. There are 18 of you slaves (including children) in four families and you share two houses near the tobacco fields. A fireplace divides each house in half. Your house has a front porch, as many houses do in Africa. The porch is a nice place to rest on a hot evening. You have your own garden, which provides corn and greens and potatoes. They have made you strong and healthy. You are 11, and you can't read and never will be taught how. But you can sing and play the banjo, and that makes you popular in church. Your faith is important to you and your family. You are Christians, and you have brought your African spirituality to that religion.

Hoeing Cotton

From the story of a former slave, Solomon Northup:

About the first of July, when [the cotton] is a foot high or thereabouts, it is hoed the fourth and last time… During all these hoeings the overseer or driver follows the slaves on horseback with a whip…. The fastest hoer takes the lead row. He is usually about a rod in front of his companions. If one of them passes him, he is whipped. If one falls behind or is a moment idle, he is whipped. In fact, the lash is flying from morning until night.

A whip used by overseers to punish and terrorize slaves ▶

Virginia's Capital

Do you remember the mosquitoes, deerflies, and snakes at Jamestown, back in John Smith's time? In 1699, someone suggested moving the Virginia capital from Jamestown to Middle Plantation—eight miles away but on higher ground. Jamestown's landowners didn't think moving the capital was a good idea, but most of the other plantation owners agreed that Middle Plantation would be a capital spot for the capital.

But Middle Plantation wasn't much of a name for a town. A new name was needed. The king of England's name was a natural choice, and the town became Williamsburg.

That little town, born at the beginning of the 18th century, danced across the stage of history for about 80 years. Then it left the spotlight and was forgotten (until the 20th century, when it was restored and rebuilt as if it were still in the 1700s).

Wide, tree-lined Duke of Gloucester Street ran down the middle of the town. At one end of the street stood the Capitol. At the other was the Wren Building of the College of William and Mary. Bruton Parish Church, with its white spire, stood proudly on the same street, along with neat houses, shops, and a grassy mall. Overlooking the mall was the finest building in the colony: the handsome, stately governor's palace. Now picture people, horses, cows, sheep, and gardens, and you have an idea of Williamsburg.

Nathaniel Bacon leads rebels as Jamestown burns. ▼

Bacon's Rebellion

In 1676 some frontiersmen, led by Nathaniel Bacon, marched to Jamestown. They had asked for help fighting Indians who were attacking their farms. The governor, Sir William Berkeley (BARK-lee), refused. Berkeley was a rich, selfish old man who taxed the small planters heavily. Since the governor wouldn't help, Bacon took matters in his own hands. He led a small army against the Indians. Governor Berkeley was furious. He gathered soldiers and planned to fight Bacon and his rebels. Bacon's army marched on Jamestown. The governor and his men ran to a warship and sailed off. Bacon burned the State House and started his own government. His actions are remembered as Bacon's Rebellion. But Bacon soon got sick and died. Berkeley came back and hanged all of Bacon's followers.

▲ In Colonial Williamsburg today, you can visit the reconstructed Governor's Palace.

The word *crown,* as it is used here, means the British government.

The Bruton Parish Church in Williamsburg, Virginia. ▶

If you stand outside the governor's palace and look at the brick fence—with its stone British unicorn on top and fancy iron gates—you will be impressed. If you are lucky you may get invited inside for a musical evening. You'll sit in the candlelit ballroom, where men in starched linen blouses and women in silk brocade gowns smile and nod at each other. A display of muskets and swords in the entry is intended to leave you awed with the crown's military might.

Most of the year, Williamsburg is a sleepy village of 2,000 souls. Half of them are African Americans. But in April and October, when the House of Burgesses and the courts are in session, the population doubles.

People come to take care of colonial business, make laws, consider court cases, see friends, and shop. You can buy a wig at the wig makers, a violin at the music shop, or a gingerbread cookie at the bakery.

One traveler writes of Williamsburg, "At the time of the assemblies and general courts, it is crowded with the gentry of the country. On those occasions there are balls and other amusements; but as soon as business is finished, they return to their plantations and the town is in a manner deserted."

For most people a trip to Williamsburg means having a good time—unless the Reverend Mr. James Blair of Bruton Parish Church happens to come by. Blair doesn't have a sense of humor. For 50 long years, he is a powerful force in the community. Blair usually gets his way, and his way is not one of tolerance. A landowning aristocracy rules Virginia and outsiders remain outside. Only Anglicans can be elected burgesses. A plan for religious liberty is hatched in Williamsburg in the second half of the 18th century, but it might not have happened if Reverend Blair had been alive.

But Blair is not typical of most Virginians. The Virginia way is gracious and courtly and easygoing. William and Mary's wise law professor, George Wythe (say *with*), will soon come to prominence in Williamsburg. He is kind and considerate and learned; some people call him "a walking library." George Wythe becomes mayor of Williamsburg. He frees his slaves long before he dies. He hates slavery. One of his favorite students is a young man named Thomas Jefferson.

If you had a magic wand that could waft you anywhere, you might consider landing at the Raleigh Tavern in Williamsburg on a day when George Washington, Thomas Jefferson, Patrick Henry, and Peyton Randolph are having a conversation. Just sit back and listen. Those Virginians and their friends have a rare talent for good times and serious thought. They are as splendid and energetic a group of leaders as any nation has ever produced.

School's Out

Virginia's governor Alexander Spotswood wanted to be friends with the Indians. He sponsored the Indian Act of 1714. It created an outpost where the colonists could meet and trade with Indians. An English school was founded to teach Indian children about Christianity and English ways.

Many colonists were angry about Spotswood's ideas. Some didn't want anything to do with Native Americans. Others were afraid the Indians would sell their furs to Virginia's governor and not to them. In 1717, at the colonists' urging, the king repealed the Indian Act. The outpost and Indian school were closed.

The colonists who wanted to teach Indians didn't give up. A school for Indians opened at the College of William and Mary in 1723. About a dozen Indians at a time lived and studied there. Today, the building is still in use as part of the college.

Ho Nee Yeath Taw No Row attended the Brafferton Indian school at the College of William and Mary. He was one of four Native American envoys sent to London to request Britain's recognition of the Iroquois Confederation as a sovereign nation and to ask for military aid against the French. ▶

They are struggling with a weighty problem: how to create a new and fair government on this gorgeous continent. And they are being pulled in two directions. There are many who think as James Blair does and want to reproduce Old England in America.

But there are others who have come to America because they are unhappy with the Old World and its society of rigid classes. They want to try something new, in what they call the New World. This little village of Williamsburg will ring with debates on the purposes of government.

Royal Colonies and a No-Blood Revolution

Here is some more English history. It is the year 1686 and James II is king of England. You met him before, when he was the Duke of York and his brother, King Charles II, gave him New York and New Jersey.

Now Charles is dead and James wears the crown. James is a Catholic, but most people in England belong to the Church of England.

King James II would like to rule without Parliament. He wants to be an "absolute monarch." He believes, as did his father, Charles I, that kings have a "divine right" to rule. That means he thinks God wants him to be king. He would like to make England Roman Catholic again. He will learn that you can't force religion on people.

The English people respond with another revolution—a civilized revolution. James isn't killed—as his father was in the English Civil War of 1649—so this revolution, in 1688, is called the "Bloodless" or "Glorious Revolution." James's Protestant daughter, Mary, and her Dutch husband, William of Orange, are asked to be rulers. (They are the couple the Virginians honored when they named the College of William and Mary.)

The English people make a deal with the new king and queen. They insist that Parliament

▲ A king and queen who helped make a peaceful revolution

have more power than the monarchs. They also demand a Bill of Rights for the people. It is a terrible time for absolute monarchs, but a great moment for freedom. In America, the colonists find it inspiring.

Read that last paragraph again. It's important to remember that *the Glorious Revolution gave Parliament more power than the king. HOORAY!*

The Carolinas

The Carolinas, North and South, were granted to eight lords proprietors by King Charles II. The lords never meant to live in America, and they didn't. They just planned to get rich by using the Carolinas to produce three products that were expensive in England: wine, silk, and olive oil.

The Carolinas worked out, but not as the lords had expected. Indigo (a plant grown for its blue dye) and rice became principal crops—not wine, silk, or olive oil. Eventually the colonies were bought back by the king. The lords lost out, and the Carolinas became royal colonies.

In South Carolina, Charles Town, named for Charles II, prospered from its beginning. No longer were there terrible starving and dying times when a colony was founded. Jamestown and Plymouth had taught the colonists what not to do.

Planting Indigo

Eliza Pinckney (born Eliza Lucas) played an important part in South Carolina's development. Her father was a British military officer who believed his daughter should have a good education. He sent her to school in England. She said that good education was the finest gift he could have given her.

When Eliza was 16 her family moved to South Carolina. Eliza had a scientific mind, and she studied and experimented. In South Carolina most planters grew rice, but there was a need for other crops, especially crops that could be sold abroad to bring money into the colonies. Eliza planted fig orchards, and then she dried the figs so they could be shipped far distances. She experimented with ginger, hemp, flax, cotton, alfalfa, and silk.

When Eliza's father sent her indigo seeds from the West Indies, she planted them and then replanted the best varieties. Indigo was much desired in Europe. In 1744, Eliza Lucas grew the first successful indigo crop in the colonies. Soon she was giving seeds to other planters. By 1747, South Carolina was exporting 100,000 pounds of indigo a year. That indigo crop, and South Carolina's rice, would become more valuable to England than the gold and silver mines were to Spain.

▲ Indigo plants produce a purplish-blue dye used for fabrics.

Charleston (which was the name Charles Town turned into) soon became the busiest port in the South. It attracted younger sons of the English nobility, who gave it an aristocratic flavor.

Many of Charleston's leaders came from the tiny island of Barbados in the Caribbean Sea. In the 17th century Barbados was the wealthiest and most crowded of all English American colonies. (In 1680 Barbados's exports were more valuable than the exports of all of the North American mainland.)

South Carolina had to find ways to attract settlers. One way was to practice religious tolerance. Religious wars were making people flee from Europe. The Carolinas welcomed them, and that led to an interesting mix of peoples. Scots settled on the coast and helped fight off Spanish attacks. French Protestants, called Huguenots (HUE-guh-nots), came and proved to be just the kind of colonists the new land needed. In France

▼ Charleston Harbor in South Carolina

▲ Slaves working on a rice plantation

they were persecuted, but France's shortsightedness was America's good fortune. The Huguenots were carpenters and blacksmiths and masons, and they believed in hard work. What John Smith would have given to have had them in Jamestown!

Field-workers were needed to plant and harvest the rice that was making the colony rich. The settlers from Barbados were used to owning slaves; they wanted slaves in America, and they encouraged it. It is an irony that Africans probably taught the white settlers how to cultivate rice, because it was rice that made slavery profitable in South Carolina. Soon there were more black people in South Carolina than whites.

South Carolina became an aristocratic colony with a few very wealthy people holding almost all the economic and political power. It was different from the other Southern colonies in many ways, but especially because it had that important city: Charleston. In Virginia and North Carolina there was no great city. For most of the year,

▲ Middleton Plantation near Charleston

plantation folk in those colonies lived isolated lives. That was not the case in South Carolina. Some plantation owners in South Carolina visited their plantations only occasionally. They spent their time in Charleston, where they lived in big houses and went to fancy parties.

The Huguenots mixed and married with the English; their tastes and ideas helped create the most elegant society in the colonies.

Those who were wealthy thought life in Charleston finer than in any place on earth. But the majority of Charlestonians were not wealthy. The majority of South Carolinians were not free. They were Africans, and they worked as field hands, craftspeople, and servants. But they had their own ideas and traditions, and they brought those African ideas, songs, stories, and habits to their new home. After a while, some of those African ideas became mixed with ideas they found in America. Brer Rabbit, who started as an African, became American. In South Carolina, African Americans developed their own language, Gullah.

Some people in South Carolina speak Gullah today. They talk quickly, without a Southern accent. Gullah combines words from English, French, and a number of African languages. You may have heard some Gullah words, such as *goober* (peanut), *gumbo* (soup with okra), *juke* (as in jukebox), and *voodoo* (witchcraft). Here is a sentence in Gullah: *Shishuh tall pass una.* It means "Sister is taller than you."

North Carolina was different. It had tough land to tame, so its settlers were apt to be free-spirited small farmers. Many were outcasts and religious dissenters from aristocratic Virginia. In Virginia the rich landholders were in control, and they were Anglicans. People who wanted to join the new religious sects—the Baptists and the Methodists—were persecuted in Virginia. Some moved south to North Carolina.

North Carolina may have been the most democratic of all the colonies. Generally, North Carolinians minded their own business and left their neighbors alone, which may be why pirates made the North Carolina coast a base for their adventuring. Although some said it was because the pirates paid the North Carolina governor to leave them alone. That could be true, because it was finally a force from Virginia that got Blackbeard—the most famous and ferocious of the pirates. His real name was Edward Teach. He braided his great black beard into pigtails, wove ribbons into them, and then hung smoking pieces of rope from his hat. At night the pigtails looked like coiling snakes, and the burning rope gave his face a glowing, eerie look. It was enough to scare anyone, and it did scare a lot of sailors.

Anne Bonney scared them, too. She was a tough pirate who sailed the Caribbean and Carolina coast, and had no trouble terrorizing seamen.

In 1677 some North Carolinians rebelled against England. They didn't like England's Navigation Acts, which forced them to pay taxes to England on goods sold to other colonies. If a North Carolina tobacco grower sold some of his tobacco to a merchant in Boston, he was supposed to pay a tax to England. Did that make any sense? The colonists didn't think so.

Some North Carolinians refused to pay. They even set up their own government and tried to get free of England. They almost got away with it. They put British officials in jail, elected a legislature, and chose their leader, John Culpeper, as governor. For two years they exercised all the powers and duties of government. But the British finally got angry. They tried Culpeper for treason. He was convicted but not punished— maybe because he was so popular.

One hundred years later, in 1776, people in all the colonies were angry about English taxes. The colonists would unite, as Popé had united the Pueblo Indians—and... well, you'll see what happened.

In 1997, some divers found a wreck off the coast of North Carolina. There were nine cannons on board and others scattered on the ocean floor. Archaeologists believe it is Blackbeard's ship, *Queen Anne's Revenge.*

How an artist imagined the pirate Blackbeard ▼

CHAPTER 49

Four and Nine Make Thirteen

If you've been counting, you know I've talked about 12 colonies. Can you name them? Cover the next sentence and see if you can. Here they are: Massachusetts, New Hampshire, Connecticut, Rhode Island, New York, New Jersey, Pennsylvania, Delaware, Maryland, Virginia, North Carolina, and South Carolina.

Finally, like a tail at the end of a kite, along came the 13th colony. Do you know what it was named? Here's a clue: it was founded in 1732, when KING GEORGE II was on the throne of England. That wasn't hard: it was Georgia.

The five Southern Colonies had plenty of good farmland as well as rivers that could be used for transportation. Few towns or cities had developed, and planters dominated political and social life. ▼

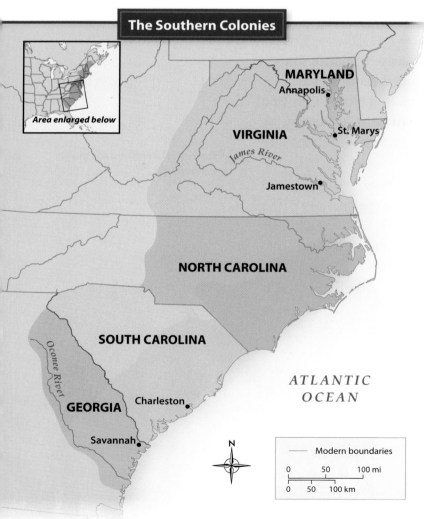

The Southern Colonies

Colony	Date Founded
Virginia	1607
Massachusetts	1630
Maryland	1632
Connecticut	1636
Delaware	1638
Rhode Island	1647
North Carolina	1663
New Jersey	1664
New York	1664
New Hampshire	1680
Pennsylvania	1681
South Carolina	1712
Georgia	1733

New England
Middle
Southern

In 1734, settlers began building the town of Savannah.

James Edward Oglethorpe, founder of Georgia

Georgia's beginning was noble, not because of birth or wealth, but because of a noble idea. Unfortunately the idea didn't work out. Still, it was inspiring.

James Oglethorpe, who planned Georgia, wanted to solve a terrible problem. People in England who couldn't pay their bills were thrown into debtors' prisons. Once they were in those jails—and they were awful places—they couldn't work or earn money, and so they had no way to pay their debts. If they were lucky, a relative or friend came up with the cash. Otherwise they just stayed there. Many died in prison.

Oglethorpe decided to found a colony where debtors could go instead of going to jail. He wanted to make it a place where people could lead ideal lives. So he had laws passed for Georgia that made drinking liquor and keeping slaves illegal. He wanted Georgians to live on small farms, and he wanted them to do their own farming. He brought experts from Europe to teach them how.

Oglethorpe helped to plan a handsome capital, Savannah, a city with beautiful parks and fine public squares. It was a shame his idea didn't work out. Not many debtors wanted to come to the wilds of Georgia. To some, even prison seemed safer.

▲ The Rock Eagle Mound is thought to have been built as many as 3,000 years ago.

Those who came were much like the settlers in the other colonies: a mixture of peoples and religions. Anglican men and women came, German Lutherans came, Catholics came, Jews came, and so did Scotch Presbyterians.

They soon discovered that Georgia was full of Indian villages. When the first settlers arrived, they found thousands of Indian mounds. The mounds were sacred sites from the Native American past. (If you get into a helicopter and fly near Eatonton, Georgia, you can see one of those earth mounds. It is shaped like an eagle with wings that spread out for 120 feet, about the size of four average classrooms.)

The local Indians had bad memories of white people. Back in 1540, the Spanish conquistador Hernando de Soto had marched through Georgia with his army. De Soto was so cruel and evil that the Indians were still telling stories about him 200 years later.

But Oglethorpe was a fine and honorable man, and the Indians learned to trust him. They made many peace treaties with him and both he and they always kept their word.

James Oglethorpe meets the Indians of Georgia in 1733. ▶

◀ Oglethorpe prepares to lead an expedition against the Spanish at St. Augustine, Florida.

It was the settlers who gave Oglethorpe problems. They wanted to drink liquor and have slaves, and eventually they won out. When Oglethorpe tried to force his laws and "good ideas" on others, it just didn't work.

Besides, life in Georgia wasn't easy. Spaniards and pirates gave the settlers a hard time. Pirates roamed along the Georgia coast, capturing ships of all nations. Spain controlled Florida and said Georgia and the Carolinas were also her territories. Because of that, there were constant border fights. When the Spaniards attacked, the Georgians were able to fight them off—luckily for them, because none of the other colonies helped out. It was a while before the colonies thought of uniting, or of helping each other.

Oglethorpe lost all his money trying to establish Georgia. Finally, he gave up. Georgians wanted to have rice plantations and slaves and the king's government, and that is what they got. The king made Georgia into another royal colony (in 1752). That made eight royal colonies: Virginia, Massachusetts, New Hampshire, North Carolina, New York, South Carolina, New Jersey, and Georgia. Each had a royal governor, appointed by the king.

Rhode Island and Connecticut had charters that allowed them to govern themselves. Their assemblies (congresses) picked their governors. Maryland, Pennsylvania, and Delaware were proprietary colonies. They were owned by individuals—the Calverts and the Penns.

All the colonies had assemblies of local leaders who made most of their laws. Later England would regret the freedom she gave the colonies and try to take some of it back. That would lead to big trouble.

But in the mid-18th century most Americans were happy to be part of the mighty British empire. The 13 colonies were like 13 children of a kindly and faraway parent. Each colony seemed to be a tiny nation, with its own government, its own habits, and its own religious ways.

Though the 13 colonies were British possessions, a significant part of the population was made up of immigrants from various European countries as well as Africans forced to come as slaves. ▼

The Colonial Population

Quebec

MAINE
(part of Massachusetts)

Montreal

Augusta

Portland

NEW HAMPSHIRE
Portsmouth

Albany • Boston
NEW YORK Providence MASSACHUSETTS
Hartford • Newport RHODE ISLAND
CONNECTICUT

Lake Ontario

Lake Erie

PENNSYLVANIA New York City
Philadelphia • NEW JERSEY

Baltimore

DELAWARE

MARYLAND

VIRGINIA Richmond
Williamsburg

ATLANTIC OCEAN

NORTH CAROLINA
Charlotte • Fayetteville

SOUTH CAROLINA

GEORGIA • Charleston

Savannah

Major areas of concentration
- Africans
- British
- Dutch
- French
- German
- Highland Scots
- Scots-Irish
- Modern boundaries

0   125   250 mi
0   125   250 km

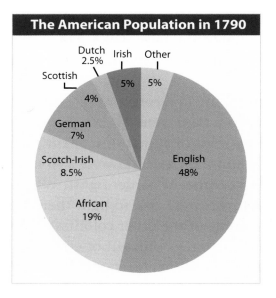

The American Population in 1790

Dutch 2.5%   Irish 5%   Other 5%

Scottish 4%

German 7%

Scotch-Irish 8.5%

African 19%

English 48%

Over the Mountains

All the early English-speaking settlements were on or near the East Coast. That's not surprising, since the settlers came by boat from Europe.

People were arriving in America every day. Much of the land on the East Coast was taken. Where could these new people go? Some headed to the tree-thick Appalachian Mountains that bordered the coastal plains—and then on, over those mountains.

They headed over the Appalachians, to the valleys or the flat lands beyond—to the frontier. They had to be brave to head into the unknown wilds. They were called frontiersmen and frontierswomen, trailblazers and pathfinders. They lived in the woods, shot the food they ate, and made their own clothes. They learned from the Indians and from each other. (You'll read more about them later in this book.)

The frontier offered something important: *land.* Land meant everything in a society that lived by farming. *Owning land made you feel really free.*

On the frontier you could be the equal of anyone. On the frontier no one cared if you were Puritan or Baptist. It didn't make a difference if your father was a lord or a pauper. Could you be depended upon? Did you tell the truth? Could you shoot straight? Were you brave? That's what mattered on the frontier.

There was no government where they went, so they were on their own. They had to fight Indians and other settlers for their land. They were a tough breed, those early over-the-mountain people.

▲ Frontiersmen had to be self-sufficient and independent.

The British tried to stop them. They didn't want settlers moving west. The British were in charge, and that meant they had to keep order. If the settlers moved into Indian territory, someone had to worry about protecting them from Indian attack. Someone had to protect the Indians from rifle-happy settlers. Someone had to make treaties with the Indians and do some governing.

That cost money. Britain would have to build forts in the western territories. She would have to send soldiers to man those forts. She would have to send governors. Parliament told the colonists to stay out of Indian territory.

But there was no stopping them.

◀ Don't be confused if you hear of White Mountains in New Hampshire, Green Mountains in Vermont, Catskill Mountains in New York, Allegheny Mountains in Pennsylvania, and Blue Ridge, Clinch, Shenandoah, and Great Smoky Mountains in the South. All these mountains are part of the Appalachian range.

A Nasty Triangle

The United States began as a collection of settlements that were not much alike. South Carolina wasn't like Pennsylvania, and Maryland wasn't like Connecticut. The people who founded the colonies had a lot to do with those differences, and so did the conditions of the land.

Massachusetts had a special problem because of its rocky soil and cold climate. It was tough being a farmer in New England, but New Englanders were tough people who liked challenges. So they did farm, although for many it was "subsistence farming." That means they grew enough for themselves; they didn't usually have extra crops to sell. A few New England farmers were able to sell their farm products abroad but, mostly, New England's land just wasn't right for large farms—or plantations—like those in the South.

And when it came to industry, the British made things difficult. They wouldn't let the colonists manufacture goods that competed with English goods. You can understand why that caused some grumbling.

New Englanders had to find ways to earn a living. Fishing was one way. Cod became New England's gold, just as tobacco was Virginia's. The Puritan settlers caught codfish and then salted and shipped and sold the fish in Europe or the Caribbean Islands. In order to do that, they needed ships. So they became shipbuilders. To make ships they needed lumber. So they harvested timber and began selling wood and wood products. They became merchants carrying goods around the world. Yankee ships were familiar sights in Singapore and Rangoon and Bristol. And New England boys, who hung around the wharfs, got a chance to touch Dutch coins, Chinese silks, or fruit from Spain. They heard tales of adventures in Tripoli and Jamaica and dreamed of becoming skippers and going to faraway places themselves.

New England cod fishermen haul in their catch on the North Atlantic. ▼

Soon Yankees were trading all kinds of things. They might take their salted cod to Barbados and trade it for cane sugar. Then they'd go to Virginia to pick up tobacco. They'd take the tobacco and sugar to England and trade them for cash, guns, and English cloth. Then on to Africa, where they exchanged the guns and cloth for men, women, and children. From there it was back across the Atlantic Ocean to the West Indies, where the people were sold into slavery. Finally they sailed home to New England (or, sometimes, New York or Annapolis). All that was called the "triangular trade." It made some people very rich.

Picture a triangle—a long one. Do you have three points in your mind? Now stretch the triangle across the Atlantic Ocean. Put one point on the New England coast, another in Africa, and the third in South Carolina. Now imagine a boat sailing along that triangle, from New England to Africa to South Carolina, and back to New England.

Stretch another triangle across the Atlantic. This one can start in England, go to Africa, and have a third point in Virginia. The Atlantic Ocean was once filled with ships sailing triangular routes. Most of them included a stop in the West Indies. (They were very jagged triangles; a few were rectangles.)

Let's pretend a triangle is starting at Newport, Rhode Island (near Boston). You can watch as a ship is loaded with rum and guns. (Rum is an alcoholic drink made from sugarcane.) The ship heads for Africa, where the rum and guns will be traded for African people.

Colonial Economic Activity

Land and climate played a large part in the development of diverse economies in Colonial America.

Map legend:
- Fishing
- Lumber
- Manufacturing
- Shipbuilding
- Furs and skins
- Cattle and grains
- Tobacco
- Rice and indigo
- Fishing banks
- Modern boundaries

0 — 125 — 250 mi
0 — 125 — 250 km

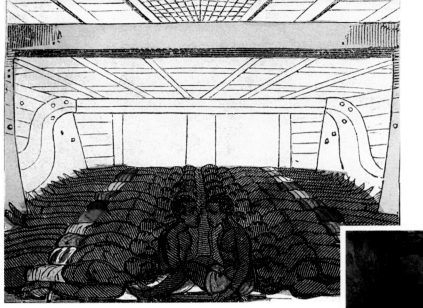

This drawing of the slave ship *Brookes* caused an uproar. It led, in 1788, to a British law limiting the number of slaves per ship's ton. The drawing was not quite accurate, but close enough: conditions were horrendous. Death rates varied, but perhaps 20 percent of the people captured died onboard the ship in the early 17th century. The death rate for crew members—from beatings and disease—was often higher. Those who owned the slave ships sat home in comfort and profited.

This statue is part of a monument in Tanzania, built to honor all those who were taken into slavery.

Chain used to shackle enslaved people in a slave market in Africa

Between 1526 and 1870, nearly 10 million slaves were shipped from Africa to

Brazil	3,647,000
British Caribbean	1,665,000
French America	1,600,000
Spanish America	1,552,000
Dutch America	500,000
British North America and the United States	399,000
Europe	175,000
Danish West Indies	28,000

The Africans have been captured by enemy tribesmen and sold to African slave traders. The slave traders bargain with the New England boat captain, who buys as many people as he can squeeze on his ship. Some of the captives are children, kidnapped from their parents.

Olaudah Equiano (oh-LOW-duh ek-wee-AHN-oh) was one of those children. He was 11 in 1756, when he was captured in Benin. He was the youngest of seven children, a happy boy in a loving home. Like many other prosperous African families, his family had slaves. Imagine that you are Olaudah as you read his words:

One day, when all our people were gone out to their works as usual, and only I and my sister were left to mind the house, two men and a woman got over our walls, and in a moment seized us both; and without giving us time to cry out or to make any resistance, they stopped our mouths and ran off with us into the nearest wood. Here they tied our hands, and continued to carry us as far as they could, till night came on, when we reached a small house, where the robbers halted for refreshment and spent the night.

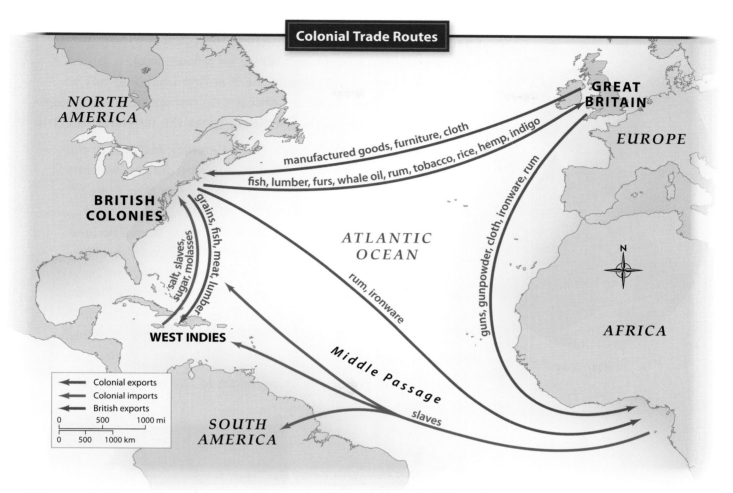

Colonial Trade Routes

NORTH AMERICA

GREAT BRITAIN

EUROPE

manufactured goods, furniture, cloth

fish, lumber, furs, whale oil, rum, tobacco, rice, hemp, indigo

BRITISH COLONIES

guns, gunpowder, cloth, ironware, rum

ATLANTIC OCEAN

grains, fish, meat, lumber

salt, slaves, sugar, molasses

rum, ironware

AFRICA

WEST INDIES

Middle Passage

slaves

Colonial exports
Colonial imports
British exports

0   500   1000 mi
0   500   1000 km

SOUTH AMERICA

▲ The network of trade routes that developed during colonial times is often called "triangular trade." There was more than one trade triangle, but all were tied up with slavery. Most of the people who made money out of slavery didn't want to see it come to an end.

Olaudah and his sister are taken on a long journey, separated, and sold. He is passed from person to person, staying a month here, a few weeks there. Olaudah sees many parts of Africa and has many adventures. He tries to run away but is unsuccessful. Then, for the first time in his life, he sees the ocean.

The first object which saluted my eyes when I arrived on the coast was the sea, and a slaveship, which was then riding at anchor and waiting for its cargo. These filled me with astonishment, which was soon converted into terror.... When I was carried on board I was immediately handled, and tossed up to see if I was sound, by some of the crew; and I was now persuaded that I had got into a world of bad spirits, and that they were going to kill me.

▲ Olaudah Equiano

Olaudah is tossed below deck, where the smell is so bad he becomes sick and cannot eat. When he refuses food he is tied down and beaten. Frightened, he is at first unable to talk to anyone because the other Africans do not speak his language. Finally he meets some men who speak the language of Benin.

I asked them if these people had no country, but lived in this hollow place [the ship]. They told me they did not, but came from a distant one...I then asked where were their women? Had they any like themselves? I was told they had. "And why," said I, "do we not see them?" They answered because they were left behind. I asked how the vessel could go? They told me they could not tell; but that there was cloth put upon the masts by the help of ropes I saw, and then the vessel went on; and the white men had some spell or magic they put in the water, when they liked, in order to stop the vessel. I was exceedingly amazed at this account, and really thought they were spirits.

Olaudah learns that he is being taken to the white men's country to work.

African Trading Kingdoms

On the west coast of Africa, near the continent's bulge, the three great kingdoms of Ghana, Mali, and Songhai rose and fell between the time of the Roman Empire and the settling of North America. In the 15th century, Timbuktu, the leading city of Songhai, was renowned for its schools and wise men.

In the late 15th century, Portugal established a trading partnership with the West African kingdom of Benin. Benin sold many people, often captives taken in battle, to the Portuguese as slaves.

When European sailing ships called at West African ports, it was trade alone that interested both peoples. The Europeans had guns, iron, cloth, kettles, and mirrors that were wanted in Africa. The Africans had workers—healthy, hardy people—who were wanted to grow crops and mine and settle the place the Europeans called a New World.

And so men and women would be traded into slavery by people, on both sides of the Atlantic, who didn't seem to worry about the consequences of their actions.

▲ These bronze sculptures were carved in Benin, the country in western Africa in which Olaudah Equiano was kidnapped.

I then was a little revived, and thought, if it were no worse than working, my situation was not so desperate: but still I feared I should be put to death, the white people looked and acted, as I thought, in so savage a manner; for I had never seen among any people such instances of brutal cruelty; and this is not only shown towards us blacks, but also to some of the whites themselves. One white man in particular I saw, when we were permitted to be on deck, flogged so unmercifully with a large rope near the foremast, that he died in consequence of it; and they tossed him over the side as they would have done a brute. This made me fear these people the more; and I expected nothing less than to be treated in the same manner.

Olaudah describes the scene belowdecks, where people are packed so closely they can hardly turn over. The smells, he says, are "loathsome." Women shriek, the dying groan, all is "a scene of horror."

One day, when we had a smooth sea and moderate wind, two of my wearied countrymen, who were chained together (I was near them at the time), preferring death to such a life of misery, somehow made through the nettings, and jumped into the sea.

Olaudah is taken to Barbados in the West Indies, where he is sold. His story is different from most. He will go to sea as a slave, have many adventures, learn to read, and write his autobiography.

He will take a European name. It is Gustavus Vassa.

Many Africans are sent to Virginia, where they are traded for tobacco. Some are exchanged for sugar and molasses in the West Indies. Others are traded for rice in South Carolina. Then the ships head back to their home ports.

In Newport, Rhode Island, where we started this voyage, the sugar and molasses are turned into rum—and the triangle begins again. That is the way the

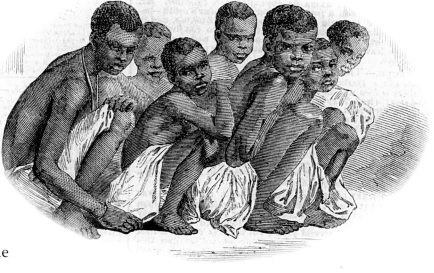

Young children, kidnapped from their homes, face the horrors of a slave ship. ▼

▲ Enslaved men in the West Indies cut sugarcane.

terrible triangular trade works. Every colony is a part of it. English ships carry the greatest numbers of Africans into slavery.

In the colonies, laws are soon passed that attempt to take away the blacks' humanity. The Virginia Black Code says slaves are property—not people. New York law says runaway slaves caught 40 miles north of Albany—on the way to Canada and safety—are to be killed.

Remember when the first black people arrived as indentured servants at Jamestown? In 1725 about 75,000 blacks are living in the American colonies. By 1790 there are more than 10 times that number.

PART 3

FROM COLONIES TO COUNTRY

Freedom of the Press

Peter Zenger was 13 when he sailed to America. He set out from Germany in 1710 with his parents and his brother and sister. They were excited when they left their home; they were looking forward to a good life in a land of freedom and opportunity.

But their voyage was long, and much worse than anyone expected. Some people died on the ship. Peter's father was one of them.

Stop and think how the Zenger children must have felt when the ship finally docked in New York. Their father was dead, they were in a strange land, they had to learn a new language, and they had no money. Their first home was a tent. How would you have felt?

Peter became an apprentice to a printer. He was apprenticed for eight years.

His brother became a carpenter's apprentice. His mother and his sister went to work in a Dutch household helping with the housework. They were indentured servants.

Zenger was apprenticed to William Bradford, a Quaker, who was one of the best printers in the colonies. The Bradfords treated Peter kindly. During the day he learned the printing trade. At night Peter went to school and Mrs. Bradford helped him with his schoolwork.

About half the people who came to America in those days became either indentured servants or apprentices. They worked for the person who paid their boat fare—usually from 3 to 10 years. If they didn't like that person it was too bad. Some indentured servants were treated just like slaves. An apprentice was usually better off; at least he or she got a chance to learn a trade.

An apprentice learns the printing trade in colonial America. ▶

When Peter was 21 he was finally free to go out on his own—and he did. First he set up a print shop in Maryland, but later he moved back to New York. There was enough work in that city for two printers.

William Bradford was now publishing a newspaper, the *New York Gazette*. It was the official royal paper; it said only what the English governor wanted said.

Now, I won't go into all the politics of the time—they were just as complicated in the 18th century as they are now—but I will tell you that William Cosby, the king's governor, was a rotten governor. He couldn't stand people who disagreed with him. Two important lawyers urged Zenger to start a newspaper that would criticize the governor and his politics. They said people should be able to read both sides of a story.

Zenger did it. He founded a newspaper called the *New York Weekly Journal*. It was full of spicy articles. People looked forward to reading it each week. Some articles said Governor Cosby took bribes, took away people's land, and made elections come out the way he wanted them to. The articles were probably written by Zenger's lawyer friends, but no one is sure because they were signed with made-up "pen" names.

Governor Cosby was furious. He wanted the paper to stop publication, but Zenger wouldn't stop. He was arrested and sent to jail. That didn't stop the *New York Weekly Journal*. Peter's wife became the new publisher. The articles criticizing the governor continued.

Peter Zenger stayed in jail for almost 10 months. A trial date was set. The court assigned him a young lawyer with little experience.

The day of the trial came. It was a hot day in August 1735. The courtroom was full of spectators. Suddenly an old man in a powdered wig entered and stood before the judge. When he said his name there were gasps and whispers throughout the courtroom. He was Andrew Hamilton, a Quaker from

▲ William Bradford, printer

British officials burn Zenger's newspapers on Wall Street in 1734. ▼

▲ Andrew Hamilton defended Peter Zenger during his trial for libel in New York in 1735.

Philadelphia, and a friend of Benjamin Franklin and William Penn. Andrew Hamilton was the most famous lawyer in the colonies, and he had come to take Peter Zenger's case.

The attorney general, who was the government's lawyer, said Zenger was guilty of libel. Libel is a crime. You can go to jail for libel.

Today in America, two things are necessary to prove you have committed libel. You must publish something you know is a lie, and that lie must hurt a person. (Let's say that you write an article stating that Mary Smith is a thief. You know that is not true. Mary Smith's boss reads the article and fires her. You have committed libel. She can sue you.) Libel laws were not very clear in the 18th century.

Zenger had printed nasty things about Governor Cosby, but most people thought the things he said were true. "So what?" said the attorney general. It didn't matter if the nasty things were true. Truth was no defense, he said.

Now, in those days it was a crime to say anything bad about the king—even if it was true. The attorney general said the governor was just like the king. He said that gave the governor special rights.

It is too bad we weren't there to hear what lawyer Hamilton said. They say he spoke very softly, and everyone listened. Some people who were there seemed to know they were hearing history being made. "Free men have a right to complain when hurt," said Andrew Hamilton. "They have a right to oppose arbitrary power by speaking and writing truths…to assert with courage the sense they have of the blessings of liberty, the value they put upon it, and their resolution… to prove it one of the greatest blessings heaven can bestow…*There is no libel if the truth is told,*" he said.

Arbitrary power is power used without considering others.

The attorney general wasn't impressed. He kept saying that the jury could only decide facts. They could only decide whether Zenger published the paper. (And of course he had.) The jury was not supposed to interpret the law, or decide if there was libel. The judge would do that, said the attorney general.

"Hold on!" said Andrew Hamilton. Juries are made up of citizens. Citizens are smart enough to decide matters of law as well as matters of fact. And so this jury was. It said Peter Zenger was not guilty.

Jubilant supporters carry Peter Zenger after he was found not guilty of libel. ▼

That case helped give juries the power to decide if the law is being broken. That is an important power, and it will be yours when you are a voting citizen. Every citizen is expected to be ready to serve on a jury. Someday, you will probably be called to be a juror.

But there is more to this case. When Andrew Hamilton spoke to that jury in 1735, he said words that are worth listening to right now. "The question before the court and you, gentlemen of the jury, is not of small nor private concern," said Hamilton. "It is not the cause of one poor printer, nor of New York alone, which you are now trying. No! It may in its consequence affect every freeman that lives under a British government, on the main[land] of America. It is the best cause. It is the cause of liberty."

Frenchmen and Indians

By the 18th century Europe had finished with hundreds of years of religious war. It had not, however, finished with war. A new kind of conflict was beginning.

This new kind of war was fought for economic gain. The fight was about land and money, not ideas or religion. For more than a century, Britain, France, and Spain would fight each other in a series of small wars on several continents. There was King William's War, Queen Anne's War, King George's War, and the French and Indian War.

In North America the French and Indian War changed the future of the continent. It was a war to answer this question: Which would be the stronger power in North America—England or France? France, the French colonists, and France's Indian allies fought against England, the English colonists, and England's Indian allies.

The war began with conflicts about land. France and England had real arguments over the same pieces of land. French explorers—Marquette, Joliet, La Salle, and others—had been the first Europeans in the region around the Great Lakes and also in the lands drained

Jacques Marquette and companions on the Mississippi River in 1673 ▼

by the Ohio and Mississippi rivers. France had sent traders and trappers to those territories and had set up trading posts as well. (French traders were at Lake Huron in 1612, eight years before the Pilgrims landed at Plymouth.)

England claimed the same land. In the original English charters, the king granted land from coast to coast—even though no one had any idea where the West Coast was. Now that the land along the East Coast was filling up, English-speaking settlers had begun pushing west. Indian hunting grounds were disappearing as the whites moved in. The Indians were alarmed. They were willing to fight to preserve their land.

The English had signed treaties and bought land from many of the Indian nations. But sometimes the treaties were signed without the Indians understanding the details. Indians thought the earth belonged to everyone. One Indian said selling land was like selling the sea, or the sky. And yet, though Indians never owned land individually, Indian tribes did claim the right to use an area of land. It was those rights they signed over to the English.

When the English colonists signed treaties with the Indians, the people who signed the treaties usually meant to honor them. The trouble was that the people who actually signed the treaties weren't the ones who lived on the frontier near the Indians. Those frontier people were often rough and rowdy. They wanted land, and sometimes they didn't mind killing for it.

If the Indians had united, perhaps they might have been able to resist the frontier people. But old feuds kept the Indian tribes apart. So when England and France started fighting each other, some Indians sided with the English. Others helped the French. They kept

▲ Fur traders in boats and wagons arrive at a Hudson Bay Company outpost.

Both the French and the English sought to buy furs from Native Americans, because furs fetched a lot of money in Europe. ▶

picking at each other—the English, the French, and the Indians—raiding and scalping and killing. Soon the hatred was intense.

New France (Canada) was different from English America, and that made for conflict, too. There was no religious freedom there. The French insisted that all settlers in their territories be Catholic and French. So when 200,000 Huguenots, who were Protestants, fled from France, many settled in the British colonies. If France had let them settle in Canada, that country would have been stronger. It is easy for us to see that now, but it wasn't so easy then.

France was more interested in the fur trade—and the money it brought—than in settling people on the land. So when English traders began buying furs from the Native Americans and paying high prices for those furs, it made France angry. It hurt their fur business.

The French were the best friends the Indians had in North America. Mostly they were trappers, traders, and fishermen—like the Native Americans. They understood and respected the land in a way the English never learned. But the Iroquois didn't care. They didn't like them. The Iroquois had been enemies of the French ever since Samuel de Champlain sided against them in their battle with a Huron tribe back in 1609. That was too bad for the French, for the Iroquois led a strong league of six Indian nations. They were the most powerful Indians in Eastern America.

Why wasn't this war called the French and English War? It was the English colonists who called it the French and Indian War. In Europe it is known as the Seven Years' War.

Remember, France and England were both claiming the same territory—especially the lands watered by the Ohio River and its tributaries. The French built forts in that area. One fort was built where Pittsburgh stands today. The French called it Fort Duquesne (dew-CANE). The English said that the fort was in Virginia and the land belonged to them. The governor of Virginia sent a 21-year-old surveyor to tell the French to move on and out.

> A *tributary* is a stream or river that flows into a larger river.

A surveyor is a person who measures and maps land. This surveyor's name was George Washington. The French told George Washington they were at Fort Duquesne to stay.

Washington and 150 men tried to make them go. They attacked a French scouting party and killed 10 Frenchmen. An English writer, Horace Walpole, said of that small battle, "The volley fired by a young Virginian in the backwoods of America set the world on fire." It was 1754; the French and Indian War had begun.

As a young man, George Washington worked as a surveyor on the American frontier. ▼

Fort Duquesne was strategically located where rivers met, on the site of what is now Pittsburgh, Pennsylvania. ▼

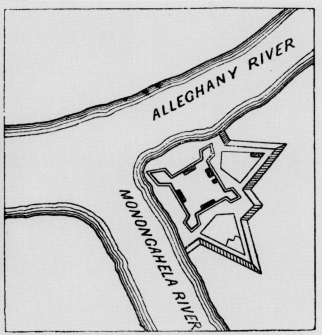

Washington built a small fort called Fort Necessity. He built it on low ground. When the French attacked, Washington and his men were outnumbered, but they held out until it started raining. Heavy rain flooded the fort, soaked all their gunpowder, and left them defenseless. The French captured the fort, but Washington escaped and learned a lesson he would remember when he became a great general: don't build a camp on low ground.

He learned even more important lessons when he fought with England's famous Major General Edward Braddock. Braddock arrived in America in 1755. He was expected to push the French out of the Ohio Territory. Braddock decided to begin by capturing Fort Duquesne, and he thought he knew just how to do that. The general had been trained in Europe, on great open battlefields, where armies lined up facing each other and shot long, clumsy guns called muskets. Braddock assumed that European methods would work in America.

George Washington wrote of the British troops in their bright red coats, and the Virginia troops in their handsome blue coats, all

European battlefield tactics did not work well in America—the French and their Indian allies would fire from behind trees at rows of exposed British soldiers. ▼

marching through the green forest. He said it was one of the most beautiful sights he had ever seen. But he realized those colorful coats were great targets. Braddock didn't. The French and their Indian allies wouldn't fight the kind of war Braddock wanted to fight. They wouldn't stand in a straight line and let the English shoot them. They hid in the woods. They wore skins to camouflage themselves. The Indians screamed blood-chilling war whoops. They shot at the British troops from the woods. The British panicked. They "broke and ran as sheep pursued by dogs," wrote Washington.

The French and Indians were outnumbered almost two to one, but they destroyed the English forces. General Braddock was killed. George Washington escaped with four bullet holes in his coat; two horses were shot from under him. But he learned lessons from Braddock's mistakes.

General Braddock was killed when the British tried to capture Fort Duquesne from the French. ▼

A Most Remarkable Man

The French and Indian War began badly for the English. The French and their Indian allies were better than the English at fighting in the wilderness. Great Britain knew it needed Indian allies if it was going to win this war.

In 1754 representatives from seven northern colonies met with about 150 Iroquois at Albany. This meeting, called the Albany Congress, was an attempt to get the colonies to form a colonial nation. It was also an attempt to get the Iroquois as English allies.

Ben Franklin took charge. He drafted a Plan of Union. But the colonies weren't yet ready to trust each other. They would not approve the plan.

While the Albany Congress failed, it got the idea of union started. It also got some colonial leaders thinking about the Iroquois way of governing. The Iroquois had united six tribes into a confederation. Everyone could see that uniting the tribes had made the Iroquois strong.

The delegates to the Albany Congress knew, as they said in a message to the English king, that "there is the utmost danger that the whole continent will be subjected to the French." England had to get

▲ William Johnson was a successful businessman as well as an Indian. As was common in the 18th century, Johnson wore fancy clothes and a wig to have his portrait painted.

JOIN or DIE

▲ Ben Franklin proposed a Plan of Union for the colonies. What do you think Franklin is saying in this cartoon, which he published in his *Pennsylvania Gazette* in 1754? It was one of the first cartoons printed in an American paper.

the Iroquois to fight on their side. There was only one man who might make that possible: William Johnson.

William Johnson had arrived in New York in 1738, at age 23, from a farm near Dublin, in Ireland. When he first moved into New York territory near Albany, Johnson met his neighbors, the Mohawk Indians, and learned their language. Johnson became a good friend of Tiyanoga, a wise sachem who was called Hendrick by the Dutch and the English. Johnson soon learned the ways of the Mohawk and was named as one of them. The Mohawk gave him the name Warraghiyagey (war-rag-ee-YAH-gay), which means "he who does much."

Johnson became a fur trader and was known to be fair and honest. That was unusual; many white traders tried to cheat the Indians. Johnson's honesty paid off. As a successful businessman and landowner, he became immensely rich.

Johnson married Degonwadonti, the daughter of a Mohawk leader. She was known as Molly Brant, and was as bold and intelligent as he. It was a happy marriage, and they had seven children.

▲ Tiyanoga was a Mohawk chief and an ally of the British during the French and Indian War.

At the Albany Congress, Johnson led the British negotiations with the Indians. As Warraghiyagey he called a great meeting. Whole Indian villages came and camped in his yard. The Iroquois had no wish to fight a white man's war. Warraghiyagey sat at the council fire. He listened carefully and spoke forcefully. He persuaded his Indian friends to fight on the side of the British. He promised that their land would be protected, and he thought he could honor that promise.

A well-trained French army was on its way to Albany. Warraghiyagey and his Indian brothers prepared for battle. William Johnson had never even seen a battle before. He was on his own with his friend Hendrick, some Indian warriors, and untested soldiers from New Hampshire, Massachusetts, and New York. There were no British soldiers.

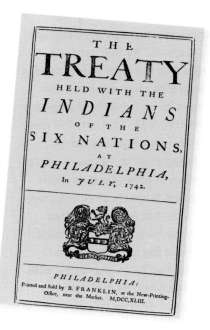

An account of the 1742 treaty between the British and six Indian nations ▶

What happened was astounding. The small army of Native Americans and American colonists beat the French, without the aid of the regular British army. In London people cheered. And they wept, too, when they heard that the old warrior Hendrick had died in the battle. The English king made William Johnson a baronet—he was now Sir William Johnson. Johnson's biographer said, "Sir William was a well adjusted European man; Warraghiyagey thought and acted as an Indian. These two personalities lived together without strain in one keen mind and passionate heart."

Major General Jeffrey Amherst (AM-urst) didn't like Sir William Johnson; he didn't like him at all. Amherst was a professional soldier who became commander of England's forces in the northern colonies. He was smart and capable, but also stuffy and haughty. Amherst didn't think much of the American colonists, and he detested Native Americans—he really did believe they were savages. When Johnson was made a baronet, General Amherst was horrified. But Amherst knew how to use Warraghiyagey's talents. He knew how to make plans and organize troops.

William Johnson once said, "If England is to become a great nation, she must go to school with the Iroquois." By that Johnson meant that the six Iroquois nations had an idea of government that worked so well that the Europeans needed to learn about it. The idea was this: each Iroquois nation governed itself but all were linked together in time of war or when there was business affecting them all. It was that linkage that had made the Iroquois the strongest Indians in the land. Benjamin Franklin had been impressed with that idea when he met with the Iroquois at Albany.

▲ General William Johnson leads his men in a battle against French and Indian forces.

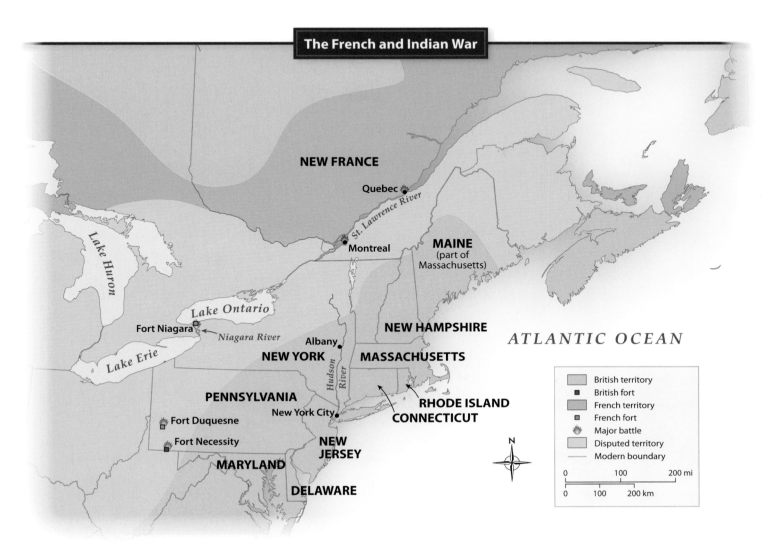

NEW FRANCE

Quebec

St. Lawrence River

Montreal

MAINE
(part of
Massachusetts)

Lake Huron

Lake Ontario

Fort Niagara

Niagara River

Albany

NEW HAMPSHIRE

ATLANTIC OCEAN

Lake Erie

NEW YORK

MASSACHUSETTS

Hudson River

PENNSYLVANIA

RHODE ISLAND

Fort Duquesne

New York City

CONNECTICUT

Fort Necessity

NEW JERSEY

MARYLAND

DELAWARE

N

	British territory
■	British fort
	French territory
▪	French fort
🔥	Major battle
	Disputed territory
—	Modern boundary

0   100   200 mi

0   100   200 km

▲ Major battles of the French and Indian War were fought on the frontier.

William Pitt understood that, too. Pitt was foreign secretary (which is the same as secretary of state) in England and one of that nation's greatest statesmen. Pittsburgh is named for him. Pitt intended that this war be won. He sent more English troops to the colonies. Then he looked at a map, and he saw the importance of the St. Lawrence and Niagara rivers. Pitt knew that the French supplied their armies through those two rivers. If the British controlled them, they could keep goods and equipment from reaching the Great Lakes and the Ohio River Valley. The French would be like bees cut off from the hive. Pitt told Amherst to take those rivers.

▲ The French surrender Fort Louisbourg to British troops under the command of General Jeffrey Amherst.

Amherst made plans. He laid siege to a French fort, Louisbourg, which guarded the mouth of the St. Lawrence. That meant he would let no one in or out of the fort. After seven weeks of being cut off, the French in the fort were starved. Louisbourg surrendered.

Then Warraghiyagey and the Iroquois won a great battle near the falls of the Niagara River. The English now had control of that river.

Everyone knew that the most important battle would be the one for the city of Quebec. Both sides were confident. Louis Montcalm, the brilliant French general, had smashed the English when he met them before. But he was pitted against England's young general James Wolfe, who was also brilliant.

General Wolfe knew that his best hope lay in surprise. So his troops did something almost impossible—they climbed the Heights of Abraham, the cliffs behind the city, in the dark. In the morning, the French were stunned to see the British drawn up on a flat plain behind the city. Montcalm and his men were totally surprised when the English attacked. Both Montcalm and Wolfe were killed in the fighting, but the English won the battle for Quebec.

When the city of Montreal fell to a force led by both Sir Jeffrey Amherst and Warraghiyagey, it was all over. New France was surrendered to the English in 1760. It took a few more years for the diplomats to get things settled, but in 1763 the Treaty of Paris officially ended the French and Indian War.

The war was very expensive. The British government's spending rose during the war from £6.5 million a year to £14.5 million. Someone had to help pay—and the English thought that the Americans should. As you will see, that was the beginning of a lot of trouble.

The English don't have dollars, they have *pounds*. A shilling was a small silver coin worth one-twentieth of a pound. The symbol for a pound is £. Do some research to find out what a pound is worth today in American dollars.

◀ The British surprised the French at Quebec by climbing steep cliffs to take up positions outside the city.

Staying in Charge

This is the way the French and Indian War came out: the English won. France was kicked off the North American continent—totally—except for two tiny fishing islands off the coast of Canada.

At the end of the war England claimed all the land from the east coast to the Mississippi. New Orleans and everything west of the Mississippi belonged to Spain. France gave all her western land to Spain in order to keep it out of British hands. That huge territory was called Louisiana. (Spain had helped France for a short time during the war. Later, France got Louisiana back—for a while.)

The British got Florida from Spain, but after a few years Spain took it back. (Does all this sound like a game? It was serious business to those involved.)

The names on the map of North America had changed, but only a few European settlers lived west of the Appalachian Mountains. Most of that western territory was still Indian land, except for some old Spanish colonies across the Mississippi in Texas and New Mexico.

What did the Indians gain from the war? Nothing. For a while there were thanks and treaties and some respect. That didn't last long. Now that France was no longer a threat on the continent, the English colonists didn't need Indians as allies.

For his part in the war, General Amherst was made a knight. He became Sir Jeffrey Amherst. He was also named governor of Virginia, but he wasn't thrilled about that. He said he would accept the post as long as he didn't have to live in Virginia, which was all right with the new king, George III.

The king offered Sir William Johnson the governorship of New York, but he turned it down. His war wounds were acting up, and he wanted to spend time at his mansion, Johnson Hall. Besides, he preferred his job as Superintendent of Indian Affairs in the northern colonies.

Did Sir Jeffrey thank Warraghiyagey and his Indian forces for their help? No. He suggested that the country would be better off if all the Indians were dead. He even tried to spread smallpox among them with blankets taken from smallpox victims. (That was germ warfare.)

Canada Colony

England got a 14th American colony out of the war. The French had called it Acadia; the English named it Nova Scotia. Many French citizens of Acadia were shipped off—against their wishes—by the English to other parts of the colonies. (Henry Wadsworth Longfellow wrote a poem about the Acadians called "Evangeline.") Some Acadians went to what is now Louisiana; they are called "Cajuns."

France lost Canada but left her language there. Today many Canadians speak French because their ancestors did. And all Canadian children learn French in school.

Amherst was now the top British military officer in America. He sent out orders to English forts to stop supplying Indians with guns and ammunition and the traditional gifts they used to get from the French. That may sound reasonable, but it wasn't. The Native Americans needed guns in order to hunt. Many had forgotten how to use bows and arrows. They were soon without food or clothing.

The situation got pretty bad. Sir William Johnson begged Amherst to treat the Indians with respect, but Amherst was stubborn. At the same time, settlers were pushing into Indian territory. They were taking tribal land and killing Native Americans. The Indians went on the warpath. Finally people in England got upset. Snobby, mean-spirited Jeffrey Amherst was called back to England in 1763. He was happy to go because he didn't like Indians or "provincials." English officials tried, as best they could, to keep the settlers out of Indian territory. But, mostly, they couldn't do it.

▲ Pontiac, an Ottawa Indian, confronts the British after learning they tried to spread smallpox among his people.

Spanish Missions in the West

While the French and Indian War raged in the East, Spaniards were settling in Texas. They were building missions (which were settlements around a church) and *presidios* (which were forts). Back in 1682 they had built a mission at Ysleta, way over in the western part of today's Texas, near El Paso. They first built at San Antonio in 1718. Soon there were five missions around San Antonio and more in some other places in Texas.

In 1769, a Franciscan priest, Father Junipero Serra, and a group of missionaries built a mission at San Diego in California. Soon there were missions and presidios at Carmel, Monterey, San Francisco, Santa Barbara, and San José, and others in New Mexico and Arizona. The priests intended to convert the natives to Christianity. They didn't intend to kill them—but that was what often happened, because of the diseases the Spaniards brought.

Father Junipero Serra ▶

253

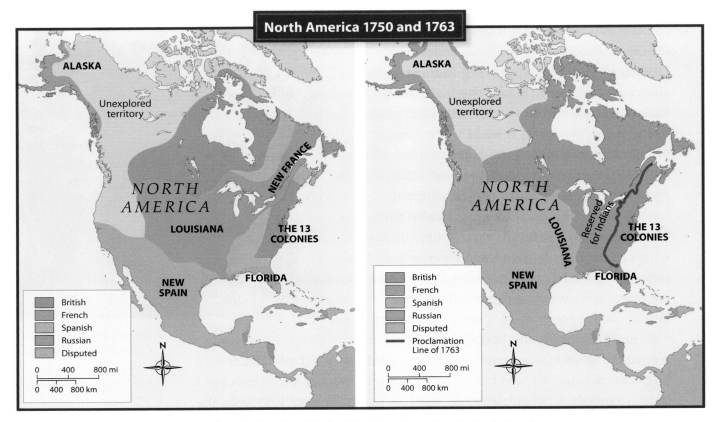

North America 1750 and 1763

ALASKA

Unexplored territory

NORTH AMERICA

NEW FRANCE

LOUISIANA

THE 13 COLONIES

NEW SPAIN

FLORIDA

British
French
Spanish
Russian
Disputed

0   400   800 mi
0 400 800 km

N

ALASKA

Unexplored territory

NORTH AMERICA

LOUISIANA

Reserved for Indians

THE 13 COLONIES

NEW SPAIN

FLORIDA

British
French
Spanish
Russian
Disputed
Proclamation Line of 1763

0   400   800 mi
0 400 800 km

N

▲ After the French and Indian War, France's territory in North America was reduced to Haiti and two small islands off the coast of Newfoundland.

England now had a big responsibility. She had to manage almost two million people in the 13 colonies, she had to take control of 60,000 French-speaking people in Canada and around the Great Lakes, and she had to keep the English colonists and the Native Americans from killing each other.

The king of England had a great idea for settling the Indian problem. Draw a line right down the crest of the Appalachian Mountains, said the king. Everything to the east of that line would be colonists' territory. Everything to the west would be Indian territory. (Settlers already in the West would have to leave.) And that was what the king ordered in his Proclamation of 1763. If the colonists could be kept east of the Appalachians there would be no more fighting between the settlers and the Native Americans.

That land to the west of the Appalachians wasn't good for much anyway, said most people in England. But that western land looked mighty good to settlers who wanted farms of their own. The eastern lands were mostly taken. It also looked good to speculators—people who wanted to make money selling land. Benjamin Franklin and George Washington were two of those who speculated in western lands. Now that the French were gone, the English settlers thought the land should be theirs. A proclamation written in England wasn't going to stop people hungry for land. They kept moving west.

Soon another line was drawn, on the other side of the Appalachians. That was in 1768, in a treaty signed by Sir William Johnson and 14 Iroquois leaders. Johnson hoped to please both sides. The Iroquois got cash and promises; the English-speaking settlers got land over the mountains—especially land west of Albany. But it was just another Indian treaty that would soon be broken. The settlers were on their way west; the Indians who lived west of the Appalachians were doomed to see their way of life destroyed.

Fort Pitt—which had been Fort Duquesne and, before that, the Indian town of Shannopin—became Pittsburgh. At Pittsburgh, two rivers come together and form the mighty Ohio River. From there you can glide to the heart of the continent. It was a gateway to the West.

Wake Up!

A religious movement called the Great Awakening began about 1739, when a spellbinding evangelical English preacher named George Whitefield arrived in America. Thousands of people were converted by Whitefield and by those who followed him. American Protestantism became split between the sedate older sects, the "Old Lights" (Quakers, Anglicans, Congregationalists), and those begun by the new revival preachers, the "New Lights" (Methodists, Presbyterians, Baptists). New Lights reached out to slaves, too; by the end of the century most slaves were Christians.

George Whitefield preaching in the countryside ▶

In 1769 Daniel Boone made his first exploring trip to Kentucky. In 1775 he led a group of settlers to that Indian hunting ground. In 1779 Kentucky became a county of Virginia.

By 1770 some 5,000 colonists were said to have climbed the mountains to Pittsburgh and then headed on west. They were pioneers, and the first of a river of people who began filling the Ohio River Valley. Mostly, these people were ordinary farm folk who just wanted to make homes for themselves.

The trailblazing frontiersman Daniel Boone may have helped build the road to Fort Pitt; we know for sure he went to Kentucky:

> It was on the first of May 1769, that I resigned my domestic happiness, and left my family and peaceable habitation on the Yadkin River, in North Carolina, to wander through the wilderness of America, in quest of the country of Kentucke.

Thousands followed after Boone cut a path through the Cumberland Gap. The Wilderness Road, as this path was called, provided a southern route to the other side of the mountains.

Those who went west were a lot like those who had come on the *Mayflower*. They were tough enough to build homes in a strange, raw world. They were able to make their own laws. They were survivors. They were independent minded. Men and women like that were not likely to take orders from a faraway nation.

Colonists begin to settle in the Ohio River Valley. This settlement will become Marietta, Ohio. ▼

Daniel Boone, Frontiersman

Daniel Boone ▶

Daniel Boone was born in 1734. He grew up in Pennsylvania, with Indians for friends, and he learned their ways along with the ways of the European settlers. Daniel became the most famous of all the American frontiersmen.

Daniel Boone's first adventures came in 1755, during the French and Indian War. He fought on the side of the British. He drove a wagon in Braddock's army, and noted the way the Indians fought. At night Boone sat around the campfire and heard tales of the western lands. He wanted some of that land for himself. He believed the Indians would have to go before he could have it; many others believed as Boone did.

As soon as the war was over, off Boone went, with a sack of salt around his neck, an ax in his belt, and a rifle over his shoulder. But he never found an easy way to get over the mountains.

Then, one day he heard of an Indian trail through the mountains. Boone searched until he found that trail. It led to a hole through the mountains, called a gap, and that led to the rich grasslands of Kentucky. In 1775 Daniel Boone and 30 woodsmen turned that Indian trail into a road that families could travel with wagons and animals. It was called the Wilderness Road, and it went for 300 miles. By 1790, almost 200,000 people had gone west on the Wilderness Road.

Three years after Daniel Boone first reached Kentucky, settlers were already pouring in. Pretty soon there was a town named after Boone—Boonesborough.

But Daniel Boone just couldn't stay settled. He was always off on one adventure or another. The stories about Boone's adventures grew and grew and grew, and some of them were true: stories about how he was captured by Indians, about how he rescued his daughter from Indians, about a buffalo stampede, about how he was adopted into a tribe. Each time the stories got told, they were bigger and better.

It was said that Daniel Boone could shoot a flea off the nose of a bear. Do you think that could be true?

◀ Daniel Boone escorting settlers through Cumberland Gap

The Rights of Englishmen

The colonies were producing strong-minded people—people who were blazing trails, building homes, and clearing farms in a wilderness. And others who were forming towns, making laws, and starting their own businesses. None of these people wanted to be pushed around. If they had to, they would stand up to England. They had seen the English army during the French and Indian War. It wasn't as fearsome as some thought.

Of course, they didn't want to fight England. Most of the colonists were proud and happy to be English. Even those who had come from Scotland, Germany, Holland, and other countries soon thought of themselves as English colonists. They just wanted the same rights that English men and women had in England.

What were those English rights the Americans kept demanding for themselves?

To understand that you need to know there was a time when kings in England could do anything they wanted to do: they could kill people, or take all their land and money, or lock them in dungeons and keep them there.

Some English history will help you understand. Way back in the 13th century, in England, there was a wicked king named John. King John believed he should have total power over everyone. John was a mean sort. He started picking on the English landholders, especially the barons and other noblemen. John, you see, felt that kings had been put on earth by God for men and women to serve.

At last the barons could stand no more. In 1215, they captured King John and took him as a prisoner to a tiny island in the Thames River called Runnymede. There they forced him to sign an agreement that gave Englishmen some basic rights. (No one thought much about women's rights then.)

The agreement said the king could not take land and money from people without Parliament's permission. The agreement also said that no person could be put in jail unless he had a fair trial "by the lawful judgment of his peers, under the law of the land." It granted other rights, too. The idea behind that great agreement was that the

It was during King John's reign that Robin Hood was said to have lived in England's Sherwood Forest, robbing the rich to help the poor.

Peers are equals, people just like you. The English barons' peers were other barons.

king's power brought responsibilities. After King John signed his name at Runnymede, kings were no longer free to do anything they wanted.

It was the lords and the wealthy landowners who made the agreement with the king, and they were the ones who, at first, benefited most, but it turned out to be a big step forward for all people. (Before long, men and women were saying that kings were meant to serve the people, not the other way around.)

That document was written in Latin, and its name means great charter; in Latin that is *Magna Carta*. Try to remember 1215. That year is important to people all over the world. The Magna Carta is one of the world's greatest documents of freedom. It provided the foundation for many of the rights we enjoy today.

Another very important right the English got for themselves is called "the right of habeas corpus." Now *habeas* and *corpus* are two more Latin words. *Corpus* means "body." (It's similar to our word for a dead body—a corpse.)

And *habeas* means "have," so *habeas corpus* means "have the body." That is what the police must do if they arrest you. They can't lose you (and your body) in a jail. In the old, old days someone could get arrested and thrown in jail, and no one would tell him what he had done wrong. Sometimes he died in jail without ever knowing why he had been arrested. If ever you are arrested, the first thing to do is ask for a "writ of habeas corpus." Then you will be brought before a judge, and he will tell you why you are being held. If there is no good reason for your arrest, you can go home. That is a very important right! In many countries today, people still get thrown in jail for no good reason.

▲ King John reluctantly signs the Magna Carta.

Magna, the Latin word for *great* or *big*, is the root of some English words connected with greatness or bigness, too—*magnify*, *magnificent*, and *magnate*, for instance. If you do very well in college, you may be awarded a degree *magna cum laude*—which means "with great praise."

Another English right guarantees that your own words can't be used against you in court. Why would you say bad things about yourself? Well, if you were tortured you might. You might even say you did something that you didn't do, just to stop the torture. So that, too, is a very important right.

Now, on with history: the English kept adding to their rights and then, in 1688, something revolutionary happened. That something was called the Glorious Revolution, because Parliament got King William and Queen Mary to sign a bill of rights that made Parliament more powerful than the king and queen. Since Parliament represented the English people, the people were now more powerful than the monarchs! (Well, maybe not more powerful, but they were headed in that direction. England was on the road to constitutional monarchy.)

The English people were very proud of the rights they had won. They had a right to be proud. The American colonists expected those same rights. The Americans thought of themselves as English citizens living in the colonies. They believed that English rights were their rights. And they would insist on them.

King William and Queen Mary listen to a reading of the English Bill of Rights, which made Parliament more powerful than the king and queen. ▶

A Taxing King

Benjamin Franklin knew that sometimes the best way to get people to think is to make them laugh. So when he was serious, he wrote a joking poem. Here is part of it:

> *We have an old mother that peevish is grown;*
> *She nubs us like children that scarce walk alone;*
> *She forgets we're grown up and have sense of our own.*

Peevish means irritable.

Who was the "old mother"? Why, England, of course! "We" were the colonists. Ben Franklin was right. King George III and his ministers didn't believe the colonists were grown up and capable of ruling themselves. The colonists knew they were. After all, they'd been running most of their own affairs from the time they first arrived in the New World. But even England's William Pitt, who was a friend of America, wrote, "This is the mother country, they are the children; they must obey, and we prescribe."

Part of the problem was that almost none of the English leaders had been to America—or cared to go. They didn't understand the country or its people. One London newspaper called Americans "a mongrel breed."

Government officials are sometimes called "ministers." They are not ministers of religion. It is confusing, but keep in mind that there are two kinds of ministers: of government and of religion. England's prime minister is the leader of the country's government.

A mongrel (MONG-grull) is a dog that is a mixture of breeds—a mutt. The London newspaper thought it was insulting us when it said "mongrel breed." Well, it was no insult. From our beginnings, we were a mixture of peoples. That was unusual for a nation.

As I've told you, most colonists (no matter where they came from) thought of themselves as English citizens, so they were hurt by sneers from London. But, to be fair, the colonists didn't quite understand themselves. Even those who had come from England weren't really English anymore. They were now Americans. The people who came to America were different from the stay-at-homes in Europe. Many had risked their lives and gone through great hardships to cross the ocean and build homes and farms in a land of thick forests. They weren't going to let anyone tell them how to run their country. King George never thought about that.

What George and his ministers wanted to do was to teach the colonists a lesson. But, almost everyone agrees, King George made some big mistakes.

To be a good king you need some wisdom, and George III didn't have much. George III wasn't a bad man. He just wasn't up to the job of being king.

Remember the Glorious Revolution that gave Parliament more power than the king? Well, George III wasn't happy with that arrangement. He wanted kings to have more power. He chose government officials who seemed to agree with him. One was Charles Townshend (TOWNS-end). Townshend enraged the Americans by sponsoring taxes they thought were unfair.

An English historian said that King George III was like "a boy whom no one could teach." ▼

Nobody likes to pay taxes. But the British government was having problems with its budget; it needed money. Foreign wars had left England with big bills to pay. The British thought the colonies should help pay some of those bills, especially the ones from the expensive French and Indian War.

And maybe we would have, but George III and his ministers didn't explain things well; they just demanded taxes. The colonists knew how European kings and barons taxed the peasants and kept them poor. They didn't want to risk that kind of treatment. People in America began to get nervous and angry.

The colonists kept talking about Magna Carta and English rights. They said Englishmen had the right to vote on their own taxes. They expected that same right. But since no colonists served in Parliament, no colonists got to vote on taxes. The colonists complained that they were being taxed without being represented. They said, "No taxation without representation." That meant they wanted to vote on their own taxes, in their own assemblies, as they had been doing.

King George and his ministers were stubborn. They wanted to show the colonists who was boss. So they levied more taxes.

It was the Stamp Tax (passed in 1765) that enraged most Americans. The colonists were supposed to buy a British stamp for every piece of printed paper they used. That meant every sheet of the newspaper, every document, every playing card—everything. The colonists wouldn't do it. They got so angry they attacked some of the British stamp agents and put tar all over them and then feathers in the tar. It was a nasty thing to do, but George III and Parliament got the idea. The Stamp Tax could not be collected. It was repealed.

Then Charles Townshend decided to tax lead, glass, paper, paint, and tea. That upset the colonists so much they decided to get even by not buying anything made in England. It was the English merchants who got angry about that—it cost them a lot of money— and they demanded that the Townshend taxes be repealed. They were, in 1770, except for the tax on tea. It was a small tax, but King George wanted to prove that he and Parliament could tax Americans if they wished to.

To the colonists, that tea tax was an example of taxation without representation. So, in 1773, some people in Boston decided to show King George and Parliament and Lord Townshend what they thought of the tax on tea. They dressed up as Indians and climbed on a ship in Boston harbor and threw 342 chests of good English tea into the water. Americans called it the Boston Tea Party, but the English didn't. They called it an outrage.

What Is Mercantilism?

If you sell more than you buy, you prosper—right? That is the theory behind a system of trade called "mercantilism." Here is its basic idea: if you export more than you import you will be rich. That economic philosophy captivated the 18th century. Many English products (such as furniture, tools, and fabrics) were made from raw materials (lumber, iron, and cotton) shipped from the colonies. Those finished products were then sold in the colonies and around the world. England wanted to keep Americans from making and trading their own finished products. For mercantilism to work well, one nation has to be in charge. When the colonies tried to make their own products and control their own commerce, relations with England turned icy.

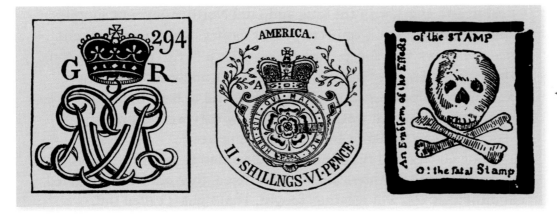

◀ At left are two tax stamps for the American colonies from the Stamp Act of 1765; on the right, one colonial newspaper's view of the hated "fatal stamps"— "fatal" because colonists worried that the Stamp Act meant death to liberty.

▲ In the Boston Tea Party, to protest the tax on tea, colonists dressed as Native Americans dumped tea from a British ship into Boston Harbor.

Today doctors think King George III was suffering from a rare disease that affected his mind and emotions. He often lost his temper and went into rages.

King George was furious! His prime minister, Lord North, ordered Boston Harbor closed.

Closing Boston Harbor meant no ships could enter or leave. That put half the citizens of Boston out of work. They weren't even able to fish in their own waters. Boston lived on its sea trade, and people worried that they might starve. Suddenly the other colonies, which had never before paid much attention to one another, all felt sorry for Boston and angry with the king and Lord North. They sent supplies and encouragement. Connecticut sent money; South Carolina sent rice; New York sent sheep. Virginia set aside a day to pray for Boston. During that day the Virginians began to talk about independence. At first the colonists had just wanted England to treat them like grown-ups. Now that wasn't enough. Now they were thinking seriously about breaking away, about being free.

King George and his ministers had wanted to teach the colonists a lesson. At first the Americans were bothered, then they were angered, and then, as you will see, they fought. That fight is called the American Revolution or the War of Independence.

The Firebrands

Can you guess what a firebrand is? Firebrands were very useful when people didn't have matches and the only heat in a house came from the fireplace.

You have probably figured it out. A firebrand is a stick of wood with a spark of fire at one end.

Now, if you look in the dictionary you will see another meaning for firebrand. A firebrand can be a hothead: someone who sparks a revolution, someone who lights a fire in people's minds and hearts.

Historians say the American Revolution had three firebrands: Samuel Adams, Patrick Henry, and Thomas Paine. That war of independence might have happened without them, but it certainly would have been different.

Patrick Henry was a great speaker; Tom Paine was a great writer. Samuel Adams could write well and think well, but what Adams really was was a super busybody. He got everyone keyed up, inspired, and moving.

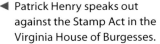 Patrick Henry speaks out against the Stamp Act in the Virginia House of Burgesses.

In 1770 the annual meeting of New England Quakers prohibited slave owning—the first American organization to do so.

Sam Adams was a New Englander from Boston with a Puritan background. Tom Paine came from England and lived in the Middle Colonies, in Philadelphia. He was a deist with Quaker friends. Patrick Henry was a southerner, an Anglican, a Virginian, and a country boy. These men were very different from one another, but alike in one important way: each understood, before most other Americans did, that a break from England was necessary.

Remember, it took a long time for the colonists to think of themselves as Americans. They thought of themselves as English colonists. Even those who came from France or Germany or Holland soon thought of English rights as their rights.

When they stopped seeing themselves as English, they began to say they were Virginians, or New Englanders, or Carolinians. It was hard for them to understand that they could all be part of the same country. To begin with, they didn't know each other. That was because overland travel between colonies was very difficult. There were no good roads and few bridges. On the fastest stagecoach you could make eight miles an hour—as long as there were no ruts in the road, or mud, or ice. For poor people, travel meant going on foot. But if you were like most travelers, you rode horseback. If you needed to cross a river you usually had to find a boat. Your horses had to swim the river. If you had a lot of baggage, it might take many trips to get it all across. If the river current was swift, you could lose everything—even your life.

On the Road

Until the middle of the 19th century, most American roads were made of dirt. Some were surfaced with gravel or oyster shells. With ice or snow on them they often became impassable. Spring thaws made them turn to mud. Even when they were dry and hard they were full of holes. A horseback rider could make his way, but for a heavy wagon or coach it was a disaster—wheels and axles broke or got mired in the mud.

The first stagecoach from New York to Boston began operation in 1772. The trip took six days. Travelers slept in their clothes at inns along the way. They could expect to be woken at three in the morning and to spend 18 hours each day traveling.

▲ A stagecoach makes its way on a snowy day on the Lancaster, Pennsylvania turnpike.

By 1760, with good winds and good luck, you could sail from Baltimore to London in four weeks. So wealthy Marylanders were more likely to go to England than to Massachusetts. And the same was true of the Virginians and the South Carolinians. London still seemed the most exciting city in their world. Now can you see why most people in the different colonies were strangers to each other?

Well, the firebrands helped change that. Sam Adams started something called "committees of correspondence." They were groups of prominent citizens who wrote back and forth between colonies and helped each other with problems. They began to be friends.

Adams started other groups, such as the Sons of Liberty. In Boston, the Sons met under an old elm tree that Adams called the Liberty Tree. As soon as the British got a chance they chopped that tree down. (A liberty tree still stands in Annapolis, Maryland.)

But mostly what Sam Adams started was trouble for the British. He was a rabble-rouser and an agitator—a real firebrand—who helped brew up the Boston Tea Party and the fight against the Stamp Act. But you never would have known that to look at him.

Sam Adams was a Humpty Dumpty-looking man: rumpled and pudgy. He came from a prominent Boston family, but he lost almost all the family money because he didn't care about business. Some people said that he was lazy, but he wasn't lazy when it came to fighting for freedom.

Samuel Adams—rabble-rouser, agitator, firebrand ▼

The English called Adams a public enemy, an outlaw, and a rebel. They wanted to hang him. He certainly was a troublemaker, but Sam Adams was different from other rebels in other times. He wanted more than just separation from England. He was inspired by a grander idea: the idea that America could be a special nation where people would be free of kings and princes. A nation where, for the first time in all of history, people would truly rule themselves.

His Puritan ancestors had described their colony as an experiment. They had hoped it would be a close to perfect society. They called it "a city on a hill," and they meant that others should see it and that it would be an example to the whole world. But the Puritan dream was only for Puritans. Sam Adams had a great dream that was for all people.

COMMON SENSE;

ADDRESSED TO THE

INHABITANTS

OF

AMERICA,

On the following interesting

SUBJECTS.

I. Of the Origin and Design of Government in general,
with concise Remarks on the English Constitution.

II. Of Monarchy and Hereditary Succession.

III. Thoughts on the present State of American Affairs.

IV. Of the present Ability of America, with some mis-
cellaneous Reflections.

Man knows no Master save creaing HEAVEN,
Or those whom choice and common good ordain.
THOMSON.

PHILADELPHIA;
Printed, and Sold, by R. BELL, in Third-Street.
MDCCLXXVI.

▲ Thomas Paine writes by candlelight. Thomas Paine's *Common Sense* roused many colonists to demand independence.

So did Tom Paine. Now, Sam Adams was a Harvard man who had old roots in the young country. Tom Paine was hardly off the boat from England, in 1774, when he became a firebrand of revolution. He didn't plan it that way. "I thought it very hard," he wrote, "to have the country set on fire...almost the moment I got into it."

He had been apprenticed to a corsetmaker when he was a boy in England. Corsets are tight undergarments that women wore to hold in their stomachs and make their waists look tiny. Being a corsetmaker was not exactly an exciting career—not for a boy with a mind like Tom's. So he ran away and went to sea. But that didn't work out. Then he tried to be a grocer, and a schoolteacher, and a tobacco seller. Nothing worked—except his fine mind, and that kept him learning. He went to lectures and he read everything he could find to read. When he met Ben Franklin in London, he knew he wanted to go to America.

He almost didn't make it. He caught a fever on board ship and was carried ashore half dead, but he was young and strong and he survived. Franklin had given him a letter that got him a job as a writer and magazine editor in Philadelphia. That was the perfect use for his talents, for he was a magician with words.

By the 1770s, the colonists were beginning to want to separate from England. But they weren't quite sure why, and they wondered if it was right to do so. Tom Paine was able to say clearly what people really knew in their hearts. He wrote a pamphlet called *Common Sense*. In it he told the colonists three important things:

- Monarchy was a poor form of government and they would be better off without it.

- Great Britain was hurting their economy with taxes and trade restrictions.

- It was foolish for a small island 3,000 miles away to try to rule a whole continent.

Well, of course, all that made common sense. But Tom Paine said it so eloquently that a whole lot of copies of *Common Sense* were sold in a very short time.

When the revolution began, Paine enlisted in the Continental army. Then he wrote a series of pamphlets about the war. He started one of them with these words: "These are the times that try men's souls."

Stop and read that line again. "These are the times that try men's souls." What do you think of that as a way to start a book about war? Tom Paine made people stop and think. He was a man of deep beliefs. He believed in the American cause. He was not rich, but he gave a third of his salary to help Washington's army, and he never took any money for his patriotic writings. He said that would demean them.

"We have it in our power to begin the world again," wrote Paine, and he really meant it.

Patrick Henry was the third firebrand, and, like Adams and Paine, he was a failure at first. He was born on a Virginia frontier farm. His father came from Scotland and had been to college there. He taught his son to read—both English and Latin. They read the Bible aloud together, and Patrick learned to love the sounds of the English language. He used English as no American speaker had done before him.

But Patrick Henry started out as a storekeeper, and then tried being a planter, and failed at both. Perhaps it was because he had a "passion for fiddling, dancing, and pleasantry." Finally, he studied law and spoke so well as a lawyer that he soon entered politics. He was elected to the House of Burgesses, which met in Virginia's capital, Williamsburg. And that was where he was when the Stamp Act was passed. He was young, but he stood up and said what he thought—that the stamp tax was a threat to liberty. Some of the older Virginians cried, "Treason!" because he was attacking the king. To that Patrick Henry is supposed to have answered, "If this be treason, make the most of it."

Some townsfolk and students from the College of William and Mary stood in the doorway of the House of Burgesses and heard that speech. Among them was a young lawyer named Thomas Jefferson. He never forgot it. He said Henry spoke "as Homer wrote," and Jefferson thought Homer the greatest of writers.

The Continental army was the American army that fought the British. It was an army raised at home—on the continent—as opposed to the king's army, which was shipped in from overseas. The revolutionary soldiers were also known as Patriots or rebels—"rebs."

To *demean* means to lower the worth of something.

Homer lived in ancient Greece and wrote the *Iliad* and the *Odyssey*, which are still among the most exciting tales of heroism and adventure ever written.

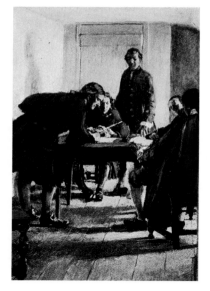

▲ Patrick Henry, Thomas Jefferson, and others meet at Raleigh Tavern.

When the English governor of Virginia heard about Patrick Henry's speech, he was furious. He dissolved the House of Burgesses. (That means he told the members to go home.) But that just made them angry. They walked over to the Raleigh Tavern, where they kept on meeting. And Patrick Henry kept talking.

By 1775, 10 years after Henry's Stamp Act speech, it was no longer safe for the burgesses even to gather in Williamsburg. So they met in a church in Richmond. It was there that Patrick Henry gave his most famous speech. The port of Boston was closed, English soldiers were in the city, and the Massachusetts Assembly had been dissolved. Would Virginia sit idly by?

Henry stepped into the aisle, bowed his head, and held out his arms. He pretended his arms were chained as he began calmly, "Our chains are forged, their clanking may be heard on the plains of Boston." His voice strengthened as he said, "The war is actually begun. The next gale that sweeps from the north will bring to our ears the clash of resounding arms. Our brethren are already in the field. Why stand we here idle?…Is life so dear, or peace so sweet, as to be purchased at the price of chains and slavery?"

Then Patrick Henry threw off the imaginary chains, stood up straight, and cried out, "Forbid it, Almighty God! I know not what course others may take, but as for me, *give me liberty, or give me death!*"

In his most famous speech, Patrick Henry exclaims, "Give me liberty, or give me death!" ▶

A Massacre in Boston

Samuel Adams had a young cousin named John. "I have heard of one Mr. Adams," said King George to the Massachusetts governor, "but who is the other?" The other—honest, serious John Adams— would become even more famous than Sam.

Sam was an agitator and an organizer who helped start a revolution. John was a farmer and a lawyer, a solid citizen who helped lead that revolution. Someone who knew John Adams said that he possessed more learning than anyone in the colonies. That may not have been an exaggeration. John had done a lot of reading and studying. And he knew how to use his mind.

Here is a story about both Adams cousins: the story of the Boston Massacre. A massacre, as you may know, is a gruesome killing. That's what happened in Boston in 1770.

The story begins in 1765, when the English Parliament passed a law that said American citizens had to provide quarters for British soldiers. The quarters they were talking about are not the kind you get when you add two dimes and a nickel. Quarters can also be houses where soldiers live. The law was called the Quartering Act. English soldiers, who were called "redcoats" because of the color of their uniforms, were to be quartered in American towns and cities.

Well, the Americans didn't want British redcoats quartered in their towns, or cities, or even in their country. So when the soldiers arrived, in 1768, the colonists weren't very kind to them. Sometimes they made fun of them, sometimes they threw snowballs or rocks, and sometimes they called them lobsterbacks, or worse names.

British soldiers occupied Boston in 1768. ▶

271

The people in Boston were especially annoyed, and, at first, wouldn't even provide quarters. So the soldiers set up tents on the Boston Common (a big grassy area in the center of town) and played their drums and bugles—loudly—at the most inappropriate times. Most of the English soldiers didn't want to be in America anyway. They were poorly paid, and many were homesick. Some ran away from the British army. (Soldiers who run away are called deserters. British deserters who were caught were shot.) A few redcoats—especially the officers—were treated well. Some married American women.

But for most of the British soldiers, the winters in Boston seemed longer and colder and more miserable than any they had ever known.

On a freezing March day in 1770, one of the king's soldiers was looking for work to earn some extra money. Someone started making fun of him and told him to get a job cleaning toilets. (Only they didn't have the kind of toilets we have today. They had outdoor "privies," which were dirt-floored holes, and they smelled.) One thing led to another, and there was a fight.

That started things. Soon a noisy, jeering group of mischief-makers gathered in front of the Boston Custom House. They began pushing and shoving and throwing stones and pieces of ice at the British sentry. He got knocked down and he called for help. Captain Thomas Preston came to the rescue with eight British soldiers.

There is some confusion about what happened next. The mob is said to have taunted the redcoats, yelling "Fire! Fire!" Captain Preston is said to have yelled, "Hold your fire!" Then a British soldier was hit with a big stick. He claimed he heard the word "fire," so he fired his gun into the crowd. The street gang moved forward; the redcoats panicked and fired at unarmed people. Five Americans died; seven were wounded.

▲ Paul Revere made this famous engraving from a drawing by Henry Pelham. It shows the Boston Massacre as the American patriots saw it (which means it isn't quite as it happened). The building called Butcher's Hall was actually a coffeehouse with a different name. The British soldiers never lined up like that and Preston didn't raise his sword. Also, it doesn't show Crispus Attucks, a black laborer who was killed. Nevertheless, it was great propaganda and made a lot of Americans fighting mad.

None of them was a hero. The victims were troublemakers who got worse than they deserved. The soldiers were professionals (the British army was supposed to be the best in the world), who shouldn't have panicked. The whole thing shouldn't have happened. Sam Adams made the most of it. He called it the Boston Massacre and had Paul Revere engrave a picture of the scene. Revere was a silversmith who made fine teapots and pitchers. He was also a dedicated Patriot, a dentist, a printer, a good horseback rider, and a friend of Samuel Adams.

The picture that Paul Revere chose to etch into a piece of copper— so it could be printed over and over again—showed British soldiers firing at peaceful Boston citizens. That wasn't the way it had actually happened—Adams and Revere knew that—but the drawing made good propaganda. It made people furious at the British. That drawing was soon seen all over the colonies. It helped start a war.

There is one hero in the story of the Boston Massacre: John Adams. John didn't want British soldiers in Boston; he wanted freedom for his country. But he was fair and he always did what he thought was right. And even though everyone in America wanted to blame the British soldiers, John Adams believed they should have a fair trial. He knew they needed a good lawyer, and he was one of the best lawyers in the colonies. So he took the case of the redcoats. Adams argued that the soldiers had defended themselves against an angry mob. A Boston jury found six of the soldiers not guilty. Two soldiers were found guilty of manslaughter—not murder; they were branded on their thumbs.

Long after the American Revolution, someone asked John Adams what the war had been about. There were two revolutions, he explained. One was the war itself. But the important revolution, he said, had occurred even before the war began. It had to do with ideas and attitudes. "The revolution was in the minds and hearts of the people," said John Adams. What do you think he meant by that?

John Adams was fighting for more than just separation from England. He wanted a chance to form a totally new kind of government: a government based on fair play and self-government.

Are people able to govern themselves? That question wasn't even being asked in most of the world. Always there were kings, or priests,

▲ John Adams

Propaganda is biased information designed to arouse emotions.

The historian Edmund S. Morgan says, "John Adams not only learned to work hard, but he always worked for something more than money....He took the interesting cases rather than the lucrative ones and spent his time studying, studying, studying."

▲ Colonial delegates met in 1774 in Philadelphia to discuss their complaints against England and how they should respond.

or a ruling class. A country where people made their own laws? That sounded strange. Could the mass of people be trusted to choose their own leaders? It was a radical idea.

Samuel and John Adams knew that people in the colonies had much experience in self-government. They believed Americans could run their own nation and elect their own leaders. The Adams cousins would convince others; they would help form an American republic.

There was much to do before it could all work out. Plans had to be made. A congress was needed. Samuel Adams's Committees of Correspondence were made up of leaders from all of the colonies. Those committees then became a congress: the First Continental Congress.

It was 1774 when the Congress met in Philadelphia, midway between New England and the southern colonies. Philadelphia

A *congress* is a group of delegates who get together for discussion and action.

was America's leading city, so it made sense to meet there. Representatives came from every colony except Georgia. Samuel Adams and John Adams were both delegates. Sam wore a new wine-red suit with gold buttons, a gift from a Boston craftsman who didn't want his representative to look shabby. Alexander McDougall and John Jay (who would later be a new nation's first chief justice) came from New York determined to see that the colonies put pressure on England by not importing her goods. John Dickinson, who lived in Philadelphia, argued that a way must be found to get along with England. South Carolina's Christopher Gadsden and Virginia's Patrick Henry didn't agree with Dickinson. They were considered radicals. "Arms are a resource to which we shall be forced," said the fiery Patrick Henry. (When he said "arms," he meant guns.) The Congress soon advised the colonists to form and arm militia (mill-ISH-uh) units and to stop buying goods from England.

▲ John Jay

Virginia's Peyton Randolph, a moderate, was elected president of the Congress. South Carolina's John Rutledge was another moderate. "There is in the Congress a collection of the greatest men upon this continent," John Adams noted in his diary.

The delegates at the Congress passed 10 resolutions listing the rights of the colonists, including the right to "life, liberty and property." But perhaps the most important thing that happened was that the colonial leaders got together and talked about their common problems. Then they wrote a polite, respectful petition and sent it to King George, urging him to consider their complaints. But George wouldn't even think about that.

The delegates made plans to meet again, if the situation in the country didn't improve.

Things got worse.

Remember, *Patriots* were Americans who wanted to be free of British rule. Sometimes Patriots were also called *Whigs*—the Whigs were an English political party that mostly believed that the colonials should be allowed to govern themselves. Americans who supported the king were called *Loyalists*—because they remained loyal to the existing government—and sometimes *Tories*. The Tory political party believed the king should keep firm control of the colonies.

One If by Land, Two If by Sea

Three men rode horseback on an April night in 1775: Paul Revere, William Dawes, and Dr. Samuel Prescott. Each carried the same message, which most people now remember as, "The redcoats are coming." You may have heard of Paul Revere, because a poet, Henry Wadsworth Longfellow, wrote a famous poem about his ride.

When Paul Revere carried his warning, he most likely said, "The Regulars are coming." *Regulars, redcoats, dragoons, grenadiers*—they're all names for British soldiers.

Listen, my children, and you shall hear
Of the midnight ride of Paul Revere,
On the eighteenth of April, in Seventy-five;
Hardly a man is now alive
Who remembers that famous day and year.

Can you hear Longfellow making his words gallop, like a horse's hoofs? Here's more of the story, this time in prose:

The Patriots were worried. It looked as if war with Britain couldn't be avoided. The Patriots were the colonists who wanted independence. They wanted to be free of British rule. The other colonists—the ones who wanted to stay British subjects—were called Loyalists. Some Patriots, like Samuel Adams, expected war. But most Patriots still hoped to find peaceful ways to settle their differences with England.

A famous portrait of Paul Revere, silversmith and patriot (painted by John Singleton Copley) ▼

It was scary to think of war. England was a great power; the colonies were scattered and had little military experience.

Still, it made sense to be prepared for the worst, so New Englanders began to stockpile cannonballs and gunpowder. They piled them up in Concord, a small town about 20 miles northwest of Boston.

When the British officers heard about those munitions, they decided to get them. Paul Revere and his Boston friends learned of the British plans. They found out that the redcoats were going to march on Concord the next morning!

Besides the gunpowder, Revere was worried about his friends Sam Adams and John Hancock. They were hiding in Lexington, right next door to Concord. The British were searching for those two troublemakers—they wanted to hang them as traitors.

▲ British soldiers were known as *redcoats*.

Someone had to alert Adams and Hancock and get a warning to those towns—and fast. It would help to know which way the redcoats would march.

Would they go by the long land route over the Boston neck? Or would they take the shorter route—by boat across the water to Charlestown and then on foot from there?

Billy Dawes didn't wait to find out. He pretended to be a drunk farmer and staggered past the British sentry who stood guard at the neck. As soon as he was out of sight of the guard, Dawes jumped on a horse and went at a gallop. He knew the redcoats would start out soon, and he shouted that message at each Patriot house he passed.

That same dark night Paul Revere sent someone to spy on the British. "Find out which way the redcoats will march," the spy was told. "Then climb into the high bell tower of the North Church and send a signal. Light one lantern if they go by land. Hang two lanterns if they go by sea."

Revere got in a boat and was quietly rowed out into the Charles River. A horse was ready for him on the Charlestown shore. He waited—silently. (Revere was a known Patriot and would have been arrested if the British had found him outdoors at night.)

> And lo! as he looks, on the belfry's height
> A glimmer, and then a gleam of light!
> He springs to the saddle, the bridle he turns,
> But lingers and gazes, till full on his sight
> A second lamp in the belfry burns!

Now he knew! The redcoats would take the water route across the Charles River, just as Paul Revere was doing. What happened next?

Back on September 11, 1774, Dr. Joseph Warren and a group of Patriots gathered in Milton, Massachusetts, where they wrote out 19 blunt statements (called "resolves") protesting Britain's actions in the Boston area. Paul Revere carried those resolves to the Continental Congress in Philadelphia, where they are said to have influenced the delegates and a declaration they were writing.

▲ Paul Revere flees from British soldiers to warn colonists of the approaching redcoats.

Well, both Billy Dawes and Paul Revere rode hard, through the night, warning everyone in the countryside that the British were coming. They met at Lexington in time to tell Sam Adams and John Hancock to escape. But before they could go on to Concord, they were stopped by a British patrol. The redcoats took their horses. Luckily, by this time, a third man, Dr. Samuel Prescott, was riding with Dawes and Revere. (Prescott had been visiting the girl he intended to marry, who lived in Lexington.) The doctor managed to escape from the British, ride home to Concord, and warn everyone there.

The American farmers were ready, and they grabbed their guns. They were called "minutemen" because they could fight on a minute's notice. (Some had been trained fighting in the French and Indian War.) Captain John Parker was the leader of the minutemen, and what he said on that day is now carved in stone near the spot where he must have stood. "Stand your ground. Don't fire unless fired upon. But if they mean to have a war let it begin here!"

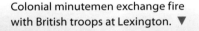

Colonial minutemen exchange fire with British troops at Lexington. ▼

▲ The British attempt to cross the North Bridge at Concord, but are stopped by minutemen.

And it did begin right there, at Lexington. Each side said the other fired the first shot. No one knows who really did, but a poet named Ralph Waldo Emerson called it "the shot heard round the world." (Can you see why?)

When the smoke cleared, eight American farmers lay dead. It was April 19, 1775. The American Revolution had begun.

But it was gunpowder that the redcoats had set out to get, so they marched on—to Concord—but they couldn't find the powder. That made them so angry they started a fire. "Will you let them burn the town down?" shouted one colonist. "No, I haven't a man who is afraid to go," said the minutemen's Captain Isaac Davis. The British stood at the North Bridge in Concord. They fired at the colonists. The minutemen fired back. Now the British were scared, and they tried to retreat. The Americans followed and whipped the redcoats. More than two Englishmen fell for every American casualty.

The stanza with Ralph Waldo Emerson's famous line goes like this:

By the rude bridge that arched the flood,
Their flag to April's breeze unfurled,
Here once the embattled farmers stood,
And fired the shot heard round the world.

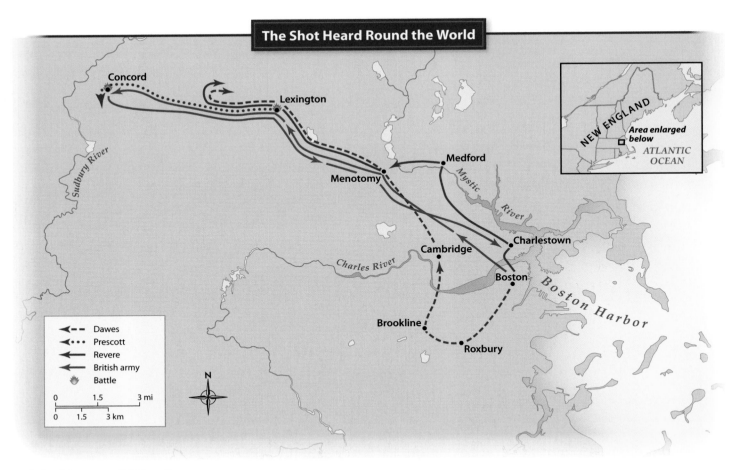

The Shot Heard Round the World

Concord
Lexington
Medford
Menotomy
Charlestown
Cambridge
Boston
Brookline
Roxbury

Sudbury River
Mystic River
Charles River
Boston Harbor

NEW ENGLAND
Area enlarged below
ATLANTIC OCEAN

◄--- Dawes
◄••• Prescott
◄--- Revere
◄--- British army
🔥 Battle

0   1.5   3 mi
0   1.5   3 km

N

▲ Paul Revere and William Dawes rode to warn the colonists that the British were advancing toward Lexington and Concord. When they were stopped by a British patrol, Samuel Prescott continued on to Concord, shouting the warning.

Do you know the song "Yankee Doodle"? Well, the British made it up to insult the Americans. They said a Yankee Doodle was a backwoods hick who didn't know how to fight. When the British marched to Concord and Lexington, they wore their fancy red uniforms, and their drummers and pipers played "Yankee Doodle."

After the battle, it was the Americans who sang that song. They said, "We'll be Yankee Doodles and proud of it!"

But that isn't the whole story. There is always more to war than winning or losing. These are words written in 1775:

Isaac Davis...was my husband. He was then thirty years of age. We had four children; the youngest about fifteen months old....The alarm was given early in the morning, and my husband lost no time in making ready to go to Concord with his company...[he] said but little that morning. He seemed serious and thoughtful; but never seemed to hesitate.... He only said, "Take good care of the children." In the afternoon he was brought home a corpse.

Henry Wadsworth Longfellow finished the story:

You know the rest. In the books you have read
How the British Regulars fired and fled,—
How the farmers gave them ball for ball,
From behind each fence and farmyard wall,
Chasing the redcoats down the lane,
Then crossing the fields to emerge again
Under the trees at the turn of the road,
And only pausing to fire and load.

So through the night rode Paul Revere;
And so through the night went his cry of alarm
To every Middlesex village and farm,—
A cry of defiance and not of fear,
A voice in the darkness, a knock at the door,
And a word that shall echo forevermore!
For, borne on the night-wind of the Past,
Through all our history, to the last,
In the hour of darkness and peril and need,
The people will waken and listen to hear
The hurrying hoof-beats of that steed,
And the midnight message of Paul Revere.

Here are some verses from a rousing patriotic song from the American Revolution:

Yankee Doodle went to town,
A-ridin' on a pony.
Stuck a feather in his cap
And called it Macaroni.

Chorus:

Yankee Doodle, keep it up,
Yankee Doodle Dandy,
Mind the music and the step
And with the girls be handy.

Father and I went down to camp,
Along with Captain Gooding,
And there we saw the men and boys
As thick as hasty pudding.

(Chorus)

And there was Captain Washington
Upon a slapping stallion,
A-giving orders to his men;
I guess there was a million.

(to tune of chorus)

Yankee Doodle is the tune
Americans delight in.
Twill do to whistle, sing or play
And just the thing for fightin'.

The Spirit of '76, by American painter Archibald Willard. ▶

Taking Ticonderoga

Ethan Allen was born in Connecticut in 1738. He was a sinewy giant of a man, rough and rowdy. In 1775, with a group of friends known as the Green Mountain Boys, he set out to capture an important British fort—Fort Ticonderoga—on Lake Champlain.

Just as Allen and the Green Mountain Boys were getting ready to start out, Benedict Arnold appeared. Arnold was a colonel in the Continental army, with a fancy uniform. He later became a traitor, going over to the British side. Despite that villainy, he was a strong leader and a good fighter. Benedict Arnold said he was going to take command of the mission, under orders from Massachusetts.

Ethan Allen couldn't stand Arnold, but they agreed to lead together, shoulder to shoulder. Into the fort they went—Benedict Arnold like a proper soldier and Ethan Allen and his men howling war whoops. An astonished British officer asked on whose authority they attacked. Ethan Allen roared, "In the name of the Great Jehovah and the Continental Congress!" It wasn't much longer before the fort, its cannons, and its rum all belonged to the Patriots.

Ethan Allen went on to help establish Vermont as an independent republic.

▲ American soldiers move artillery pieces captured at Fort Ticonderoga.

Looking across Lake Champlain to Fort Ticonderoga ▼

On the Way to the Second Continental Congress

Pretend it is 1775. You are a British subject living in the American colonies in Philadelphia. At least that is the way you have been taught to describe yourself. But now you are confused. You have overheard violent arguments. Some people are calling the Bostonians "heroes"; others call them "rabble." Politics is making people angry. Your parents are no longer talking to some of their old friends.

Your parents are Patriots; some of your neighbors are Loyalists. If there is war, the Loyalists hope Britain will win. They don't see any need for independence. England is the greatest nation on earth, they say. They remember the good old days before the French and Indian War. England didn't bother the colonists with many taxes then. They expect those times to return again. Benjamin Franklin's son William is a Loyalist. He is sincere in his beliefs, but he will break his father's heart.

Being a Patriot may mean going to war. That worries you—and it should. What side will you be on? In May, when the Virginia delegation arrives in Philadelphia, you make a decision. You will stick with the American Patriots' cause.

Back in the 18th century there were no TV stars and no big sports figures, which may explain why, in 1775, everyone in Philadelphia seemed to want a glimpse of Virginia's political leaders when their carriages rolled into town.

Delegates gathered at the Pennsylvania State House, later renamed Independence Hall, for the Second Continental Congress in 1775. ▼

Philadelphians remembered the Virginia delegates to the First Continental Congress, and eagerly awaited their arrival at the Second. ▶

The Virginians had been in Philadelphia the year before, when the First Continental Congress met. Now they were back for the Second Congress: heroic-looking men who rode their horses proudly, who danced with energy and grace, and who thought and spoke as well as any Americans anywhere. Even John Adams of Massachusetts said that they represented "fortunes, ability, learning, eloquence, acuteness, equal to any I ever met with in all my life."

Take George Washington, for instance. He was more than six feet tall, big-boned, muscular, lean, and very strong. Once he came upon some young men who were throwing weights as far as they could. They had their shirts off and were sweating from the effort. George Washington asked if he could try. He took a weight—didn't even take off his jacket—and outthrew them all. Does that sound as if he was a show-off? He wasn't. Everyone agreed about that. He was modest, and only spoke when he had something to say.

His adventures during the French and Indian War had made him famous, even in England. In America both men and women admired him. One friend called him "the best horseman of his age and the most graceful figure that could be seen on horseback." He had gray-blue eyes, auburn hair, and hands and feet so large that several people of his time remarked about them. He loved to dance and he dressed with care. He wore his military uniform to Philadelphia—bright blue with brass buttons—and they called him Colonel Washington. When John Adams's wife, Abigail, met George Washington she found a poem to describe him:

> *Mark his majestic fabric; he's a temple*
> *Sacred by birth, and built by hands divine.*

(John Adams was always jealous of George Washington.)

Washington rode to Philadelphia with another Virginian, Richard Henry Lee. The fingers on one of Lee's hands had been shot off in a hunting accident; he kept a silk handkerchief wrapped around that hand and pointed with it when he spoke. That gives you an idea of the man's style. He was good-looking, he wore elegant clothes, and he talked smoothly.

Lee was full of surprises. He was a slave owner who hated slavery and spoke out against it. Though he was dashing and aristocratic, he got along well with rumpled Samuel Adams. It was Richard Henry Lee (with Patrick Henry and Thomas Jefferson) who organized the first Committee of Correspondence in Virginia.

Lee came from a talented family. His brothers were all outspoken leaders. That means they said what they believed. So did his sister Hannah. She was furious when she was turned away from the voting polls because she was female. It was taxation without representation, said Hannah Lee.

▲ George Washington, said his friends, was serious but never stern, and always cheerful with his soldiers.

A Virginian described Washington as "sensible, but speaks little." Washington spoke up when something mattered. In 1785 he wrote about slavery: "There is not a man alive who wishes more sincerely than I do, to see a plan adopted for the abolition of it." He believed slavery should be ended by "legislative authority" (laws), because slave owners would not willingly give up wealth and property. Washington remained a slave owner himself. He freed his slaves in his will.

▲ The city of Philadelphia welcomes delegates to the Second Continental Congress.

As Lee and Washington rode toward Philadelphia, they were joined by other members of the Virginia delegation. Farmers along the way took off their hats and cheered. Then, six miles from Philadelphia, 500 soldiers on horseback appeared to escort them. By the time they entered the city, a military band was playing and infantrymen were marching—it was some parade.

The Virginians were the same seven men who had been at the first congress in 1774 (although some would leave almost immediately and others would take their place). Three were the best orators in the state, perhaps in the nation: Patrick Henry (who looked like a country boy, and seemed to want it that way), Richard Henry Lee (who asked this congress to declare for independence), and slim, graceful Edmund Pendleton (who debated with cool logic).

Virginia's Benjamin Harrison was the biggest man at the convention. He was six feet four inches tall and was said to weigh

400 pounds. (Many of the delegates were big—it was normal to be heavy. Meals were large: soup, fish, meat, vegetables, potatoes, pie and cake, fruit and cheese—all at one sitting. John Adams, just five feet six inches tall, grew to weigh 275 pounds.) Harrison told a friend he would have come to this convention on foot, if he'd had to, rather than not come. He became governor of Virginia; his son and great-grandson became presidents of the United States.

Popular Peyton Randolph, another giant of a man, had been president of the First Continental Congress and was expected to preside again. But he did not stay long. Nor did Patrick Henry. They were needed in Williamsburg. Virginia's House of Burgesses had been called back into session. State business seemed more important to them than anything that might occur at this experimental gathering.

Peyton Randolph's cousin, who was just 33, came to take his place in Philadelphia. The cousin was a thoughtful, quiet man who was known to be a good writer. His name was Thomas Jefferson.

Meet Some of the Delegates

Delegate Philip Livingston lived like a prince in New York. His family had been prominent in the colonies for five generations, but Philip Livingston made his own fortune as a trader and privateer during the French and Indian War. In spite of his wealth, he identified with ordinary people and opposed the colony's royal governor and the Stamp Tax. Livingston believed in political and religious freedom.

Joseph Hewes, who came from North Carolina, was opposed to separation from Britain—even when people in North Carolina told him to vote for it. Then, in a debate at the convention, something happened. "He started suddenly upright," reported John Adams, "and lifting up both his hands to Heaven, as if he had been in a trance, cried out, 'It is done! and I will abide by it.'" Hewes was now for independence!

Stephen Hopkins, who was elected governor of Rhode Island 10 times, attended the Albany Congress in 1754 with Benjamin Franklin, Sir William Johnson, and Hendrick (the Mohawk sachem, Tiyanoga). Stephen Hopkins helped Ben Franklin write a plan for a union of the colonies. Most Americans weren't ready for that in 1754. Now it seemed that they were.

Georgia's Button Gwinnett had an unforgettable name and just a year to live. Gwinnett—Georgia's governor—was killed in a duel. Afterward, no one could remember what the duel was about—except honor, they said.

▲ Delegates gather outside the Pennsylvania State House in Philadelphia.

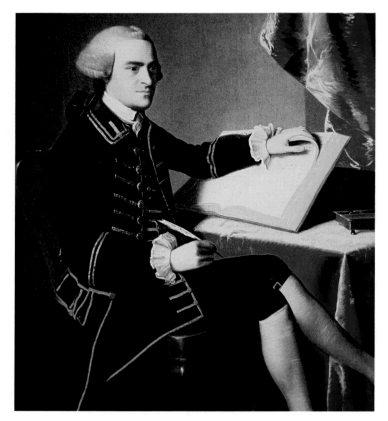

▲ John Hancock, president of the Second Continental Congress

The Virginians were the crowd pleasers, but the congress as a whole was so extraordinary it would still inspire awe 200 years later.

The Adams cousins—Sam and John—were back from Massachusetts, along with rich John Hancock, who became president of this Second Continental Congress. John Witherspoon, a Scotsman who had needed persuading to come to America to head Princeton College, was a delegate from New Jersey. So was Francis Hopkinson, an inventor and scientist who wrote poetry, composed music, and painted.

Of Caesar Rodney, the delegate from Delaware, John Adams wrote: "[He] is the oddest looking man in the world; his face is not bigger than a large apple, yet there is a sense of fire, spirit, wit, and humor in his countenance."

Benjamin Rush was a doctor and a teacher. He'd learned medicine as an apprentice to a doctor and then had gone to Scotland to learn more. Rush had ideas that seemed strange to some people: he hated slavery, tobacco, and capital punishment. He thought girls and blacks should go to school and that they could learn as much as white boys. Rush was one of Pennsylvania's representatives, and remarkable. Pennsylvania's Ben Franklin was even more so.

Men of the Middle Colonies

Benjamin Rush served as an army surgeon during the Revolutionary War. He set up the first free clinic in America and became the country's most famous medical professor. When Rush was studying medicine in Edinburgh, Scotland, he helped persuade John Witherspoon, a famous Scots clergyman, to come to America to be president of Princeton, where Rush had gone to college. Dr. Witherspoon was the only minister to sign the Declaration of Independence. Charles Carroll of Maryland was the last signer to die (in 1832) and the only Roman Catholic.

No American was better known than Benjamin Franklin. He'd come to Philadelphia from Boston as a penniless boy and soon made his fortune as a printer and publisher. He made his fame as an inventor, scientist, philosopher, and political leader. Franklin had spent years in London as an agent for several of the colonies. No one tried harder than he to avoid a break with England. He proposed the idea of a British commonwealth of independent nations, each with its own parliament, but all with the same king. The leaders of Britain's Parliament rejected that idea and treated Franklin with contempt.

Franklin changed his thinking; he began to favor independence. He arrived home from England on May 5, 1775, just in time to attend the opening of the Second Continental Congress.

The following March he was off again, this time on a wild goose chase to Canada to try and convince the Canadians to join the other colonies and fight Britain. Franklin and the two Maryland delegates—Charles Carroll (said to be the wealthiest man in America) and Samuel Chase (a leader of the Sons of Liberty in Annapolis)—headed north. It was an exhausting trip, especially for 69-year-old Benjamin Franklin. (In Albany they noted that most people still spoke Dutch. In upper New York, they had to sleep in the snowy woods.) When they finally arrived at their destination, they couldn't persuade the Canadians to join the revolution. (Religion had something to do with it. Catholic Canada feared an alliance with the mostly Protestant colonies.)

Benjamin Franklin ▼

In June Franklin was back at the convention, where he was asked to serve (with John Adams and Thomas Jefferson) on a committee that was to write an important declaration. Some people say this was the most important political statement ever written. It was addressed to King George III. Hold on for a few chapters and I'll tell you all about it.

Naming a General

At first the Continental Congress found itself in a strange situation. Americans were in fighting mood, but war had not been declared. Should they prepare for war? Should they work for peace? Could they do both?

People were calling for a Continental army. The minutemen who fought at Lexington and Concord were gathered near Boston. Others had come from the countryside with rifles and muskets. If someone didn't take charge they would all go back home.

The Continental Congress couldn't ignore the problem, especially after a letter arrived from the Boston Patriots pleading for the Congress to take over their forces.

John Adams spoke up. He called for a "Grand American Army" to be made up of volunteers from all of the colonies. The guns fired at Lexington and Concord might be heard next in Charleston, or Baltimore, or even in Philadelphia, Adams told the delegates. They must have shuddered, because they knew he spoke the truth.

In each of the colonies, citizen soldiers—militia—were ready to fight. Someone had to organize the militias and the minutemen into an army. A general was needed, said Adams.

A recruiting poster for the Continental army ▶

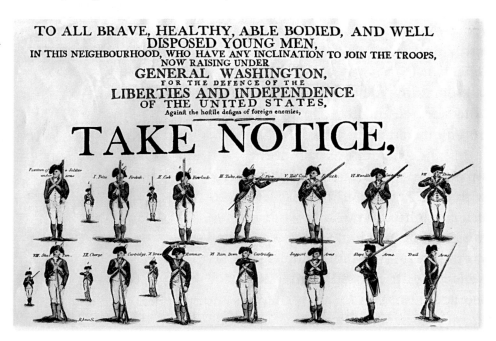

◄ The Second Continental Congress appointed George Washington as general of the Continental army.

John Hancock from Massachusetts believed he was the man for the job. He had done a bit of soldiering, and it was his money that was paying some of Congress's bills. So when John Adams stood up to nominate a general, almost everyone—especially John Hancock—thought it would be Hancock. But, as you know, John Adams always did what he thought was best for the nation—not what would make him popular at home.

"There is but one man in my mind for this important command," said Adams, and Hancock looked pleased. "The gentleman I have in mind…is from Virginia." When Adams said that, John Hancock's face fell, and Washington, who realized he was the man from Virginia, rushed from the room.

John Adams continued, "[His] skill as an officer…great talents and universal character would command the respect of America and unite… the Colonies better than any other person alive." The congressmen agreed. George Washington was elected general unanimously.

The Second Continental Congress is best known for two things:

1. Naming George Washington as general of the American armies.

2. Producing the Declaration of Independence. (It took more than a year to get that done.)

The Congress did more than that, but those two accomplishments were enough to make any body famous. (Yes, a congress is a body—a legislative body.)

He accepted—on one condition. He would take no salary. And that was part of Washington's greatness. He was willing to serve without pay for a cause he thought noble.

Washington knew that the general's job could lead to disaster. England was the greatest power in the world. Its army was well trained and supplied with the latest guns and cannons. Its navy was the finest in the world.

The American army was made up of a raggedy bunch of men— farmers, shoemakers, carpenters, blacksmiths—who had few guns, no cannons, and no military training. George Washington knew that he had an almost impossible job. He said to Patrick Henry, "Remember, Mr. Henry, what I now tell you: from the day I enter upon the command of the American armies, I date my fall, and the ruin of my reputation."

And that, too, is part of what made Washington great. He was willing to do what he thought was right and important even if it might bring his own ruin. (Of course, we know it didn't bring his ruin. It made him famous for all time.)

George Washington set out for Boston to take charge of the soldiers gathered there. In the meantime, the Continental Congress tried once more to patch things up with England. They sent another petition to King George III. This one was called the Olive Branch Petition. An olive branch is a symbol of peace. The colonists asked the king to consider their problems. But George wouldn't even read the petition.

Now all this may seem strange. The colonists were petitioning England and at the same time they were getting ready to fight. But most members of the Congress weren't ready to break away from England. Those who were—like Washington and Adams and Jefferson—were wise enough not to rush the others. People thought of separation from England as different from revolution. They wanted a revolution. That word had a splendid sound to it. Everyone knew of the Glorious Revolution of 1688. Englishmen and women were proud of that peaceful revolution and of the rights it gave them. For a long time many Americans thought they could have the rights of free people and still be part of the British empire. (And they might have, if the king and Parliament had been wiser.)

Meanwhile people in America were getting angry and saying and doing wild things. Soon there would be no turning back.

The Spread of Ideas
Some English citizens were rooting for the Americans. They knew that George was not a good king, and they didn't like his ministers, either. They realized that some of their own precious English rights were being threatened because the king wanted more power for himself.

As it turned out, the American Revolution helped bring better government to England. Indeed, as the revolution's ideas of freedom and equality spread, monarchs and despots everywhere began trembling. Some kings and queens would lose their jobs because of those ideas. In France they would lose their heads. But that's another story—and a good one, too—that you'll have to read on your own.

The War of the Hills

England's Major John Pitcairn to the Earl of Sandwich (Boston, March 4, 1775):

> *I am satisfied that one active campaign, a smart action, and burning two or three of their towns, will set everything to rights. Nothing now, I am afraid, but this will ever convince those foolish bad people that England is in earnest.*

And so there was war. It seemed to begin almost by itself. Some people—on both sides—wanted to fight, and that was enough.

Two days after the Second Continental Congress appointed George Washington commander in chief of the Continental army—before anyone in Boston even knew there was a general—redcoats and Patriots were killing each other. They were fighting the first major battle of the Revolutionary War.

Two hills, Breed's and Bunker, lie just across the Charles River from Boston. Like Boston itself, they are on a peninsula connected to the mainland by a narrow neck: the Charlestown peninsula.

The British were asleep on that June night in 1775 when the Massachusetts soldiers began to dig fortifications on Breed's Hill. The Americans worked all night. They must have worked with great speed and ability, because by morning it was done. Those hills that looked out on Boston were filled with troops and trenches.

The British couldn't believe it. For months they had tried to get the colonists to work for them. They needed barracks, and there were other construction jobs to be done. But nothing got finished. Americans are lazy, the British thought. And then they saw this amazing feat, accomplished overnight. Breed's Hill

Continental soldiers prepare to do battle against advancing British troops. ▼

Guns and Swords

Revolutionary soldiers were issued big, clumsy muskets with bayonets attached. The bayonet was a sharp sword. Muskets weren't very accurate, and they took time to reload; the bayonet was ready and deadly and could be used at close quarters. Many American farmers and frontiersmen brought their own rifles to war and understood their value before the officers did. Muskets and rifles look a lot alike, but the grooving inside the barrel of a rifle makes a bullet fly straight as aimed. It took a long time for the officers to catch on. Muskets were still being used in the Civil War, nearly a century later.

was swarming with men and covered with impressive earthworks. Bunker Hill was dark with men. The British—especially the four British generals in Boston—were dumbfounded.

If they had thought a minute, they might have sent troops to capture the neck of the Charlestown peninsula—and perhaps trap the colonial soldiers. But they didn't think. They reacted.

Before long, barges filled with English soldiers were splashing their way from Boston, across the Charles River to Charlestown. Fifers played, drums pounded, and cannon blasted.

The British troops made ready to attack—head on. The Massachusetts men, dug in at the top of the hill, must have been scared—really scared. They had no training for this; they were fighting Europe's best soldiers; and they had very little gunpowder. They knew they had to use that gunpowder carefully. They had few bayonets; the British soldiers all had bayonets. The American officers told the volunteer soldiers to wait until the British soldiers were almost on top of them before they fired. "Wait until you see the whites of their eyes," they said.

Firing a Revolutionary Cannon

Firing a Revolutionary War cannon isn't easy; six or seven men are needed to do the job. And it is dangerous: sometimes the monsters explode. Firing begins when the officer in charge shouts, "*Worm!*" A wormer—a soldier with a long, corkscrew-shaped iron

▲ Revolutionary War cannon

worm—twists the worm and cleans out the barrel. Next comes the call "*Sponge!*" and a sponger sticks a wet sheepskin into the gun barrel. That cools it down and puts out sparks. "*Load!*" says the officer, and a bag of powder is stuffed into the barrel, followed by a big iron ball, or grapeshot (clusters of small balls that scatter with great force, killing or wounding men over a broad area). "*Ram!*" Now a rammer, holding a pole with a wooden disk on its end, pushes and packs the ammunition. "*Pick and prime!*" A gunner sticks a pick into the barrel and breaks open the ammunition sack. He adds powder in a vent hole, and puts a pinch of powder on top of the cannon barrel. "*Give!*" shouts the officer, and the gunner lights a slow fuse. "*Fire!*" The gunner uses the fuse to light the powder on top of the barrel. The flame skips through the vent and sets off the powder inside the cannon. The ball explodes out of the gun's mouth at a speed of about 1,000 feet a second. *Watch out!*

And that is what the Massachusetts men did. Can you imagine the strain? It is said that those who saw the Battle of Bunker Hill never forgot the sounds, the smells, the ferocity, and the fear of that day. Pretend you are up there with them on the top of Breed's Hill. Watch the redcoats advance toward you, bayonets pointed. Don't panic, and don't fire until you hear the order to do so.

It was eerie, they say. All those soldiers climbing and no one firing.

Then, all at once, the hills seemed to explode. Bullets tore through the redcoats and left the ground covered with bodies and blood. The British would not consider defeat or retreat. They landed more troops, and again the American fighters held their fire until it could hurt the most. The English soldiers kept coming, and falling, until "some had only eight or nine men a company left; some only three, four or five."

> A *company* is a group of soldiers usually led by a captain and made up of at least two platoons. A *platoon* is a subdivision of a company, commanded by a lieutenant.

Colonists watched the fighting at Bunker Hill from Boston rooftops. ▼

▲ Low on gunpowder, colonial militiamen advance in the Battle of Bunker Hill.

In this 19th-century painting, Peter Salem, one of the black minutemen who fought at Bunker Hill, is shown at the lower right loading his gun. Salem is said to be the marksman who killed Britain's Major Pitcairn. Shortly after the battle, he was almost pushed out of the Continental army when Congress decided to limit it to free men. Salem's owners gave him his freedom. ▼

Suddenly it was quiet. This time the British made it to the top of the hill. The Americans were gone. They had run out of gunpowder. The British captured Breed's Hill and Bunker Hill, too. But what a price for two unimportant hills! More than 1,000 British soldiers were killed or wounded that day. The Americans lost 441 men.

Dr. Joseph Warren was one of those who died. He was a leader of the Boston Patriots. They say he was cool and brave under fire and that he inspired those around him. The same kinds of things are said of the handsome Major John Pitcairn, who fought for the Royal British Marines at Bunker Hill and didn't live to tell of it.

How the New World Changed the Old, and Vice Versa

The 18th century would come to be called a time of "Enlightenment." Why? Because lights were going on in the minds of the thinking people.

In England, a scientist named Isaac Newton had shown that the universe was not as full of mystery as people had supposed. It could be understood with study and observation and by people using their brains. That was an astonishing thought in a world that had often been guided by superstition and fear. Suddenly there seemed to be all kinds of brilliant thinkers who were using their minds and encouraging others to do the same thing.

An Englishman named John Locke and a Frenchman named Jean-Jacques Rousseau (jahn-jahk-roo-SO) were two of the most important Enlightenment thinkers. They thought about politics and the way governments were run. They got some of their ideas by considering the American Indian and the "New World." Jean-Jacques Rousseau called Indians

John Locke wrote, "Wherever Law ends, Tyranny begins." ▶

"noble savages." John Locke said, "In the beginning, all the world was America." (What do you think he meant by that?)

John Locke wrote about natural rights. He said that governments should be run for the people, not for their rulers. Locke made people think about democracy.

The colonists in America read what Locke wrote. They read about the ancient democracies in Greece and Rome. They knew that most American Indians seemed to live a free, democratic life in self-governing tribes.

The colonists knew something else: they knew they could govern themselves. They didn't need kings or nobles to make decisions for them. Americans had been running their own assemblies for years. There was the General Court in Massachusetts and the House of Burgesses in Virginia, and there were lawmaking bodies in each colony. Nowhere in Europe did people have that kind of experience in self-government.

An article published in England around 1776 said, "The darling passion of the American is liberty and that in its fullest extent; nor is it the original natives only to whom this passion is confined; our colonists sent thither seem to have imbibed the same principles."

Americans were sending raw materials to England—like lumber and tobacco—and getting them sent back as finished goods—furniture and cigars. Well, another raw material got sent back and forth across the sea: the idea of freedom and democratic government.

▲ Isaac Newton uses a prism to separate white light into a spectrum of colors.

Declaring Independence

Unless you like to memorize dates, there aren't many that you need to remember. But here are a few that are important:

1215, 1492, 1607, 1620

What happened in those years? You can't remember? Go ahead and try. You might be surprised and find there is more in your brain than you realize. (Then, if you need to check, look on page 301.)

A draft of the Declaration of Independence, in Thomas Jefferson's handwriting ▼

Now I have another date for you to remember, and this one is the most important of all. Something happened on that day that changed America—it even changed the whole world. (It was a day that King George III didn't think important. He would find out how wrong he was.)

The date is July 4, 1776. That was the day the members of the Second Continental Congress approved a Declaration of Independence. It was a year after the Battle of Bunker Hill, and, finally, the Americans had made up their minds to be free of Great Britain.

But that wasn't why the world was changed. It was the words they used in that Declaration that made all the difference.

The delegates believed that if they were going to vote for independence, they should have a good reason. They knew that when they signed the Declaration they became traitors to England. They would each be hanged if England captured them.

If they were going to take that big risk, they wanted to make it worthwhile. And it would be worthwhile if they could help create a free nation, a great nation, a nation run by its citizens—something that had never before been done.

◄ Thomas Jefferson designed this portable writing desk, upon which he wrote drafts of the Declaration of Independence.

So they thought it important to explain exactly what they were doing and why it was necessary to be free of English rule.

That's why they asked Thomas Jefferson, one of the members of the Congress, to write a paper—called a "declaration"—that would

- tell their beliefs about good government;
- tell what King George had done wrong; and
- announce that the colonies were now free and independent states.

Some people thought it surprising that Thomas Jefferson was asked to write the declaration. Jefferson was one of the youngest members of the Continental Congress. He was a

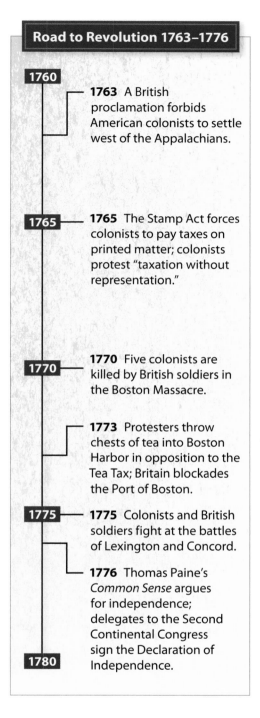

Road to Revolution 1763–1776

1760

1763 A British proclamation forbids American colonists to settle west of the Appalachians.

1765 — **1765** The Stamp Act forces colonists to pay taxes on printed matter; colonists protest "taxation without representation."

1770 — **1770** Five colonists are killed by British soldiers in the Boston Massacre.

1773 Protesters throw chests of tea into Boston Harbor in opposition to the Tea Tax; Britain blockades the Port of Boston.

1775 — **1775** Colonists and British soldiers fight at the battles of Lexington and Concord.

1776 Thomas Paine's *Common Sense* argues for independence; delegates to the Second Continental Congress sign the Declaration of Independence.

1780

◄ Benjamin Franklin, John Adams, and Thomas Jefferson meet to review a draft of the Declaration of Independence.

tall, shy redhead who loved to read, run, ride horseback, and play the violin. He had a reputation for writing well. John Adams said of him, "Though a silent member in Congress, he was so prompt, frank... and decisive upon committees and in conversation—not even Samuel Adams was more so—that he soon seized upon my heart."

Jefferson had left his wife behind on his Virginia farm, and he missed her. He wasn't sure he could write a good declaration. But John Adams and Benjamin Franklin had faith in him. They talked Thomas Jefferson into trying. Adams told him, "You can write ten times better than I can."

Adams and Franklin were right. Thomas Jefferson knew just what to say, and he said it in a way that inspired people all over the world.

The whole Declaration is something to read and think about, but one part will ring in your ears with its greatness. Jefferson wrote:

We hold these truths to be self-evident, that all men are created equal, that they are endowed by their Creator with certain unalienable Rights, that among these are Life, Liberty and the pursuit of Happiness. That to secure these rights, Governments are instituted among Men, deriving their just powers from the consent of the governed.

That was plain language in the 18th century, but you might have to read it a few times to understand it. It is worth doing. Those words are worth memorizing.

All men are created equal.

Just what does "equal" mean?

Thomas Jefferson thought John Adams should write the document about independence. This is how Adams remembered their conversation:

"Why will you not?" Jefferson asked. "You ought to do it."

"Reasons enough."

"What can be your reasons?"

"Reason 1st. You are a Virginian, and a Virginian ought to appear at the head of this business. Reason 2d. I am obnoxious, suspected, and unpopular. You are very much otherwise. Reason 3d. You can write ten times better than I can."

▲ Words from the Declaration of Independence are etched in stone at the Jefferson Memorial in Washington, D.C.

Are we all the same? Look around you. Of course we aren't. Some of us are smarter than others, and some of us are better athletes, and some of us are better looking, and some are nicer. But none of that matters, said Jefferson. We are all equal in the eyes of God, and we are all entitled to equal rights: the right to live, the right to be free, the right to be able to try to find the kind of life that will make us happy.

And that is the whole reason for having governments, he said. Governments are not made to make kings happy. They are for the benefit of the people who are being governed. Governments should have "the consent of the governed."

Sometimes, when ideas are written down, they take on meanings that go beyond what the writers intended. Jefferson's Declaration of Independence was great from the moment he wrote it, but it has grown even greater with the passing of time. He said "all men are created equal." He didn't mention women. Did he mean to include women? No one knows. Perhaps not. We do know that in the 18th century the words "men" and "mankind" included men and women. But very few people, except for Tom Paine, thought much about women's rights. It was the 20th century before women in America had the right to vote.

Some Dates to Remember

1215: Magna Carta

1492: Columbus sails to America

1607: Jamestown settled

1620: the Pilgrims land at Plymouth

1776: the Declaration of Independence!

Here's another date for your memory bank:

1610: Spanish speakers found Santa Fe, New Mexico

Did Thomas Jefferson mean to include black men when he said "all men"? Historians sometimes argue about that. You'll have to decide for yourself.

In 1776, when Jefferson wrote the Declaration, he included a long section in which he described slavery as a "cruel war against human nature." Yet Jefferson lived in a slave society and owned slaves himself.

He thought slavery was wrong, and he said so. "Nothing is more certainly written in the book of fate than that these people are to be free," wrote Jefferson. Many congressmen agreed. John Adams spoke out strongly against slavery. Benjamin Franklin and Benjamin Rush founded the first antislavery society in the New World. But South Carolina and Georgia would not sign the Declaration if it contained the antislavery section. So Jefferson's antislavery words were taken out. The delegates compromised.

Should they have gone ahead without those southern colonies? That would have meant that the Deep South would not have joined in the fight against England. It might have meant defeat for the proposed union of states.

Jefferson and Adams and Franklin and others thought the Union was more important than the issue of slavery. They knew that staying with England would not bring freedom to the slaves. They thought slavery could be dealt with later. Do you agree with them?

Those were tough decisions the delegates were making.

It took a civil war to end slavery. Do you think that war could have been avoided? Do you think the delegates should have acted differently in 1776?

Of one thing you can be sure. Today, when people all over the world read Jefferson's words, they understand them to mean all people—men, women, and children—of all colors and beliefs.

◀ A bronze statue of Thomas Jefferson

Signing Up

On July 4, 1776, the Declaration of Independence was officially approved by the delegates.

It took courage to sign that Declaration. John Hancock was first to put his name down. He did it with a big, bold signature. "So the king doesn't have to put on his glasses," he is supposed to have said. (Because of that, today, when you sign a document, people sometimes call your signature a "John Hancock.")

John Dickinson of Pennsylvania wouldn't sign. He believed the Declaration was foolhardy. He thought the colonists should work to gain the rights of free citizens within the British Empire. Independence! To Dickinson that was "like destroying our house in winter…before we have got another shelter." But he loved America dearly, so after he refused to sign the Declaration of Independence, he enlisted in the Continental army as a private and fought for his country.

◀ Standing by the table *(left to right),* John Adams, Roger Sherman, Robert Livingston, Thomas Jefferson, and Benjamin Franklin present the Declaration of Independence to the Second Continental Congress.

John Hancock's famous signature ▼

IN CONGRESS, JULY 4, 1776

The unanimous Declaration of the thirteen united States of America.

◀ The Declaration of Independence

▲ Cheering colonists outside the Pennsylvania State House in Philadelphia on July 4, 1776

The Pennsylvania State House was soon to be called Independence Hall. Why?

New Yorkers pull down a statue of King George III. ▼

The citizens outside the red-brick Pennsylvania State House, where the delegates voted, were now screaming for independence. That didn't make it easy for the men inside. They knew they would pay with their lives if the colonial army was squashed by Britain. And all the power seemed on Great Britain's side.

It was John Adams, perhaps more than anyone else, who got the delegates to sign the Declaration. Adams was a talker as well as a thinker. At the Second Continental Congress he kept talking and talking and talking until finally he convinced the delegates.

Copies of the Declaration were still warm from the printing press when they were put on coastal vessels or stuffed into saddlebags so they could be sped on their way to each of the 13 colonies.

On July 9, the document reached New York and was read to General Washington's troops, who shouted hurrah and tossed their hats in the air. That night a gilded statue of George III was pulled down from its pedestal on Manhattan's Bowling Green. (The statue was soon melted and turned into bullets.)

On July 19, the Declaration arrived in Boston, and Tom Crafts, a house painter, stepped out on a small square balcony in front of the Massachusetts State House and read it aloud. "When, in the course of human events," he began in his flat New England tone. When he finished a voice rang out, "God save the American States," and the crowd cheered mightily.

Benjamin Banneker to Thomas Jefferson

Fifteen years after the Declaration was proclaimed, Thomas Jefferson received a letter from Benjamin Banneker.

Banneker was an African American, but he was not a slave. He grew up on a small tobacco farm in Maryland and learned to read and write at a nearby Quaker school. After that, he borrowed books from a neighbor and eventually taught himself calculus and trigonometry and astronomy and surveying (an incredible feat of self-education).

Like Jefferson, he was an Enlightenment thinker, with broad interests and a lot of curiosity. He published yearly almanacs—calendars—with weather predictions, projections of tides, information on the moon and stars, and daily comments. Banneker sent Jefferson a copy of his almanac, along with a letter reminding the writer of the Declaration of Independence of his now famous words—*all men are created equal*. Here is part of Banneker's letter:

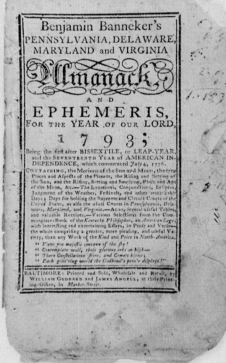

▲ Benjamin Banneker published yearly almanacs.

> *Now, sir,...I apprehend you will readily embrace every opportunity to eradicate that train of absurd and false ideas and opinions, which so generally prevails with respect to us [blacks], and that your sentiments are concurrent with mine, which are that one universal Father hath given Being to us all, and that he hath not only made us all of one flesh, but that he hath also without partiality afforded us all the same sensations, and endued [endowed] us all with the same faculties, and that however variable we may be in society or religion, however diversified in situation or color, we are all of the same family, and stand in the same relation to him.*

And here is Thomas Jefferson's reply:

> *Sir,—I thank you sincerely for your letter..., and for the Almanac it contained. Nobody wishes more than I do to see such proofs as you exhibit, that nature has given our black brethren talents equal to those of other colours of men, and that the appearance of a want of them is owing only to the degraded condition of their existence, both in Africa and America. I can add with truth that no one wishes more ardently to see a good system commenced for raising the condition both of their body and mind to what it ought to be.*
>
> *I am, with great esteem, Sir, your most obedient humble servant, Th: Jefferson*

Revolutionary Women and Children

Well, that Declaration did it! We Americans announced that we were free, and then we had to make it real. England wasn't going to give up her colonies without a fight. In 1775 King George had proclaimed that the colonies were in rebellion. But that Declaration of Independence in 1776 changed the nature of the conflict. It said that we no longer wanted to be colonists. This wasn't a little family squabble anymore. It had become a war to found a nation. It was war for a revolutionary idea: the idea that people could rule themselves. And so it was called the American Revolution. It was a people's war—and people means men, women, and children. It wasn't only the men who would do battle.

A British officer told his general that if all the men in America were killed, "We should have enough to do to conquer the women." One British soldier wrote home to England, "Even in their dresses the females seem to bid us defiance…on their shoes [they wear] something that resembles their flag of thirteen stripes."

Margaret Corbin was 23 when her husband went to war; she went with him. When he was killed, "Molly" Corbin took his cannon and kept firing.

Another Molly, Mary Hays, also helped fill her husband's place at a cannon. But she is most remembered for dodging shells as she carried a water pitcher to thirsty soldiers. She was known as Molly Pitcher.

◀ Sybil Ludington, known as "the female Paul Revere," was 16 when she rode eight hours through the New York countryside to warn colonial forces of approaching British troops.

Deborah Sampson disguised herself as a man. She served as a soldier for three years and was wounded twice, but took care of her own wounds to avoid being found out. Then she came down with a fever and ended up in a field hospital. That's where an amazed doctor learned the truth.

The doctor took Deborah Sampson to his house to care for her. When his niece decided she wanted to marry the handsome "soldier," the doctor decided he would have to tell Sampson's general the truth. In later years, Sampson went on a speaking tour telling of army life.

Anna Marie Lane was the only woman to receive a Revolutionary War soldier's pension from the Virginia Assembly. She enlisted in the army with her husband, but only he knew she was a woman. It wasn't that hard to keep it a secret. Soldiers rarely bathed, and they slept in their uniforms. Lane fought in four major battles until she, too, was discovered by an army doctor after being wounded.

How many women fought and weren't discovered? Well, if they weren't discovered, and didn't write it down later, we'll never know.

▲ Mary Hays, known as Molly Pitcher, takes her husband's place at a cannon.

Abigail Adams never stopped reminding her husband, John, about the inequality of opportunity for women in America compared with men. But he didn't listen.

Most women stayed home during the war, but they did things they hadn't done before. They had to do all the men's work as well as their own. They ran farms and businesses, sewed clothes for soldiers, and helped make gunpowder and cannonballs. When battles were fought near their homes, women fed and cared for the wounded. Some women followed the army, acting as cooks and laundresses.

Children were part of it, too. An observer in Massachusetts watched "Children making Cartridges, running Bullets, making Wallets [soldiers' bags], and baking biscuit [soldiers' food]."

"The men say we have no business with political matters," Eliza Wilkinson wrote to a friend, "[but] I won't have it thought that because we are the weaker sex (as to bodily strength my dear) we are capable of nothing more, than minding the dairy."